IN ENGLAND—a young couple flees from the presence of an unearthly being

IN ARGENTINA—a businessman is instantaneously transported over 900 miles

IN JAPAN—a car is engulfed in a cloud of vapor and mysteriously vanishes

IN AMERICA—spectral figures are seen near several UFO landing sights

IN FRANCE—a farmer is temporarily paralyzed by two extraterrestrials

IN RHODESIA—a driver is accosted by aliens and given a view of a spaceship's interior

For twenty-two years, *Flying Saucer Review* has been seeking out, documenting, and reporting bona fide encounters with UFOs. Now their most noteworthy cases have been gathered together in one book to present a conclusive argument for the actual existence of UFOs. How long they have been among us and why they are here can only be guessed at. But that they are, indeed, here can no longer be denied. The next move may be up to us. . . .

ENCOUNTER CASES FROM *FLYING SAUCER REVIEW*

EDITED BY

Charles Bowen

A SIGNET BOOK
NEW AMERICAN LIBRARY
TIMES MIRROR

SIGNET TRADEMARK REG. U.S. PAT. OFF. AND FOREIGN COUNTRIES
REGISTERED TRADEMARK—MARCA REGISTRADA
HECHO EN CHICAGO, U.S.A.

SIGNET, SIGNET CLASSICS, MENTOR, PLUME AND MERIDIAN BOOKS
are published by The New American Library, Inc.,
1301 Avenue of the Americas, New York, New York 10019

FIRST SIGNET PRINTING, DECEMBER, 1977

1 2 3 4 5 6 7 8 9

PRINTED IN THE UNITED STATES OF AMERICA

Contents

Introduction: UFOs, Occupants, and the *Flying Saucer Review*

For more than thirty years, reports of unidentified flying objects (UFOs) have excited interest and stirred the imagination of people all around the world. From the outset of the modern reporting on the subject in June, 1947, there were many who assumed that our planet was under surveillance by extraterrestrial "spacemen"—a claim for which irrefutable proof has yet to be produced. There were also many who seemed to let their imaginations run riot, and the growth of a highly vocal lunatic fringe—not to mention an uncomfortable number of hoaxers—brought the fledgling subject into instant disrepute. Almost everywhere reports of the phenomenon were either treated with scorn or with outright levity. The views of the small band of serious devotees were rudely brushed aside.

It was into this unfavorable and uninviting climate that *Flying Saucer Review (FSR)* was launched at the beginning of 1955, a time when even the epoch-making events described in the great autumn wave of UFO reports from France and Italy in 1954 were little known beyond the frontiers of those countries. (And that is how they remained until Aimé Michel's famous study, *Flying Saucers and the Straight Line Mystery*, to give it its English title, was published by Criterion Books of New York in 1958.)

FSR hung on through the storms of its first decade and lived vigorously during the last twelve or more years to witness a gradual change in the climate, a change exemplified by a handful of significant events:

1. The United States Air Force, more than a little conscious of the unfortunate public image that its explanations of the phenomenon had earned for it, apparently decided to shed the responsibility that it had acquired for the examination and explanation of UFO reports.

2. A growing fraternity of scientists and technologists is now looking into a subject where, some of them realize, there could be an overlap with other interesting phenomena.

3. A member of the French government, the defense minister, in a radio interview on February 21, 1974, confirmed that his department was very interested in UFO reports, that it had been interested since the great wave of 1954, and that in its records there were accounts of some baffling radar/visual incidents (UFOs *seen* at the same time that they are recorded on radar scopes).

4. Researchers everywhere—albeit many of them cautiously, or even covertly—recognize that a most important aspect of "ufology"* could be the reports of observations of, or even contact with, humanoid-type occupants, however ethereal these might appear to be.

In this anthology we are largely concerned with the substance that has brought about the last of these significant changes, so a comment at this point would seem appropriate.

UFO and Occupant Reports

UFO reports are a global phenomenon, and the reports mostly come in waves (surges of reports of "peaking" activity) from individual countries, or from groups of countries, or from whole continents; even sometimes covering the whole world. Accumulation of data reveals that many of the waves include reports which describe the "pilots" or occupants of the objects or craft—if indeed they be craft. More often than not, these are seen at close range; such reports fall within the category, called by some, "close encounter" reports. This book contains a selection of these types of report from many parts of the world.

Let us for the time being put aside the notion, attractive to many, that those who have reported an observation of an unidentifiable flying object and its occupants have witnessed a

* A word coined to embrace studies pertaining to UFOs, and all aspects of UFOs, reported or discovered, past and present.

landing or low-level approach of extraterrestrial explorers—however ludicrous the reported activities of those "crewmen" may have been. There remains a very good reason for studying this type of report, and that is that glowing or metallic objects seen on or near the ground, with or without undercarriage, ladders, or companionways, and whose "pilots" are encountered, can under no circumstances be explained away as misidentifications of stars, the planet Venus, meteorite showers, aircraft, satellites, weather balloons, temperature inversions, or flights of wild geese.

Returning to the adherents of the extraterrestrial hypothesis, it should be noted that the group of devotees is split down the middle to form two distinct sides: those who believe that our home planet is being surveyed by unknown interlopers from space, yet at the same time prefer largely to keep the reports of occupants at a distance; those who believe and support the claims of others that they have met with, and perhaps even conversed with the denizens of flying saucers. Right from the outset of modern interest in the UFO phenomenon the latter type of claim has been anathema to many who insist that they are serious researchers of the UFO phenomenon. Not without cause those seriously interested in UFO reports throw up their hands in horror at the cultist activities of those who long to meet these visitors from outer space, bringers of good tidings and carriers of messages of hope and instructions as to how we can save ourselves from ourselves and so on—messages often with technical details which anyone with a modicum of scientific, technologic, or engineering training will recognize instantly as gibberish . . . or are they?

Little by little, *FSR*, its friends and contributors, and a few amateur organizations and journals have tried to demonstrate to those who will look and listen that the phenomenon consists of much more than extraterrestrials with golden hair and no dental caries who allegedly contact humans for the purpose of taking them on space trips or reeducating them. It consists also of encounters with beings, humanoids, occupants, entities, creatures—call them what you will—who go about their tasks and seldom give signs that they are observed, or that they are observing; that it consists of reported encounters with decidedly unpleasant creatures, or of encounters spoken of in an almost dreamlike way, and about which we think we have learned a little more by using, when possible, the skills of a hypnotist.

All of these, and we must also include the oft-derided "contactee" encounters with their tales of "messages" and "trips" as well, fall into the category defined by Dr. J. Allen Hynek as *close encounters of the third kind.* Somewhere among them we may one day find a clue as to what goes on, be it experimental surveillance by extraterrestrials, preparations for invasion and possible takeover, control of the human race, or just a sick joke perpetrated by something somewhere.

The Colorado University Study

In January, 1969, after more than two years' study at a cost of something over $500,000, the U.S. Air Force-sponsored group of investigators at the University of Colorado at Boulder, under the late Dr. Edward U. Condon, issued its report, the general tenor of which was that UFOs weren't worth bothering about. In fact, Dr. Condon *implied* from the outset that they don't exist, for he wrote in his conclusions, with which he *opened* the 900 (plus)-page Bantam Books version of the report: ". . . Careful consideration of the record as it is available to us leads us to conclude that further extensive study of UFOs probably cannot be justified in the expectation that science will be advanced thereby." This statement was made even when the report contained a high proportion of inexplicable and puzzling incidents in the case histories to be found in its pages.

And so the U.S. Air Force achieved what must surely have been its aim in being relieved of the responsibility of logging and explaining the tiresome UFO phenomenon. Its small investigating and explaining group, Project Blue Book, was disbanded, and its civilian scientific consultant on UFO reports, Dr. J. Allen Hynek, at last found himself free to write a valuable book *The UFO Experience* (Chicago: Henry Regnery Company, 1972; London: Abelard-Schuman Ltd.). He then set about forming his institute, the Center for UFO Studies (924 Chicago Avenue, Evanston, Illinois 60202) with a band of scientists of varied disciplines giving support. In September, 1974, Dr. Hynek associated himself with *Flying Saucer Review* as a consultant.

The British Attitude

The official British attitude to UFO reports has long been one of intransigence, and until recently the media generally accepted any opportunity to "knock" the subject. For instance, on a BBC-TV program, *Man Alive*, in February, 1972, the writer was describing the remarkable 1956 events over Lakenheath and Bentwaters Air Force bases. This was a USAF/RAF radar/visual case, involving USAF ground control radars and ground observers, and a Royal Air Force night fighter which had gun-lock radar contact and pilot visual observation. The existence of this hitherto secret incident was revealed, and left unexplained, in the Condon Report. Viewers of the *Man Alive* program later saw an officer of the RAF at Fylingdales, who denied that there were any radar recordings of UFOs. Then, in response to a question from the audience, a Ministry of Defense official stated that the RAF had destroyed its records of the Lakenheath case—this statement, and the question that prompted it, were edited out of the final broadcast.

All of which is interesting in view of the third of the significant events we outlined earlier.

The French Attitude

French official acknowledgment of the existence of radar/visual cases was revealed by M. Robert Galley, Ministre des Armées, on February 21, 1974, in an interview broadcast over the France-Inter radio network. He discussed the topic with reporter Jean-Claude Bourret, whose interest in ufology had been aroused by an incident at Caselle Airport, Turin, Italy, on November 30, 1973. This involved the airport control tower, the pilot of a light aircraft making its landing approach, the captains of two jetliners, and the commandant of the adjacent military airfield who announced that he had followed the UFO on his own radar screens.

Monsieur Galley admitted there had been French interest in UFO reports since the great wave of 1954, and spoke not only of the radar cases but also of the massive nature of the phenomenon. He also told of the collaboration of the Gendarmérie in gathering information, and of the channeling of all information to Dr. Claude Poher of the Centre National d'Etudes Spatiales at Toulouse, who himself is on record as saying that some 10 percent of all cases studied officially are radar cases.[1]

Dr. Poher, who has contributed to the pages of *Flying Saucer Review*, and who is a member of Dr. Hynek's center, works together with several other French scientists, including Aimé Michel and astrophysicist Dr. Pierre Guérin.

Flying Saucer Review

Twenty-three years ago, in January, 1955, *FSR* first saw the light of day in London, England. It was a small issue, a quarterly, and that for the first and only time in its existence. It appeared under the editorship of Derek Dempster, aviation journalist and former RAF pilot. One of the items that appeared in that issue has been selected to open this anthology.

FSR[2] never aspired to a mass circulation on the newsstands. It was not that kind of publication, for its financial backing at the outset was limited and was little more than the support that could come from the pockets of a few dedicated enthusiasts and a small subscription list. To the best of its ability, an ability severely restricted by the shortage of funds for advertising, it sought out those who wished to know the truth about this controversial matter of UFO reports, which by then had been recognized as a global problem. *FSR* managed to keep its head above water by being a subscription magazine, and that method of distribution is employed to this day.

The leading light in the founding of the magazine, and the managing director of the private, limited company which was formed to run it, was Waveney Girvan who, in private life, was a director and editor of a firm of London book publishers. Waveney, who was to become a good friend of mine, took over editorship of *FSR* in 1959 from the honorable Brinsley le Poer Trench—now the Earl of Clancarty—who had succeeded Derek Dempster late in 1956.

In August, 1964, Waveney Girvan was battling against the onset of the vicious illness that was to end his life (he died on October 22, 1964). Nevertheless he managed to write a piece entitled "Ten Years Old" for inclusion in *FSR* Volume

10, Number 6. It was the last thing he was to write for his beloved magazine, and it was published posthumously.

Literary ability and editing skill of a high order, together with a native charm—and a biting wit when necessary—were the strengths of Waveney Girvan. He was also a chartered accountant, and he needed all his financial skill and doggedness to guide *Flying Saucer Review* through what Dr. Jacques Vallée has called the dark ages of ufology—the period 1960 to 1963. Waveney underlined this in "Ten Years Old" and I quote here from two paragraphs of that article:

> To have survived ten years of publishing in an era of adverse economics and without subsidy or patronage of any sort would normally be regarded as an achievement for a small magazine dealing with any other interest, but as flying saucers are generally believed to lack both existence and significance, the achievement should appear much greater to the skeptic than to the believer. But the *Review* will not look forward with any confidence to a general acclaim and wishes for a happy birthday. The occasion will no doubt be allowed to pass with customary silence—customary, that is, to all who know the truth about the saucers, and who patiently await the day when the subject can be intelligently and fearlessly discussed in the columns of the national press. That day is not yet with us.
>
> The *Review* can look back on its particular decade with mixed feelings (one of which, of course, is gratitude born of survival) upon a unique publishing experience. It is impossible to think of any other topic that would have brought a publisher similar problems. To begin with, as officially there is no such subject, strictly speaking the *Review* should never have been able to start, let alone pass its tenth milestone . . .

Well, that was in 1964, and *Flying Saucer Review* has now passed its twenty-second milestone, and is going better than at any time in its history, thanks to the obstinacy and skill of Waveney Girvan, and to the determination, talents, and resourcefulness of the editorial assistants, consultants, and directors, and the brilliance of our contributors and their devoted support all around the world. Our aim is to present the worldwide news, and views on that news as it comes in, and detailed and interesting reports of investigations and reinvestigations, as and when they can be arranged. A tall order for a small magazine which appears six times a year? Certainly, but a taller order still when one realizes that that task has been achieved without a break for close on twenty-three years by four editors and their helpers on a spare time, part time, and largely voluntary basis. For it should be remembered that *serious, unsensational* (impossible almost of achievement in such a sensational subject!), and *responsible* UFO journalism allied to a high-quality production has never been a field in which the response has been capable of supporting well-paid, full-time staffs.

The *Flying Saucer Review* Team

I have been fortunate to have a fine and devoted team of co-workers and consultants on *FSR*. Miss Eileen Buckle, author of *The Scoriton Mystery*, is assistant editor and helps with layouts and artwork, not to mention correspondence. Then there is Gordon Creighton, my right-hand man, scholar, researcher, and linguist extraordinary who translates from more than a dozen languages including French, German, Spanish, Portuguese, Italian, Flemish, Dutch, Russian, and Chinese. Formerly a diplomat who has served in several posts around the world, Mr. Creighton has a prodigious memory which makes him a formidable "think-tank" as well as a remarkable "electronic interpreter."

The rest of the team in England consists of Dr. Bernard E. Finch, physician and surgeon, who saw service as a doctor in the Royal Air Force during World War II, and was aware at that time of the foo-fighter mystery; C. Maxwell Cade, physicist and electronics expert who is a radiation medicine specialist and inventor of the Pyroscan diagnostic equipment and treatment; Charles Gibbs-Smith, the eminent aviation historian and keeper emeritus of the Victoria and Albert Museum, London; R. H. B. Winder, widely traveled engineer and university lecturer; Dr. Ivor Grattan-Guinness, mathematician, historian of science, lecturer, author, and editor of *Annals of Science*, whose wife Enid organized the distribution of the magazine for four years; Percy Hennell, photographic expert and businessman; and Jonathan M. Caplan, barrister-at-law and free-lance journalist.

Overseas consultants to whom we are greatly indebted are Aimé Michel, the doyen of French researchers, indeed of researchers the world over, mathematician, science writer, parapsychologist, radio and television broadcaster, and author of several books including *Lueurs sur les Soucoupes Volantes* (known in English as *The Truth about Flying Saucers*) and *Mystérieux Objets Célestes* (English-language version: *Flying Saucers and the Straight Line Mystery*); Dr. Berthold Eric Schwarz, M.D., psychiatrist, and consultant, Brain Wave Laboratory, Essex County Medical Center, Cedar Grove, New Jersey; and Dr. J. Allen Hynek, astronomer and head of the Department of Astronomy at Northwestern University, former civilian scientific consultant to the U.S. Air Force on UFO reports, and now founder and director of the Center for UFO Studies.

A debt of gratitude is also owed to John M. Lade, who has been company secretary for twenty-two years, and also a well-known contributor throughout that time. Many thanks are due also for the vast amount of work behind the scenes that is done by Mrs. Betty Revell, who handles distribution; Mrs. E. Spencer, the first distribution secretary, who still takes phone calls for us; and Mrs. Jo Hugill and Tim Good who help with correspondence. Without the help of these stalwarts, the efforts of the rest of us would be in vain.

CHARLES BOWEN
Editor, *Flying Saucer Review*,
West Malling,
Maidstone,
Kent, England

NOTES

1. J. C. Bourret: *La Nouvelle Vague des Soucoupes Volantes* (Editions France–Empire, Paris).
2. FSR Publications Ltd., West Malling, Maidstone, Kent, England.

Flight Lieutenant Salandin's Encounter

This report was included without by-line in the very first issue of Flying Saucer Review, *Volume 1, Number 1 (Spring, 1955). As it was the story of an alarming encounter by an Air Force Reserve pilot on a weekend training flight in his jet fighter, we were lucky to have been able to have printed it in* FSR. *Shortly before that, there had been a clamp-down on the revealing of details of UFO encounters to the press and the public by service personnel. No doubt this was due to the effects of the report of an investigative panel which sat in the United States of America during 1953. Possibly this particular cat got out of the bag because Flight Lieutenant Salandin was a "weekend flyer" of the reserve.*

The Salandin incident occurred in 1954, a year in which many UFO phenomena were reported in France and neighboring countries.

If Flight-Lieutenant J. R. Salandin, a weekend pilot of Number 604, County of Middlesex Squadron, Royal Auxiliary Air Force, had not been skeptical about flying saucers before his near collision with one last October, the Air Ministry might have had one of the first authentic cine records ever taken and been closer to solving the riddle of the unidentified flying objects than ever before.

Reporting for duty after lunch on October 14, 1954, Jimmy Salandin climbed into a Meteor Mk. 8 jet fighter and at 4:15 took off from North Weald, Essex.

The sky was blue and cloudless, and as he climbed in a

southerly direction toward the Thames Estuary he spotted two Meteors in formation high above him, leaving vapor trails behind them.

As his aircraft climbed, Salandin kept his eyes on the two fighters and every now and then checked his instruments and position.

The altimeter was reading just over 16,000 feet and Southend was just looming up beneath him when he saw two circular objects streaking between the two Meteors, traveling in the opposite direction.

He watched them until they reached nine o'clock high—a position high on his port beam—when they disappeared beyond his range of vision. Reporting the incident later, Salandin said: "One was silvery and the other gold in color."

But the shock was yet to come. When he turned to look through his windscreen he was horrified to see another object coming straight for him at his own level.

"The thing had a bun-shaped top, a flange like two saucers in the middle and a bun underneath," he said, describing it later. "It was silvery in color and could not have been far off because it overlapped my windscreen."

A Meteor fighter's 37-foot-span wings just fill the windscreen at 150 yards.

As it closed in, the object changed direction and passed Salandin on his port side.

"It was traveling at a tremendous speed," he reported and added: "I was so shaken I had to fly around quietly for about ten minutes to recover. I told control over the R/T (radio/telephone) what had happened."

What gripes Jimmy Salandin now is that he did not press his camera-gun button. "The thing was right in my sights," he says wistfully. "Next time I'll be on the ball."

UFO Seen from a Trident near Lisbon

by Omar Fowler

This recent radar-visual incident occurred during the long, hot summer of 1976, and received its first publicity in the pages of Flying Saucer Review *in November of that year (see Volume 22, Number 4).*

Mr. Fowler's report should be read with certain pronouncements and statements in mind, notably those of the French defense minister in his radio broadcast of February 21, 1974, and of the Royal Air Force officer on a BBC-TV program in February, 1972, both of which are discussed in the Introduction to this book. Also the Condon Report (Scientific Study of Unidentified Flying Objects, *Bantam Books, pages 248 and 163–164), discussing the great Bentwaters/Lakenheath radar-visual group of incidents observed: ". . . the preponderance of evidence indicates the possibility of a genuine UFO in this case." (See Flying Saucer Review, Volume 16, Number 2, March, 1970.)*

Our contributor is chairman of the Surrey Investigation Group on Aerial Phenomena (SIGAP), which is based thirty miles to the southwest of London. He is also a member of the UFO Investigators Network, which works in close collaboration with FSR.* *He and his SIGAP colleagues have set up a system of communication with the public by the simple but effective means of maintaining, first, a telephone directory entry under the name "Unidentified Flying Objects," and secondly, an entry in the telephone directory's Yellow Pages*

* See Appendix.

of classified advertisements. One of these was seen by one of the pilots of the British Airways Trident who knew that the passengers who had seen the UFOs might conceivably give a garbled report to the press. Wishing to keep the record straight, he called Mr. Fowler on the telephone. The rest followed.

We have interviewed the captain, and the first and second officers of a Trident 2 (G-AVFG) following their reported UFO sighting off the coast of Portugal on the evening of Friday, July 30, 1976. The officers have asked for their full names to be withheld.

The skipper, Captain D.W., who has been flying for British Airways for 20 years and has more than 10,000 hours of flying to his credit, describes the incident:

"We were about 40 miles south of Lisbon when Lisbon Control (Air Traffic) called up a TriStar that was above us and said: 'We have reports of a UFO. Could you confirm the sighting?' We looked up and there, sure enough at 90°, was this very bright light; I drew a sketch as we flew along. The time at night was 2000 GMT, nine o'clock local time. It was still light, the sun had just set, there was no cloud, and we could still see the ground. The crescent moon could be seen, but it was daylight to all intents and purposes at 29,000 feet.

"(As) we looked up, there was this brilliantly white, incredibly bright object. Relative to us, it was at 90° and looked about 30° in elevation. It was an incredible thing to see just sitting there, so I said (to his crew), I think we will just tell the passengers, so I made a cabin address and said: 'If you look on the starboard side, you will see what we believe to be a UFO.'

"Then as we were looking, a long cigar-shaped, or sausage-shaped brown affair appeared below it and to the starboard side of it. It just materialized, just appeared there, and then another one appeared next to it. Certainly, I saw this very bright light which Lisbon had asked me to confirm and the TriStar had already said: 'Yes, we have this UFO in sight.' I confirmed that (to Control) and I said: 'There is no way that this is a star or planet.' This is all on tape.

"We saw the bright one for eight minutes, but (as for) the other two, I think the first one appeared two minutes later and the third one at the same time. It was then that I thought

I was looking at something very unreal. I think the bright light was fascinating, but the other things were also extraordinary, and something that I cannot possibly explain. It certainly was not natural. If natural is what I have been accustomed to for the past 20 years, then this was not natural and the other members of the crew agreed with me.

"Apart from ourselves and the TriStar, there was also a T.A.P. (Portuguese State Airline) 727. I had been speaking to the TriStar captain, and then the T.A.P. pilot started speaking to Lisbon and it was then that they said they were going to 'scramble' some fighters. Whether they did so or not I don't know but they were getting excited about it and completely blocked the 'air' (radio band). This was difficult as we wanted descent clearance. Finally we were able to clear with Faro (airport)."

The first officer, C.T., who has been flying for 20 years, including 12 years as a Royal Air Force fighter pilot, recorded his version of the events, and his impressions:

"The Trident 2 aircraft (C-AVFG) flying from London to Faro on Friday July 30, 1976, was in a position 08° 30′ W., 38° S., just Southeast of Lisbon at 29,000 feet, heading 195°. The speed was 500 knots, the time 2000 GMT.

It was a beautifully clear sky, a newish moon had appeared and the sun was setting. A very bright light appeared, well above the horizon, bearing 30° from our position. The light was really incredibly bright; dazzling and very large indeed. Its shape was very difficult to discern. Rather like an enormous headlamp in the sky. It was not a star, planet or satellite.

"Whilst watching this light an incredible occurrence was witnessed. At a much lower level, a large rectangular object suddenly materialized. It had the appearance of a thick, foreshortened condensation trail. The periphery was of a vaporish appearance and colored, probably by the setting sun. The center was very dark, solid looking, somewhat cigarlike and appeared stationary.

"Approximately 30 seconds later another of these objects suddenly appeared just behind the first. I watched the objects continuously for some five minutes: they appeared to be stationary although the shape did alter slightly, probably due to our own southward progress. They were not aircraft condensation trails: vapor was present, but it was all embracing the dark centers. I was under the impression that a third one appeared underneath the second but couldn't swear to it.

"Another light then appeared at 'seven o'clock' (relative position) to the headlamp, but was lower on the horizon, not so intense, and maybe unrelated to this situation.

"The sighting was also observed by a British Airways TriStar en-route to Faro, and by Portuguese Airlines. The Portuguese controller became very excited and talked about sending up fighters to have a look. Whether they did or not I don't know.

"I have been flying at high altitude now for 20 years, 12 of them in the RAF, and have never witnessed the like of this before."

The second officer, S.S., has been flying for five years. Confirming that the Trident G-AVFG was flying from London to Faro, Portugal, on the evening of July 30, 1976, he went on:

"The first we saw of the object was when 'Air Traffic' called up to the TriStar that was right above us and said that they had a 'contact' at about 3 o'clock (area of the sky) and was there anything there? So we turned around (in our seats) and had a look. There, at 3 o'clock or slightly higher, was this bright light. It was daylight and the sun was setting, and it certainly appeared to have form rather than being a point source. It was far too bright to be a star, or anything explainable, no matter what effects the atmosphere may have had.

We watched this thing for a while and then, below it to the right, a fat sausage shape appeared, then behind that another one appeared. I am not sure about those; the thing that was totally unexplained was the light. The sausage shape could at a stretch of the imagination have been contrails caused by an aircraft, but they were too short and besides that they could only have been made by a very large aircraft, or whatever, and in any case the atmosphere was very dry and there were no contrails being produced by any aircraft, so it is very unlikely that it was a contrail.

"Really that is all there was. This thing, the light, was stationary but I wouldn't like to say what happened to the brown things as they were getting farther away all the time behind us.

"We carried on down over the coast, turned in to descend and could still see the light in the distance.

"The thing that interested me was the light, for it was totally inexplicable. I have a physics degree, so I am not completely 'lay' about it.

"Anyway we came back to London Airport and reported it to 'Air Traffic' and filled out a report on the UFO forms.

"The light was of several orders of magnitude brighter than any star. As far as I am concerned it wasn't any star; it was a very bright white light."

The crew questioned the passengers at Faro Airport after the landing. Nobody had had a camera available, but one witness had binoculars, and had viewed the bright light. He described seeing an object like "crinkled silver paper" in the middle of the light.

Return Flight Radar Surprise

After the initial contact made on the flight from London to Faro (Portugal) at 2000 GMT on July 30, 1976, the aircraft landed, refueled, and took off for the return flight to London. The crew decided to switch on the radar and scan the area where the initial contact had been made . . .

Here is Captain D.W.'s report:

"We took off an hour and a quarter later. We came up to this area (of the sighting) again—we had a note of the latitude and longitude on a card—and I decided I would turn on the radar. I tilted the radar. It is in the nose of the aircraft and can be tilted up and down.

"To see airplanes on the radar, you really have to know where they are. For instance, we saw the TriStar going down, because we knew exactly where it was. We knew it was two minutes ahead, so we were able to look about eighteen miles ahead on the radar scanner; you could see a tiny speck, and that was the TriStar.

"I turned on the radar and in the same position where we had seen these objects. I got a return with the radar, at 5° tilt up. I was climbing through 28,000 feet, going for 31,000 feet. With the radar 5° tilt up, it scans then from about the lateral attitude of the airplane upward. First I got this big 'blip' and then a couple of others close to it. The big 'blip' was much bigger than any ship I have ever seen . . ." [*Question*: By ship, you mean an aircraft?]

"No, I mean a ship, because you can pick up the ships as you come over the Channel. They produce much bigger 'blips' than airplanes do. I know how big these things are and a ship, say a big tanker, a 200,000-ton tanker, would produce a 'blip' an eighth of an inch long. This thing (the radar blip) was three times . . . at least three times as big as that, and then there were others that were not as clear. You had this sort of elliptical image on the radar screen which was just solid, and there was no way that this could have been an airplane, there was no question of that. The lights in the cockpit were dimmed and there was just a backdrop of stars; the moon did not seem to be around anymore, there were just stars and nothing to see at all.

"We had the radar return at 20 miles, and stationary, and we passed climbing. Gradually they disappeared on the starboard side, which is what one would have expected, as that is where they were and the closest that we reckon we got was seven miles. As the image gets close to the bottom of the radar screen, it gets rather diffused and you can't really read it, but that was the last straw as far as I was concerned. It was good radar—they vary a bit—but this was a good one. At night of course you can see the radar screen very much better than you can during the day. Because the lighting in the cockpit is very dim, you can read the details much more clearly and that's about it . . ."

First officer C.T. stated:

"On the way back, it was dark, very dark, (although) quite clear with a completely cloudless sky. We thought we would have a look on the radar when in the same position (as the earlier sighting) so when we got within about 50 miles, we turned the radar on and pitched it up. Of course we were still climbing and blow me if we didn't get some enormous returns on the 20 miles scale. There were no clouds in the sky, and these were ten times the size of any aircraft returns that you ever get on any aircraft radar. Very large, and there appeared to be a cluster of them. We turned the lights down and started to look for them, but we couldn't see anything, and yet we had this completely positive 'ident.' It was about 10° off to the left and it went down the left-hand side as we passed. We went within seven miles of it and never saw a thing. Any doubts that we had about these things having solid middles well . . . that confirmed it, that sold us at that stage."

Second pilot S. S. added:

"We took off again and about two hours later we passed the same spot, we returned on the same track; the skipper had turned the radar on just to see if anything was there and we got these very strong returns (blips) at about twenty miles away, about 5° up from our position. You can get this information ref. distance and inclination from the airborne radar.

"The returns appeared stationary and we closed with them as we flew along. We came down their port side and passed about six or seven miles away from them. They were very strong returns, and if they had been aircraft we probably would have seen 'nav' lights as it was a very clear night. They could have been military for they don't always carry 'nav' lights, but they were very strong returns and it is surprising that we didn't scc anything."

Postscript to the Trident Report
by Charles Bowen

Since Mr. Fowler's article with the statements of the crew members of the British Airways Trident was published in *FSR*, two important things have happened.

First, *FSR* has received, through Omar Fowler, a corroborating report from Portuguese investigator Vitor Santos, who obtained a valuable interview with Commander A. Cavalheira of the Portuguese Air Transport (T.A.P.) who had just taken off in the Boeing 727 referred to in the preceding article. I quote from the report (which at present is being translated for inclusion in *Flying Saucer Review*, Volume 23, Number 1):

> It was when, at 3,000, we passed over [from Faro Tower] to the Lisbon Control Tower, that I heard their conversation with the BEA Trident [BEA—British European Airways—was merged with BOAC to form "British Airways"—C.B.] and I began to pay attention to what the pilot was saying. Then the Trident asked me if I could see anything. I replied that I was listening to their conversation and that I could indeed see something, and also something else, which was the shadowy shape, for which my explanation was . . . namely that it was the trail of an aircraft.

Indeed, Commander Cavalheira had been watching the light *before* he took off, thinking it might be an approaching aircraft, which was why he had not at that time been given clearance to take off. Then he and his crew considered, after takeoff, that it might be the planet Venus, until they saw from their position that it was *rising* and not setting as the planet would have been doing.

Secondly, Captain D. W., the skipper of the British Airways Trident, appeared with Professor John G. Taylor of Kings College, London University, and myself, on an Independent TV network program on April 12, 1977, and described the incident. He was introduced to the public as Captain Denis Woods.

The incident has been given belated media publicity. One explanation offered was that the Trident flew close to a research balloon released by Southampton University. While this would satisfy *some* of the data, I must observe that if the radar is to be believed in this case, the object was only a few seconds flying time from the jetliner whose captain had had no warning of its presence. However, the *three* "blips" on the radar tube—enormous ones, remember—would seem clearly to contradict the "explanation" that was broadcast. I sincerely hope, particularly for the sake of air travelers, that the object over southern Portugal that evening was indeed only a UFO.

Vehicle Stoppage at Hook

by R.H.B. Winder

Hook is a small village near Basingstoke, in Hampshire, England, and the strange event that was alleged to have happened close by was investigated by two of the FSR *team of consultants, Mr. Winder, an engineer, and Dr. Bernard Finch, a medical practitioner.*

The incident was part of the short, sharp wave of UFO reports that posed a few puzzles in England during the fall of 1967. Short and sharp, one suspects, because of the mode of reporting, particularly on television, which could well have dissuaded people who had had an unusual experience from coming forward with their stories. One example of this concerned the police, for this was a time when there were a number of well-publicized sightings by police officers, notably in Devonshire, where police in a car chased an object, and in Sussex. The senior police officer at Brighton, Sussex, was seen by millions of TV viewers as he addressed a parade of policemen and told them, in no uncertain terms, that those among them who had been reporting UFOs had been watching the planet Venus.

The witness in this interesting vehicle stoppage and time-lapse case was so worried and puzzled by what had happened to him, yet so fearful of the ridicule he might attract by approaching the press (and having little faith in either the police or the Ministry of Defense after reading their pronouncements), that he took the trouble of seeking out the editor of Flying Saucer Review. *Fortunately the magazine is listed in the telephone directory, so he was quickly in touch with Messrs. Winder and Finch, whose account and comments appeared in* Flying Saucer Review, *Volume 13, Number 6 (November–December, 1967).*

At the witness's request a nom-de-plume was used (B. J. Colley), but in a television program soon afterward it was revealed that his proper name is W. Collett.

During the late October rush of sightings an important incident occurred that did not reach the newspapers because the witness did not want publicity. He rang the editor of this review only because he saw the journal mentioned in a newspaper the next day and was seeking an explanation of what he saw. He would not have bothered if he had merely seen the lights in the sky that were then being reported so frequently.

Mr. B. J. Colley* directs a small transport company somewhere in Sussex. He is an intelligent and versatile but down-to-earth and busy man, always looking for rational explanations. He is a skilled engineer with considerable experience of vehicles and aircraft. He is also a linguist, understanding French, Spanish and Portuguese.

On Wednesday, October 25, he went to bed early after carefully studying a route from his home to Redditch—near Birmingham—by way of Odiham, Hook, Reading, Oxford, and Stratford-on-Avon, over which he intended to carry a ton of machined titanium castings in his 2½-ton, 1966 model, Ford Transit bus. The four-cylinder petrol engined vehicle normally has twelve seats and is used to carry aircrews on or between airfields. When not required for such purposes the seats are removed and the bus is used to carry freight. Mr. Colley was particularly anxious to pioneer this particular route himself because a lucrative contract hung upon timely delivery.

At about 4:30 A.M. (B.S.T.) on Thursday, October 26, 1967, Mr. Colley found himself making good progress, at around 45 mph northward along the A.32 toward Reading, 10 minutes after crossing its intersection with the A.30, at Hook in Hampshire. The road was level, reasonably straight, and well lit by the moon, now in its last quarter, shining in a clear sky. It was dry but not frosty. Confident of a timely ar-

* Fictitious name to cover identity.

rival, Mr. Colley had the radio tuned to a Spanish station and was enjoying his trip. The radio had faded slightly a few minutes before, not exceptional for a foreign station, but it was free from any interference.

The prospect of a successful trip receded sharply when the electrical system of the vehicle failed suddenly and completely. Confident that everything was in good condition, Mr. Colley could only suppose that a battery lead had worked loose and could think of nothing else that would cause lights, radio, and engine to fail simultaneously. He was, therefore, surprised, upon getting down into the road and looking under the bonnet, to find the 12 volt battery in apparent good health with its negative earth lead and positive power lead secure and undamaged. Somewhat baffled, and growing anxious about the delay, he inspected the fuses, distributor, and all other accessible leads, including those to the exposed sparking plug terminals, without finding any fault. He could then think of nothing else to do but to return to the driving seat and try the engine again.

Whilst climbing the step he caught sight of, but paid little attention to, a dark object clearly outlined in the sky and motionless over the road ahead. It was not far away, but too high to be seen from his seat when he reached it. Mr. Colley tried the starter but got no response, so he sat for a short time wondering what to do next. He was too preoccupied to think further about the shape in the sky. A few minutes later, (he is not very sure about the lapse of time), he tried again and the engine started without difficulty. The starter switch also brought on the radio. With considerable relief, Mr. Colley switched on the lights and went on his way—all systems functioning well.

Four hundred yards down the road the same total and baffling failure occurred again.

Stepping down on to the road once more, Mr. Colley noticed a change of pressure on his eardrums, an effect familiar to him in aircraft but inexplicable in his current predicament. He actually applied the standard cure of holding his nose and blowing. In the road, he also noticed an all-pervading, quite powerful, and rather oppressive smell which he likens to that produced by an arcing electric motor. We discussed this smell at some length and eventually classified it as a combination of hot insulating material, which he describes as bakelite, and of electrical sparking. The witness is not familiar with ozone, which is a by-product of ionization, but he felt no irritation. He found the smell of film floodlights in a small room similar but far less intense.

Mr. Colley again inspected the engine and again found nothing wrong. He is certain that the smell did not come from under the bonnet. Baffled and now very worried, he straightened up, looked around, and once more saw the object in the sky in much the same relative position as before. He reckons it was no more than a hundred yards away and 50 to 100 feet up, dark and motionless above the trees bordering the road ahead. This time he paid more attention to it but did not connect it with his problem: he had no knowledge of vehicles being stopped by UFOs and, indeed, did not think of this thing as one, since it did not manifest the well-publicized illumination. He did, however, notice a glint of reflected moonlight from its right-hand upper surface, the moon being on the right-hand side of the road ahead. He was also able, later, to sketch the shape which was clearly outlined against the moonlit sky. The sketch . . . with the witness's estimate of size: 60 feet wide by 30 feet high . . . shows a shape that is best described as that of a squat ice cream cone with a flange or rim at the junction between the curved upper works and conical underpart. No further details could be seen, although judging from the reflection he supposed that the surface had a dull rather than a bright finish. He estimates that he watched the object for several minutes until, still in complete silence and without any warning tilt, it began to move horizontally away to the right at a moderate speed and soon went out of sight over the trees. Turning once again to his immediate problem, Mr. Colley returned to his seat, tried his engine, and found everything back to normal. He immediately resumed his journey.

A few more points remain to be noted: Mr. Colley's recollection of the remainder of the trip is not entirely clear; he was worried over the delay and a little alarmed by the object, but he does know that he completed the journey without any reference to roadsigns or map, and without stopping. In retrospect this surprised him because the route was strange to him and he would normally have been very careful to avoid risking wasted time in a wrong turning and would have stopped frequently to check his position. He is particularly surprised at finding the correct turning off the main road, about six miles before Redditch without apparently thinking about it. After an estimated delay of 20 minutes, he actually arrived 15 minutes early. We must, however, note that he had taken care to study the route before setting out. He also mentioned unusual difficulty in operating the gear lever and accelerator, which could be attributed to some lack of coordination after his experience. After returning home, he noticed some throbbing in the fingertips and an unexpected absence of the toothache that had pestered him for some days before the event. He also finds that he now dreams when asleep, which is apparently an uncommon experience for him. However, such matters are properly the province of Dr. Finch who deals with them in his comments on the case. Of possible engineering significance is Mr. Colley's contention that he used three gallons of petrol, equivalent to about sixty miles, more on the return journey by the same route, than he did on the outward run, but this might be attributable to some ordinary cause such as the difference in driving conditions by day and by night.

Mr. Colley was, and still is, skeptical about flying saucers, particularly the extraterrestrial theory of their origins, although he is now showing interest in the literature and may well change his mind. Nevertheless, he insists that the object he saw was real and under intelligent control, because he saw it move off, and further reasons that it must have followed him deliberately between the two stops. At the time, three days later, when Bernard Finch, Gordon Creighton, and I talked to him he was still trying to rationalize the experience in terms of some military device or the like. It is worth mentioning that the location is in the vicinity of several military installations and not far from the Royal Aeronautical Establishment at Farnborough.

This is a valuable sighting by a credible witness, particularly in view of his competent examination of the vehicle's electrical system and his quite precise account of the smell. The shape of the object is conventional except for the conical base which is not common. The complete absence of illumination is also unusual and at least enables us to discount Venus! It is also as well to note that there was no interference with the vehicle's valuable load.

We remain in touch with Mr. Colley, to whom we are very

grateful for the information supplied, and will write again if anything further transpires.

Physiological Effects on Witness at Hook
by Dr. Bernard E. Finch

Three days after Mr. Colley told Charles Bowen about his encounter with a flying saucer near Hook I was able to cross-examine him closely and to draw certain conclusions.

In the first place I found Mr. Colley an intelligent and co-operative witness. He was able to give me a convincing story of his experiences.

When he alighted from his driving cab he stated that he noticed a strong smell rather like burning bakelite or insulation—yet this did not come from his lorry's engine or dashboard. He next had a feeling of oppression, the kind of sensation that we all get before a thunderstorm.

This "feeling" has often been described by other witnesses in the vicinity of UFOs, and closely resembles the sensation felt near high-tension electrostatic condensers when being charged, or ready to discharge.

Mr. Colley also described a peculiar clicking in his ears. On further questioning it appeared that this clicking was really his eardrums popping in and out—rather like the sensation in an airplane or rapidly descending lift. Obviously there must have been considerable air pressure changes in the vicinity of the object.

When Mr. Colley resumed his driving, he found that he had considerable difficulty in coordinating the movements of his hands and feet. It was "as if he had to learn the movements of driving all over again," and that all involuntary movements had to be carried out with deliberation. These symptoms have occurred in other witnesses who have been near UFOs, and one can only assume that the "force field" has interfered with the peripheral nerves and their connections in the spinal cord so that the reflex-arc has been temporarily "knocked out." In support of these findings, we learned that Mr. Colley later complained of a strange "tingling, numbness, and crawling feelings" at the end of his fingers—a very descriptive account of regenerating nerves.

One remarkable feature was that Mr. Colley, who had complained of toothache some time before this incident, now stated that it had completely disappeared. In fact, when I spoke to him today, a fortnight after the incident, he confirmed that it had still not returned. A dentist colleague of mine commented that this would tie up with a suspected disruption of the nerve impulse, but that an abscess could develop now that nature's warning has been interfered with.

All in all, it appears that Mr. Colley was affected by the periphery of a force field which we assume was contracted down to its minimum. The saucer was hovering, there was practically no glow nor sound, and we may assume the "engine" was obviously at low "thrust."

Had the engine been on full throttle it would have been a different kettle of fish. The saucer would have been surrounded by a brilliant violet glow, the force field would have extended outward several hundred yards, and Mr. Colley would have been knocked unconscious, his skin being rendered erythematous. And when he recovered, would he have been the same man? Would his cerebral neurones have acted as before? I doubt it. I suspect his memory and concentration would have been impaired, and the auditory and visual cortex recovering from its "stunning process" would begin to show various activities. For, as the peripheral nerves in recovering give rise to "tingling," so the auditory and visual cortex in recovering give rise to "sounds" and "visions," respectively. And, as we have seen with previous witnesses, there would be auditory and visual hallucinations.

Therefore, in all contact ground-level sightings, one must bear in mind the considerable side effects of the "force-field" on the physiology of the human body.

London, November 9, 1967

Teleportations

by Gordon Creighton

The UFO lore is studded with alarming tales of humans who are carried almost instantaneously from one place to another, and with tales of abductions too—but that aspect will be covered later on. It would seem that historic times also contain records of such events.

This contribution was published in Flying Saucer Review, *Volume 11, Number 2 (March–April, 1965).*

On the morning of 25th October 1593, a Spanish soldier suddenly appeared on the Plaza Mayor (the principal square) of Mexico City. He was wearing the insignia of the regiment which at that moment was guarding the walled city of Manila, in the Philippine Islands, more than 9,000 miles away on the other side of the Pacific Ocean. How did this soldier come to be in Mexico City? The truth is that he had no idea. All he knew was that he had suddenly found himself no longer in Manila but in Mexico. But there was something else that he said he *did* know. He said that His Excellency Don Gòmez Pérez Dasmarinas, governor of the Philippines, was dead. A preposterous rumor of course. But one that spread through the Mexican capital like wildfire.

Although puzzled as to how precisely the soldier could have traveled so far without so much as soiling his uniform, the Spanish authorities in Mexico jailed him as a deserter from the Manila garrison. An awkward Fortean "damned fact" was thus safely swept under the carpet, and no doubt folk breathed again with relief.

And so the weeks passed, while our soldier languished in the brig; the long, slow weeks necessary for news to travel by galleon along the regular sailing route from Spain, which runs via Manila to Acapulco, the port on the west coast of Mexico. From Acapulco the news would pass by messenger up across the great sierras and into the sky-girt Valley of Mexico.

And then suddenly Mexico City was full of the news. His Excellency Don Gómex Pérez Dasmarinas, governor of the Philippines for King Philip II, *was* dead—murdered by a mutinous Chinese crew off Punta de Azufre just as he was setting sail on a military expedition against the Molucca Islands! And, moreover, he had been murdered on the very day that the mysterious soldier from the Manila garrison had appeared on the Plaza Mayor of Mexico City.

The Most Holy Tribunal of the Inquisition, always alert for signs of witchcraft and *"diablería,"* took charge of the case. But still the soldier could not tell them how he had traveled from Manila to Mexico. All he could tell them was that it had been "in less time than it takes a cock to crow."

The Inquisition ordered that the man be returned to Manila for further investigation of the matter, and on his arrival there it was established beyond question, on the word of not a few witnesses, that the soldier had indeed been there on duty in the city of Manila on the night of 24th October 1593, just as it was proven beyond any peradventure that on the following morning he had been apprehended on the Plaza Mayor in Mexico City, over 9,000 miles away.

There are reliable records of this episode.[1] It is no fabrication. And the best term with which we can label it, is one already familiar to us from the annals of psychic research: teleportation.

We possess records of numerous disappearances, apparent abductions, apparent teleportations. In the *Flying Saucer Review* for July–August, 1963, I reported the case of the Swedish student Olaf Nielsen who claims that he was swept up and carried off by a saucer near Halmstad, Sweden, on the afternoon of 25th August 1960, and taken to a secret base. I suggest that the Manila/Mexico case and many others are all *UFO phenomena.* And I shall give some further recent examples.

In his book *The Case for the UFO*, the late M. K. Jessup (and, by the way, his death was just one of many mysterious deaths) dealt with a number of classic cases, including this one of the Manila soldier and some of the more extraordinary disappearances, such as that of Oliver Lerch in 1890 and that of the RAF officers Day and Stewart whose footprints came to a sudden end in the sands of Iraq one day in July, 1924. Space does not permit me to deal here with the fantastic problem of disappearances and abductions. My purpose in the present article is only to examine some of the evidence for *teleportation*, that is to say, evidence of cases in which a UFO may have picked a person up in one place and set him down again elsewhere. (Perhaps this is how our peripatetic pumas get here?)

I shall, of course, be told immediately that the Manila Soldier Story—if indeed it ever happened—is almost four centuries old; that they were capable of cooking up all sorts of tales in those days; that there has never been a whit of evidence since that pointed to a repetition. I regret that I cannot agree, and for the record here are two more cases which I have selected.

The Buenos Aires Businessman

One day in 1959, an important Argentine businessman[2] was driving back to the south of that country after a visit to Buenos Aires. He stopped for a night en route at a hotel in Bahìa Blanca, with the intention of continuing his journey next day.

On the following morning he got into his brand-new car and was just about to drive off from the hotel when he became aware of a "cloudy mass enveloping the whole car." He felt later that he must have lost consciousness at this point, and the next thing he knew was that he was alone, *sans* car, in some deserted spot in the countryside. Seeing a lorry coming along the road toward him, he hailed the driver, and asked him for a lift into Bahìa Blanca. An astonished lorry-driver replied that he wasn't going to Bahìa Blanca, that this place was Salta, and that Bahìa Blanca was over a thousand kilometers away! (It lies 1,155 kilometers southeast of Salta.) The businessman then looked at his wristwatch and found, to his amazement, that only a few minutes had elapsed since he had stepped into his car at Bahìa Blanca. Bewildered, he climbed into the cab beside the lorry-driver, and they went off to report the matter to the local authorities. The authorities, equally dumbfounded by the story, telephoned to the police at Bahìa Blanca, giving the registration number and description of the businessman's car, and after a brief investigation the Bahìa Blanca police phoned back to say that the car in question was still there, just a few meters from the hotel, with the engine still running!

I have translated this from a clipping taken from a 1959 issue of the Argentine daily paper *Diario de Córdoba*. It is unfortunate that the newspaper did not give the name of the Argentine businessman who had this experience, but the clipping was sent to us by Señor Oscar Galìndez who is the *Flying Saucer Review*'s correspondent in the Argentine, and who himself lives in Córdoba. We are most grateful to him for this as well as for an enormous number of other press clippings for the period 1947–1964, and I am writing to ask him whether he can give us the name of the businessman and any other details, such as the date of the occurrence, and so on.

We turn now to the second case:[3]

On the Road from Tokyo

Shortly after 8 A.M. on 19th November 1963, a Mr. Kinoshita. acting manager of the Kashika branch of the Fuji Bank, Tokyo, Japan, was driving along the Fujishiro bypass. He had just gone through the towns of Matsudo and Kashiwa, on the Mito road, and was headed for a golf course at Ryugazaki, Ibaraki-ken. (This region lies a little north of Tokyo.) In the car with him were two passengers. These were a Mr. Saito, vice-director of the bank's Kashika branch, and another man who was a client of the bank.

Ever since passing through a place called Kanamachi, they had had in view another car, which was about 150 yards ahead of them and traveling in the same direction. It was a black car, of a type known as the Toyopet New Crown, and it had a Tokyo registration number (which, of course, most unfortunately none of them memorized). In the left-hand rear seat of this black car was an elderly man, who was reading a newspaper. We are given no information about the driver or any other occupants.

Suddenly, "a puff of something gaseous, like white smoke or vapor, gushed out from somewhere around the black car," and when this cloud dispersed (a matter of not more than five seconds) the black car had vanished.

Not having memorized the registration number of the black car, Mr. Kinoshita and his companions felt that there was no way of tracing it, nor of finding out who had been in the car and what had become of them.

This affair was reported in the evening edition of the *Mainichi* (one of Japan's two leading papers) of 4th March 1964. The newspaper stated that hallucination had been suggested as an explanation, but that all three witnesses vehemently denied that there could have been any question of hallucination.

Well, there you are. There seems to be a link between each of these four cases. I suggest that the link is that they are all cases of teleportation by UFOs.

I have written to Japan in the hope of finding out whether there was any sequel to the last case, and whether the "missing" car and its occupants ever turned up. If the answer is negative, then of course it looks as though this is a case not only of teleportation, but of abduction too.

NOTES

1. From *Las Calles de Mejico,* by Luis Gonzalez Obregón, quoted in Part III of M. K. Jessup's *The Case for the UFO*. According to Jessup, further corroboration of the case is in the records of Santo Domingo, and also in the book *Sucesos de las Islas Filipinas* (An Account of Events in the Philippines) by Dr. Antonio de Morga, High Justice of the Criminal Court of the Royal Audiencia of New Spain.
2. Extract (precise date not for yet available) from Argentine daily newspaper *Diario de Córdoba,* 1959, kindly supplied by Dr. Oscar Galíndez of Córdoba, representative of the *Flying Saucer Review* in the Argentine Republic.
3. Report in Tokyo evening paper *Mainichi* of 4th March 1964, furnished by courtesy of Mr. Jun-Ichi Takanashi of the Modern Space-Flight Association, Osaka, Japan, and reproduced on page 11 of the *Journal and Bulletin,* Volume 1, Number 1 (Summer, 1964) of the British UFO Research Association, to whom I am much indebted for the item.

Postscript
by Charles Bowen

As far as I know, Mr. Creighton never received any satisfaction with regard to his inquiries about the missing Japanese car and its occupants.

He suggests that not only teleportation but abduction also could have been involved. And thereby a point is made, for the cases selected for this anthology thread their way through a whole cross-section of encounter and contact cases, leading to finales of abduction and teleportation on the grand scale, with broad hints as to what might have happened during those alarming incidents.

The Specter of Winterfold

by Charles Bowen

Here is a report of a creature encounter which occurred toward the end of the British UFO wave of 1967. This, together with other reported features, prompted its inclusion in this collection despite the fact that no craft or UFO was seen by the witness. Could this have been a solid creature, or something more ethereal? Perhaps a vision projected onto the scene from a distant or hidden object? Perhaps an image projected into the mind of the witness? What a pity Philip Freeman's girl friend was too scared to look: she smelled the foul odor but we cannot say whether, if she had looked, she would have seen the spectral shape.

There is an early reference in the article to other comparative cases: these can be summarized here.

The Saltwood affair was a UFO case with creature observation reported in 1963 which was described in our book The Humanoids *Chicago: Henry Regnery; London: Neville Spearman, 1969.) Four young people aged 17 to 18 watched a glowing ovalloid descend over wooded ground near the village, on the outskirts of Hythe and Folkestone in Kent, England. In sudden alarm the witnesses began to run, but stopped when the object emerged from the trees and hovered 80 yards away. When, almost instantaneously, a shambling human-sized figure with no head but with batlike wings emerged and moved toward them, the four ran for dear life.*

Flatwoods, West Virginia, in 1952 was the scene of a UFO landing, and when the witnesses surged forward to see what had happened, a monstrous spectral-like figure with blood-red face and glowing greenish orange eyes floated down the hill toward the by now terrified observers.

Casa Blanca, near Riverside, California, was the scene, in August, 1955, of a weird encounter with unpleasant overtones, for the witnesses were a group of children playing in a garden, who, fortunately enough, had the sense to keep away from the things they saw. One of the children made the initial discovery of a disc-shaped object which was spinning overhead. Then he and others saw a recurring series of spectral-like shapes appearing. The shapes had heads, eyes and mouths, and arms, while some had belts. They were semitransparent. Other flying objects were seen, one of which landed in a field nearby. Then an "arm," which was independent of any body, appeared and beckoned. Now thoroughly scared, the children ran inside the house to alert the grownups, but when they returned to the garden the objects and specters were gone.

All three of these incidents—like that of Oscar Iriart described by Gordon Creighton in "A South American 'Wave' "—seem to fall within the bounds of the "projection" idea and have caused deep concern among some researchers as to what really is happening.

The report on the Specter of Winterfold appeared in Flying Saucer Review, *Volume 14, Number 1 (January–February, 1968).*

On the night of November 12–13, 1967, two young people of Woking, Surrey, had the fright of their lives. I first heard a whisper of the incident on the morning of Sunday, November 26, through a friend—who in turn knows the mother of the young man involved in the affair.

"It is a very strange story," said my friend, "but as it is not connected with UFOs I didn't hasten to tell you."

Which is a pity, because it so happened that when I heard the gist of the account I became very interested, with my thoughts ranging from Saltwood[1] to Flatwoods[2] and Casa Blanca.[3] I arranged immediately to interview the witnesses, and first met them on the afternoon of November 26. I am grateful to them for their cooperation.

At about 12:30 A.M. on November 13, on a damp, cloudy night—there had earlier been some drizzle following a very pleasant autumn Sunday—Philip Freeman and his friend Angela Carter left the house of Philip's married brother Leslie Freeman, who lives in Cranleigh. They were not sure of the precise time, but just before leaving they had been watching the Eamonn Andrews show on ATV (London). Philip was driving his red Triumph Vitesse convertible. The hood was up.

Aged 22, Philip is one of two partners in a small subcontracting carpentry business. He lives with his parents in a comfortable flat in Loder Close, Sheerwater, Woking. He says he has no knowledge of, or interest in, flying saucer literature: his time for reading is limited, but he has read some science fiction (*The War of the Worlds,* the Woking-based novel by H. G. Wells, was quoted as an example). He was surprised when I showed him a copy of *Flying Saucer Review*; surprised to see such a well-turned-out magazine on the subject. Miss Angela Carter, 20, of Devonshire Avenue, Sheerwater, works locally.

The route which the couple took from Cranleigh was up over hilly, forested country, to Shere. The narrow, twisting lanes make their way through rocky cuttings and the woodlands of Hurtwood Common, between Winterfold and Pitch Hill, which is the third highest point in the county of Surrey. From Shere, they were to take the A25 road to Newlands Corner on Albury Down, where they would join the road down to West Clandon and Send, and then on to Woking. This is a much shorter route than that by the main roads through Shamley Green and Guildford to Woking: it is also a wilder, and much more lonely route—to which I personally can testify, for I know the district very well.

There was no other traffic about, and, as the windscreen and windows of the car were misting over—the heater had not at that time warmed up sufficiently to keep them clear—Philip stopped the car at a place which he thinks was about two miles from Cranleigh.

Dousing the headlights, but leaving the side lights on, with the engine running, Philip got out to leather the windscreen. As he did so, he became aware of a very unpleasant odor. When I asked him to describe the smell, he said it was something like food being cooked, and burning badly. Then, as an afterthought, he suggested it could even have been like a "stink bomb."

I questioned Miss Carter separately, and she confirmed the

details of their movements. She also said that she became aware of the smell as soon as Philip got out of the car, and that it was not in any way like the smell from an overheated car engine (I had not mentioned that possibility). Philip agreed with this when I spoke to him again, and pointed out that the car had not run long enough for it to overheat.

The night was pitch black, and there were no lights in sight other than the car's side and rear lights.

As Philip returned to the driver's seat he looked round to Miss Carter, on his left, and was alarmed to see a "face" through the near-side passenger window. He estimated it to be about 10 inches long and 8 inches wide, and stated that it was close up to the window. There were no visible features like eyes, nose, or mouth; it was blank, and white, and sharply defined. As there was little or no light for it to reflect, he suggests now that it may have been faintly luminous. There was also something that looked like an "arm" which was reaching up to the top of the car's hood. He was suddenly terrified and felt very cold.

Miss Carter was looking at Philip as he got back into the car, and was mentioning the revolting smell. She observed the look of fright which came over his face and instinctively dared not look around to the side window.

"There was an 'atmosphere' which alarmed me," she said. "I knew by the look on Philip's face, and by my own 'feeling' that something horrible was out there."

Continuing his description, Philip Freeman said that the little he could see of the rest of the "body" was not white at all, but dark.

By now very frightened, his companion urged him to drive away.

Philip is a driver who always starts in first gear. As, with the majority of cars, there is no synchromesh on the first gear of his car, he usually eases into gear by putting the lever into the position for second gear, and then slipping it up into the position for first gear. In the time—perhaps a second or two—taken to perform this operation, the apparition apparently moved to the back of the vehicle, for Philip glanced around as he switched on the headlights preparatory to moving off, and saw the same white "face" close to the perspex rear window. As he drove away, he caught a glimpse of the rest of the "body" in the light from his rear lamps, and he has a distinct impression of a dark bell shape surmounted by the two white, or luminous, parts. He cannot recall seeing any "legs."

The "creature" appeared to be approximately level in height with the top of the Vitesse (4½ feet).

The whole experience, from the stopping of the car to the hurried departure, was estimated to have occupied less than two minutes.

As soon as the vehicle moved away from the site of the encounter, the smell—which had been stronger inside the car than it was outside—disappeared.

A few hundred yards up the road, Philip asked Miss Carter if she was agreeable to turning round and going back with their twin headlights full on. She would not hear of it, and urged him to drive home as quickly as possible.

Philip's parents were abed when he arrived home. He roused them and blurted out his story. Their reaction was one of surprise, which changed to mild amusement.

"Maybe it was a traffic warden," suggested Mr. Freeman, senior.

However, they quickly saw that their son was adamant, and in no mood for joking, and when I spoke to them they assured me that his agitation was such that he must have seen something real and very alarming. This does not surprise me, for I found both Philip Freeman and Angela Carter to be down-to-earth, matter-of-fact, and likable young people.

It seems, furthermore, that Philip's friends and employees also found the story to be a "bit of a giggle," but it quickly flitted through the bush telegraph to reach telegraph to reach the ears of a reporter who works for the monthly *Woking Review*. Late one evening the route was retraced by Philip and the reporter, but nothing was seen. . . .

When I met the witnesses, Philip was understandably fed up with the reaction of other people to his factual account of something he had seen.

There have been a number of somewhat vague flying saucer reports from the Ewhurst-Hurtwood-Cranleigh district during the past three years or so. My daughter Pauline is endeavoring to trace a former fellow student at Guildford who mentioned seeing two luminous objects rise from a field at the edge of the forest area one evening in 1965. Again, elsewhere in this issue (*FSR*, Volume 14, Number 1) will be found Squadron Leader Shipwright's account of his sighting (from the Downs close to Newlands Corner) of an unusual object near the village of Albury. This is no great distance from the place where the Winterfold specter was seen.

Nor should we forget that the Ewhurst-Hurtwood Common district has been the scene of many sightings of the mystery "Puma," reports of which so interested Waveney Girvan and myself during 1963 and 1964. Accounts of the "Puma" have often contained references to the strong ammoniacal smell present at a sighting.[4] In fact my main reason for bringing this latest Winterfold account to the attention of *Review* readers is the report of the strong smell. Philip Freeman mentioned "stink bombs": could the odor have been akin to the "bad egg" smell of hydrogen sulfide (H_2S)? Just such an odor was reported at the site of the Flatwoods landing and monster case of September 12, 1952, where marks on the ground were later found by investigators.

Again, our contributor Jerome Clark reminded us of the incident—mentioned by Donald Keyhoe—of the aircraft which, with a dead and mutilated crew, was miraculously brought back to base by the dying second pilot. The smell of hydrogen sulfide was found to be strong inside the cabin when the aircraft was examined after landing.[5]

An obnoxious smell was also mentioned by the claimant in the Ohio contact case reported by John A. Keel elsewhere in this issue.

When I discussed this new Winterfold case with Gordon Creighton, he reminded me that in medieval times, tales which told of manifestations of the devil often told also of the smell of brimstone. Had such a thing as the specter—as seen by Philip Freeman and Angela Carter—been reported 600 years ago, I feel sure it would have been interpreted as a manifestation of the devil: certainly the Flatwoods monster would have fallen into the same category, and, as we know, a UFO was also reported on that occasion.

NOTES

1. "The Saltwood Monster," *Flying Saucer Review* (March–April, 1964).
2. For *FSR* record of this case, see Lorenzen, Mrs. C., "UFO Occupants in United States Reports," *The Humanoids,* special issue for October–November, 1966 (reprinted July, 1967).

3. Creighton, G., "The Extraordinary Happenings at Casa Blanca," *Flying Saucer Review* (September–October, 1967).
4. Bowen, C., "Mystery Animals," *Flying Saucer Review* (November–December, 1964).
5. Clark, J., "Why UFOs Are Hostile," *Flying Saucer Review* (November–December, 1967).

The Cyrus Case

by G. Cattiau et al.

Two French cases which take their place in this collection come from the industrial northeast of the country (although Warneton, strictly speaking, is on the Belgian side of the border with France); another (Valensole) took place in the southeast; this present intriguing affair of Monsieur Cyrus was reported from another corner of the country, having taken place in the southwest. As far as can be ascertained, it seems to be independent of any major wave.

No entities were observed during the encounter which must surely be one of the closest auto encounters on record! It underlined in no uncertain fashion the attraction that vehicles, particularly automobiles, and their occupants have for UFOs, a fact further demonstrated by other reports elsewhere in this collection.

Monsieur Cattiau, together with his colleagues Messrs. R. Gayral and D. Lacenal of the Toulouse research group, carried out this investigation for the excellent French organization Lumières dans la Nuit (LDLN)* *which publishes a journal under the same name. The report appeared in issue Number 153 (March, 1976), and Gordon Creighton's translation was published in* Flying Saucer Review, *Volume 22, Number 2, March–April, 1976.*

This case occurred in August, 1975, in a country district near Muret in the Département of Haute-Garonne (Southwest France).

* For address, see Appendix.

Monsieur R. Cyrus is aged 48, a man with a sound head on his shoulders, and no nonsense about him. Formerly a gendarme, he is now in business and his mind is more likely to be on his shop than on "queer goings-on." If he considers himself to have been successful in his life so far, it is precisely because of this direct, realistic, even materialistic, side to his nature, for which, indeed, his wife takes him to task from time to time, as he laughingly confessed during our investigations. However, Monsieur Cyrus is not known in Muret simply as a reliable and responsible businessman but also as the president of the town's group of majorettes. So the witness is well known and very honorably regarded. He even went so far as to confess to us later that it wasn't the first time that he had seen this sort of "thing," that it had not worried him over-much except perhaps on this latest occasion, when he had been pretty close to the "thing."

The August, 1975, Sighting

As stated, it is August 29, 1975, and the time is 10:45 P.M. The witness, at the wheel of his car (Peugeot 404—petrol engine type) is on the departmental route D 10 which runs from the village of Longages to National Highway (Route Nationale) No. 125 to the south of Noé.

When three quarters of the way along the D 10, the witness suddenly perceives—about ten meters distant on the right-hand side of the road, in a field slightly above the level of the latter—a dark mass, an aluminum-gray colored "machine." (It was a moonlit night, and the moonlight seemed to be reflected by the "machine," giving it a metallic appearance.)

M. Cyrus estimates the object to have been about seven meters long, a bit more than that in width, and about three meters high. At this stage the body of the machine is dark, emitting no light.

Just as he arrives abreast of the machine, however, the underpart of it lights up (up to about one third of its height) with a phosphorescent glow, and it "glides" toward the car at the level of the bonnet, and then shoots forth a dazzling light which the witness describes as being as bright as the sun. Monsieur Cyrus pulls up, takes his hands off the wheel, and instinctively throws up his arms to protect his head. The car ends up in the ditch, which very fortunately is not deep at that spot (about 20 centimeters).

The whole thing has been a matter of four seconds or so. Then the "object" shoots straight up into the air directly above the car and, without the slightest sound, takes up a stationary position there. At this stage it is emitting an irregular light; gradually its intensity diminishes, and then it starts to shine more brightly again. This fluctuation happens several times. Its light is now reddish. It is to be noted that the sky was clear, the temperature mild, and a gentle southeast wind was blowing.

Meanwhile, Monsieur Cyrus does not get out of the car immediately. He seems to have a gap of half a minute or so in his memory. He remembers getting out of the car only when another motorist, who has come from the other direction, starts to open the door for him. This other motorist is a direct witness of Monsieur Cyrus's adventure, since he was only about 150 meters distant when the object swooped at Cyrus's car and poured the flood of blinding light over the bonnet. As this second motorist explained later, he thought that Cyrus's car was exploding.

So now Monsieur Cyrus gets out of the car, and the first thing he does is to touch himself, feel himself. He recalls precisely this gesture, and recalls saying, as he did it, "Good heavens—is this it!"

The fact that this is Monsieur Cyrus's first action puzzles him greatly: touching himself in fact to see whether he is still alive! But he remains in a state of severe shock, and when people urge him to go straight away to the Gendarmerie to make a statement, he says: "Look, fellows, you all know me. I'll go to the Gendarmerie tomorrow. Now, I'm going home." When he arrives there, his wife finds him distraught and manifestly in a state of shock.

Monsieur Cyrus only noticed the object when he came abreast of it. All he saw at first was a dark metallic mass (effect of the moonlight). Then the object lit up suddenly and glided toward his car at bonnet level, and as it did so, it seemed to tilt backward and display its under-face like a vast lightning flash, so that Monsieur Cyrus now thinks that when we see a fireball in the sky we are seeing its underside!

It seems, therefore, that the object deliberately made for his car and there, at a height of less than 50 centimeters from the bonnet of his Peugeot 404, tilted back sharply. Then it shot straight upward till it was no more than a point of light which seemed to keep fading and then becoming brighter again. He stood there watching it for about fifteen minutes. The light beam directed down from it still seemed to be aimed solely onto the spot where his car stood, without lighting up the rest of the countryside (as a searchlight would have done). And all the time it was emitting pulsation flashes.*

Effects on the witness:

Seeing the object right on top of his car, he abandons the wheel and instinctively throws up his arms to protect his head.

1. He no longer remembers whether he was paralyzed by it, but he does remember "that he still had all his mental faculties, but that his throat was jammed up." His voice was also "jammed up." He was unable to speak. The ability to speak only returned to him suddenly when the other motorist came up to his car door.

2. Disturbance to his watch (it has gained five minutes daily since the occurrence).

3. Increased sleepiness, even when at the wheel of his car. As soon as he stops any activity in which he is engaged during the day, he drops off to sleep in a fashion that is not habitual for him.

4. Troubles with his eyesight: two days after the UFO sighting, he woke up in the morning with black patches before his eyes. They gradually faded away and vanished after he had had his dinner.

Peugeot 404 (petrol engine). No anomaly has been noted in the car. No scratch marks, no signs of burn, or changes in the paintwork.

The engine did not stall.

The lights remained on.

No signs of overheating on the body of the car or on its interior.

(It is to be noted, incidentally, that no steps were taken to test the car for radioactivity.)

* One of the photo captions in the *LDLN* article mentions that the UFO was still visible, as a point of light, hours later, but there is no discussion of this in the text—G.C.

There were other witnesses who came forward later and confirmed the statement made by Monsieur Cyrus.

The first was Monsieur L. Gain, a night watchman at the CUMA-SICA plant, who lives at Longages, and who saw a bright glow which vanished suddenly.

Madame G. Tegedor, a lady residing on the route de Noé at Longages, says she saw the glow over in the direction of the spot where Monsieur Cyrus experienced his "happening," and then later, at about 1:00 o'clock in the early morning, she saw another intensely bright glow, close to the ground, in a field quite some distance from the scene of Monsieur Cyrus's experience, and consisting of two big lights bigger than car headlamps. The glare was blinding, and her eyes were painful next morning. The light seemed to illuminate the whole countryside around as though it were daytime.

Finally, there was also another witness—namely the motorist who came and helped Monsieur Cyrus, but apparently he is unwilling to make any statement.

Then there is the Gendarmerie at Carbonne too, but the gendarmes on this occasion showed themselves very unwilling to cooperate with our investigator.

No marks were found in the field where the UFO had presumably landed, despite the efforts of several people who went there to investigate. Aerial photos of the place were also taken, but these showed no marks.

Needless to say, we were astonished when Monsieur Cyrus all of a sudden informed us that the episode had not greatly astonished him, seeing that it was the *third time* that such a phenomenon had been good enough to manifest itself before his eyes. The details of his two previous episodes are as follows . . .

Earlier Sightings

This was in the Quillan district of the Departement of Aude, in 1957, at the time of the grape harvest. It was about 8:30 one evening, in mid-September. While the other vineyard workers are all still sitting at their dinner, Monsieur Cyrus steps outside to answer a call of nature, and sees two elongated objects (orange-colored cigars) at a distance of about 200 meters or so from him, just as though "sitting there" above the vineyard while a cart was passing below them between the rows of vines. He called to some of the other workers, who came and also saw the objects. Then they decided to approach the "objects," but when they had gone half of the way toward them the "cigars" departed silently and without changing color.

This occurred at the village of Ox, in the same region, in September or October of 1974. The witness, who was with his wife, was driving along the main national highway linking Noé to Muret. The time was about midnight, the weather was clear, and they were headed toward Muret.

They were traveling along at a moderate speed when, after passing through Martes-Tolosane, they spotted a light to their left. They paid at first little heed to it. It seemed to take the form of a series of low flashes, seemingly "vibrating," almost at ground level. After they had passed through Noé the real phenomenon started, when the flashing lights were succeeded by an enormous orange ball which lit up the whole countryside around. The fact that it did not seem to them to be moving suggests that it was in fact traveling parallel to the car, away out to the left from the road.

For a distance of eight kilometers the object continued to accompany them in this fashion. When they arrived at the village of Ox, they became aware of the extent of the phenomenon, for they saw the village church, situated some two kilometers from their road, silhouetted against the glow as though "on the screen of a Chinese shadow-theater."

By now they can see that the disc is enormous, lighting up the whole countryside. The tower of the church is thought to be about 35 meters high. The vast ball was bigger than that. Still moving along parallel to their route, it now vanished from their sight behind a service station beside the highway. The service station's lights blinked three times and then remained extinguished. Then the ball reappeared again and came back toward the church tower and passed behind it. The ball flared up brilliantly and suddenly, and then died down. The transformer situated near the church appeared to explode in one vast arc of light. Then, with the explosion in the transformer, all the lights in the village went out. Monsieur and Madam Cyrus meanwhile continued on their way to their home in Muret.

Next day, they asked the electricity authorities in Muret whether anything extraordinary had happened in Ox. (It turned out that the Ox transformer's circuit-breaker had indeed tripped for some unknown reason that night. However, the EDF—French Electricity Board—would not let us have a copy of their report on the matter.)

Remarkable as it may seem, the "ordinary extraordinary" adventures of Monsieur Cyrus were not to end there. For he, along with two other persons, was to witness a further curious phenomenon which—this time—was to puzzle him vastly.

This next episode took place in the summer of 1975, and prior to the happenings of August 29 described at the beginning of the article.

The first manifestation of the phenomena was at 11:00 P.M. on the square in Muret. Monsieur Cyrus had just sat down in his car in order to put it away in the garage for the night when, to his astonishment—since his car radio was not switched on—he hears sounds coming from it. He could not believe his ears; surely, he thinks, this beats everything! The sounds from the radio lasted about half a minute. He checked three or four times and made quite sure that the radio was definitely not switched on, and he also established positively that the voices were coming from its amplifier. (As an indication of the wave-length, he told us that he always kept his radio tuned to Radio-Andorra.)

These seemed gutteral, and do not appear to be identifiable with any known language. The pitch was flat and monocordant. Several "voices" seemed to be present, and taking part in a "discussion."

Despite the fact that it bore no resemblance to any language, Monsieur Cyrus insists on using the words "speech" and "phrase" in describing it. And he does, however, make one comparison: he has been in Africa (where he served in the Gendarmerie) and he tells us that it could conceivably by likened "to the language of apes." It had the same sort of abrupt, jarring sounds. This comparison returns several times later, and most cogently, to his mind. (It should be noted, incidentally, that he knows one foreign language, German, and so is able to cut out categorically any possibility that it can have been that.)

Once his initial astonishment had passed, he went on with his job of garaging the car, and meanwhile the incoherent conversation began again from his radio, leaving him in a state of the most utter bafflement.

Moreover, there was to be a second manifestation of this voice phenomenon. The next time, it occurred on the road to Saint-Gaudens, when he was driving to that place from Muret. His wife was with him, and they were just passing the little place known as Marquefavres. This time, it started with a noise comparable to that of a continuous, drawn-out sounding of a klaxon (like the way country bakers sound their horn in France, for example). Thinking that they were being hooted by another vehicle behind them, they looked back, but there was no sign that any other driver was doing it. Then it began again, and this time with the same voices mingling with the noise of the klaxon. They checked to see where it was coming from, and once again there was no question about it: it was definitely coming from the loudspeaker of the car radio, and with the radio well and truly switched off. The phenomenon continued for about ten minutes, until they got to the village of Cazères. And that is the end of Monsieur Cyrus's remarkable adventures!

It seems that at the moment when all this was going on, there was a burst of intensive UFO activity over the whole region around Muret and Cazères. The case of Monsieur and Madame Cyrus with the voices was no isolated phenomenon. At least two other investigations conducted in the area mention similar phenomcna happening to other persons, all quite unknown to each other.

At present we feel that a thorough investigation in the whole area is likely to show that we are by no means done with our surprises from that quarter.

So far the following cases have come to light:—*Cazères*, 1974: an object was seen, plus humanoids. *Aspet*, 1975: two women report that over a period of ten days an object was seen in the midst of a herd of cows. *Auterive*: There was a sighting in 1972.

Further reports are still arriving, and this encourages us to push on with our project for an intensive study of the whole Departement—indeed even of this whole southwestern region of France. We have just formed our group, the Toulouse Regional UFO Investigation Group (Groupement Regional de Recherches sur les OVNIs) in Toulouse. So it seems that as the reports flow in, we shall secure a clearer picture.

Points to be borne in mind in any investigation of this area include the following:

1. There is a radio transmitter at Muret.
2. There is a Herzian Wave station at Venerque.
3. There is a military installation at Venerque. All these are within a radius of thirty kilometers.

We must express our thanks to Monsieur Cyrus for his good-natured collaboration and assistance to our members in their task of investigating—not always an easy one.

Comment
by Gordon Creighton

Once more we see an interesting report with many of the "classic" features with which we are now becoming so familiar—the physical paralysis of the witness and his temporary loss of speech and shock; the overwhelming luminous phenomenon of the close approach; the EM effect and electrical disturbances (can they be so sure that the car's engine did not stall?). Highly interesting too is the resultant "sleepiness" and visual disturbance of the witness, so reminiscent of the cases of Antônio Villas Boas, Aveyrou, and others. And, last but not least, we have the zany business of sounds and voices coming from the loudspeaker of a car radio that is not even switched on (see my article "Gobbledygook," in *Flying Saucer Review,* Volume 18, Number 6 [November–December, 1972].

A South American "Wave"

by Gordon Creighton

The year 1968 produced a mass of UFO reports in South American countries at a time when Dr. Condon and his team were preparing their negative conclusions for the much-publicized U.S. Air Force-sponsored report. Such a mass of incidents is known to researchers as a "wave," and these occur at varying intervals and in varying places around the world.

As is nearly always the case, this South American wave contained a good cross-section of all that ufology has to offer the interested inquirer: UFO "flyovers," daylight observations, nocturnal observations, close-range observations, teleportations, landings, landings with occupants encountered out of their craft (see also "One Day in Mendoza"), and in one remarkable case actually in a house in Córdoba. In his opening paragraph, Mr. Creighton refers to this reported Córdoban incident as "strong meat," and as one of the "peak features" of the wave, as was also the report of the teleportation from Chascomús to Mexico. Hopefully we will be able to present these cases on some other occasion. Suffice it to say that they, and Mr. Creighton's article, from which we here present extracts, made compelling reading in Flying Saucer Review, *Volume 14, Number 5 (September–October, 1969).*

The astonishing reports from Chascomús and Córdoba—both towns in Argentina—are strong meat indeed. But they are only the "peak" features of a truly extraordinary situation now developing, which looks likely to surpass both in quantity of reports and in general weirdness, the "bumper" South American year of 1965. I give below in outline the principal reports that have recently come to *Flying Saucer Review* from its Argentine representative, Señor Oscar A. Galíndez of Córdoba, from Señor Guillermo J. Gainza Paz in Buenos Aires, from Mr. Nigel Rimes in São Paulo, from Senhor Jáder U. Pereira in Pôrto Alegre, and from Dr. Walter Buhler in Rio de Janeiro. To all these gentlemen we express our hearty thanks for the mass of newspaper reports received from them.

1. Punta Arenas, near Magellan Strait, in the far southern part of Chile, June 4, 1968. (As usual the "wave" starts in Tierra del Fuego—close to Antarctica—and moves north.)

At 9:17 P.M. on June 4, two veteran pilots of Argentine Air Lines, and many of their 18 passengers, saw a shining reddish cylinder flying at an estimated height of from 1,800 to 2,000 meters—roughly twice the height of their own aircraft. The UFO was in sight for five minutes and, on landing at the Chilean airport of Chavunco a little later, they learned that it had been seen from there and had also been photographed. In a press interview (*La Razón*, Buenos Aires, June 8) the senior pilot, Comandante Humberto Raúl Guardabassi, refused, as did his co-pilot, to budge from the view that they had seen a UFO. Guardabassi spoke of his absolute belief in the events now occurring, including the Chascomús teleportation, and concluded: "powerful interests are opposed to the divulging of the facts."

2. Buenos Aires, Argentina. *La Razón* of June 4 and the *Correio do Povo* (published in Pôrto Alegre, southern Brazil) of June 11, gave details of an extraordinary recent happening to the well-known Argentine painter and sculptor Benjamin Solari Parravicini. This gentleman claimed that some time after midnight (precise date not given) he was walking home from the theater in Buenos Aires, a copy of the program in his hand. The night was foggy, he tells us, and in view of the "fog" or "mist" mentioned in teleportation cases we should take careful note of this point. The streets hereabouts were deserted.

Arriving at the corner of Avenida Belgrano and Avenida 9 de Julio, Parravicini was suddenly confronted by what he took at first to be a madman, a fair-skinned Nordic type of man, "whose eyes were so light in color that it looked as though he were blind." This individual detained him and addressed him in an unintelligible guttural language, but his manner was "kindly and even gentle." Looking upward, on this man's instructions, Parravicini then beheld through the "fog," and at a distance of only about 50 meters, close to the tower building of the Argentine Ministry of Public Works, an extraordinary aerial ship, with no lights.

Parravicini was overcome by dizziness, and when he recovered he found himself along with three other individuals inside the machine, which was in flight. One of these people, very handsome, was questioning him in a language which was unintelligible to him and yet his mind understood, or seemed to understand, the thoughts of the alien being. In other words, as Parravicini said, it was a case of direct telepathic communication.

The alien told him not to be alarmed; they would merely take him for one trip around the earth and would then put him down again at the precise spot where they had taken him aboard. A few minutes later, Parravicini found himself observing surface features of what he recognized as Japan, and then France, and then Chile. And when he had returned, as he said, from this "dream," he found himself back on the corner of Avenida Belgrano and Avenida 9 de Julio—and there on the pavement nearby was his theater program which had fallen from his hand before the experience . . . Parravicini, for many years director of the art gallery owned by the Banco Municipal, concluded by saying that the alien beings had now contacted him several times. He said they told him that they were watching and patroling our planet to see that no catastrophe befalls it.

Commenting upon this case, in a lengthy interview in *La Razón* (June 4), Professor Alejandro Erú, a member of the faculty of humanities at the University of La Plata and secretary of the Argentine College of Parapsychology, told this paper that Parravicini's case was only one of a number of "contact" and "teleportation" cases that the college has in its files. Professor Erú mentioned specifically the cases of the Argentine businessman who was instantly teleported from Bahìa Blanca to Salta in 1959 (see my article "Teleportations" in

Flying Saucer Review, March–April, 1965)* and of the Brazilian professor, João de Freitas Guimarães (see *The Humanoids,* Latin American case 19, and *FSR* for November–December, 1957 and September–October, 1961).

3. Colón, Uruguay. According to *La Razón,* Buenos Aires, of June 15, four people at Colón near Montevideo saw two saucers fly over on the evening of June 14, traveling very fast and headed toward the east.

4. Buenos Aires, and vicinity, June 15. According to a France-Presse report in the Brazilian *Correio do Povo* (Pôrto Alegre) of June 20, the passage of a UFO near Buenos Aires recently had caused marked disturbance of the earth's magnetic field. Radios, clocks, and other domestic electrical equipment were stopped, and the needles of compasses were reversed.

Residents of the Buenos Aires suburbs of Boulogny and San Martín said that they saw a saucer land during the night of June 15–16. A railway worker named Juan Carlos Barros said that the passage of the UFO caused the roof of his house to collapse. According to eyewitness reports received by several police stations, the maneuvers of the saucer "were accompanied by a continuous noise of thunder and by a strange smell and a strange light."

5. El Choro, Bolivia, May 29, June 16, June 19. *La Nación* (Buenos Aires) of June 28 published a Reuters report of the 27th from Oruro in Bolivia. It stated that Bolivian police authorities had revealed that unidentified flying objects had recently been seen on three occasions in the vicinity of El Choro, a town in the Departmento of Oruro (some 200 kilometers south of La Paz).

The sightings were on May 29, June 16, and June 19, and all at late hours of the night, said Germán Rocha, chief of the provincial police, who was himself a witness, along with Police Major Nicéforo León. In their own particular sighting, they were amazed to behold a round object, with a most vivid blue light, which object landed and left behind it a strange and powerful odor. The surrounding grass and shrubs were burned by it.

* Reprinted in this anthology on page 18.

The report relating to June 19 said that, at a place called Cabrería, near Choro, a settler named Rómulo Velasco, aged 25, saw a bright object land and from it there emerged a strange "tall slim being" who tried to approach him, but Velasco fainted.

6. Catamarca, Argentina. According to the *Correio do Povo* (Pôrto Alegre, Brazil) of June 22, the pilot of a light airplane (his name was Jorge Scassa) was at a height of about 200 meters or so, at a place some 25 miles from Catamarca (in the Andes, northwest of Córdoba) on June 18, when he saw what he at first took to be a "gray cloud," but which he soon saw was a dish-shaped object in rapid flight. He mentioned that it was not rotating. He called the Catamarca airport, but they did not answer. He then sent out a general message, which was picked up by an aircraft of Argentine Air Lines, which in turn notified the control towers at Córdoba and Catamarca. The personnel of the tower at Córdoba later confirmed that they had lost contact with Scassa's plane.

7. *Correio do Povo* of June 22 also reported that, on the same night, i.e., June 18, an Argentine taxidriver was driving along with three passengers when suddenly the engine stopped and he was unable to restart it. Then he and the passengers noticed a strange object hanging stationary beside the road and at a small distance above the ground. Then the object rose into the sky and vanished. Various telephone calls to police during the same night mentioned an unknown object seen flying over the region. (The paper does not quote the name of the area in Argentina.)

8. Miramar. According to the same paper, a chauffeur at Miramar (450 kilometers due south of Buenos Aires, and near Mar del Plata) was cycling home one night recently when he found himself confronted by a mysterious object stationed right on the road. The chaffeur, named Oscar Vivas, aged 24, said it was elliptical in shape and very large. The upper portion of it was rotating rapidly, and the object was only about half a meter from the ground. From the lower part there came, "as though supporting it," a vivid beam of light. On receiving this report from Vivas, "a man of excel-

lent reputation who does not drink," the police went to the spot and found that the soil was scorched.

9. *Correio do Povo* of July 3 reported that at 9:40 A.M. on June 25, Senhor Edson Elop, manager of the Radional installations at Florianópolis on the island of Santa Catarina off the coast of southern Brazil, with one of his workmen, watched a UFO for 40 minutes. The object, circular and domed, arrived from the south, flying very slowly. Above the island it turned west and headed inland. Both observers, with their long experience of observing aircraft, felt that its apparent size was "comparable with that of a Boeing aircraft flying at 3,000 meters."

On June 27, again at 9:40 A.M., the two men saw two more objects, flying side by side and coming over from the east, very fast. Their color was "dull leaden." The two UFOs changed course again in precisely the same area over Santa Catarina Island, and vanished toward the north after being in sight for only four minutes.

Similar objects were again seen, at the same time on the following day, June 28, by the same two observers and by many other people.

10. Rosario and vicinity, Argentina. According to the Buenos Aires paper *La Crónica* (July 4), flying saucer reports were now daily affairs in Rosario, and the witnesses, usually serious steady sort of folk, unlikely to be avid for publicity.

At 10:45 A.M. on June 25, José Juan Racoski, an employee of the Carmal Chemical Plant at San Lorenzo, near Rosario, was leaning on a rail at the plant, above the gorge of the River Paraná, when suddenly something unknown dazzled and paralyzed him. He was found by workmates unconscious, grasping a torch in his left hand. Coming to his senses half an hour later, he shouted in terror: "I can't see a thing!" His eyes were in fact bulging and badly swollen and his skin had turned red. It took him three days to recover. Speaking of his experience, he said: "It was a flying saucer that bedazzled me. Then I lost consciousness."

Covering the case in greater detail, the Buenos Aires *La Razón* (also of July 4), mentions that the Carmal Chemical Works are situated in Bouchard, a suburb of San Lorenzo, and at a distance of 1 kilometer from National Highway No.

1. The account continues: "It was at about 10:45 A.M., when the plant's electrician Jorge Ribles noticed that the engines driving the fermentation machinery and the grinding mills were at a standstill and the whole surroundings were lit up with an intense reddish light. He checked, but could find no mechanical faults or damage in the electrical machinery.

"Another employee, José Juan Racoski, aged 52, who lives in Calle Fray Luis Beltrán and has worked at the Carmal Chemical Plant for many years, had a strange experience. He states that he was leaning on a rail checking the level of a vat, when suddenly he was enveloped in a vivid light that dazzled and paralyzed him. His strength ebbed away and he fell unconscious. Fellow workers ran to his aid and it was a while before he recovered consciousness, and when he did so, it was to find that for some time he was without the power of sight. His mates say moreover that his body turned a reddish color and his eyes were misshapen and seemed to be about to leap from their sockets.

"It was three days before Racoski could move his paralyzed left arm. He continued, however, to suffer from extreme nervousness and severe pains all over the body as though he had been badly beaten with a cudgel.

"Nobody can explain this strange affair. Racoski is considered a decent, serious fellow, not given to believing in phenomena of this sort. He is a man of vigorous build and constitution, and not a man easy to affect.

"It is reported that personnel at the Duperial Factory and at the Petroquímica Plant (situated in Bella Vista, a suburb of San Martin) as well as residents of the nearby district of Ricardone, have also seen flying saucers."

11. Santa Fé, Argentina, June 27. *La Nación* (Buenos Aires) of June 28 reported that at 6:50 A.M. on the previous day, a worker named Luis Gulicovich was engaged in loading cases on to a truck in front of his place of employment, a soft drinks plant on Calle Ayacucho in Santa Fé (north of Rosario). Looking up suddenly, he beheld an object, shaped like a silver dish and emitting flashes of red flame around its rim. It was at some distance, apparently level with the top of the local LT 3 radio transmitting tower, and was moving toward Alvear. In fear and astonishment he called his workmates and four of them also saw it. All five witnesses told the

press that they thought the object definitely far bigger than an airplane and described it as an inverted hollow silver plate, flying very slowly at first, and then accelerating and vanishing at great speed. It had a bright light that flashed intermittently.

12. Laguna Paiva, N.E. of Santa Fé, Argentina, June 23. According to the Buenos Aires *La Nación* (June 28), two young women students, Beatriz Fernández and Elda Paredes, were visiting a friend in the suburb of Villa Rosario, at Laguna Paiva, when they heard a humming noise and, looking toward the west at an elevation angle of 45 degrees, they saw a strange object flying slowly on a north-south course. It was shaped like a spinning top with a flattened base, and flashes of light were coming from the under part of it. On the upper part, which was rotating, there were beams of light directed downward toward the ground. The object was visible for about one minute before accelerating sharply and vanishing.

13. Mar del Plata, Argentina, June 28. According to *La Razón* of July 2, an eminent lawyer of Mar del Plata, his wife, herself a professor, his daughter, and various other people, all saw a UFO stationary over an open piece of terrain near their home at El Sosniego, 15 kilometers from Mar del Plata, on June 28. Arriving at the house, the lawyer, Dr. Marcelo Anibal Betnaza, found the whole family observing the object. Getting out his binoculars he saw that it was shaped "like a mushroom or a spinning top." Stationary, not far from the ground, it was emitting flashes of light that changed color constantly. From the cupola came a steady vivid green light, while from below it was emitting red and yellow flashes that were constantly changing.

After a while, the saucer began to climb, halted when observed at an angle of approximately 25 degrees, then dropped again abruptly. It also performed wobbling movements and other movements which, as the lawyer said, "would be regarded as signs of intelligent control."

Dr. Betnaza and his family had driven in their car to a point estimated to be about 1,000 meters from the "craft," and thought it prudent to observe from there without approaching more closely. His wife, professor of geography at an important local college, had seen the same type of craft behaving in the same manner the previous day, and the paper adds that a man named Raúl Frías of Miramar had recently seen precisely the same type of object too.

14. Córdoba, Argentina. According to the *Correio do Povo* (Porto Alegre, southern Brazil) for July 3, quoting an Agence France-Presse report of July 2 from Buenos Aires, some children at Córdoba recently saw two "Martians" emerge from a flying saucer.

The children aged 12, 11 and 10, respectively, said the beings came out of an egg-shaped craft, wore luminous clothing, and "were holding hands, just like two newly married people." After walking around their machine a few times, the "Martians" got in again and the craft flew away at a terrific speed.

The children told their parents. The latter believed them sufficiently to inform the police authorities, who at once launched an investigation.

15. Province of Corrientes, Argentina, June 29. The Buenos Aires daily *La Crónica* of July 4 reported that on the night of June 29, three men named Eduardo Sánchez Aguilar, Pablo Pastor Ortega, and Damián Vega were driving a car along National Highway No. 5 in the district of San Luis del Palmar in Corrientes Province (north of Buenos Aires), when they saw a circular flattened object that emitted an intensely bright orange light. At one moment the object seemed to approach dangerously close to them, so they turned out their lights. As the UFO passed near, the car was shaken by a most powerful vibration and the gears went into reverse.

16. Ricardone, suburb of Rosario, Argentina, July 1. According to the Buenos Aires daily *La Razón* of July 4, the district of Rosario and neighboring areas of Ricardone and San Lorenzo were all agog with stories of flying saucers, apparitions of weird and strange beings, "and even incomprehensible phenomena that have caused fear and commotion . . . Although no official reports have been lodged with the police, the general talk among the public indicates that in these past few days many folk have seen luminous objects flying through the skies above San Lorenzo, and have also seen extraterrestrial beings."

The paper goes on to describe how, at 4 A.M. on July 1, a

17-year-old youth named Raúl Salcedo was returning home from a dance in Ricardone when, just before reaching his home, he met two strange beings at the corner where Calle Hipólito Yrigoyen crosses Calle San Juan. The beings were almost three meters high. The youth "felt himself drawn toward them by the powerful magnetism irradiated by them, which well-nigh immobilized him."

Finally, he managed to break loose from his difficult situation and fled in terror. Just before reaching home he ran into his father and some friends at a spot two blocks farther on, but was too frightened to stop and rushed on home past them.

17. San Lorenzo, near Rosario, Argentina, July 2. According to the Buenos Aires dailies *La Crónica* and *La Razón* of July 4, a married woman named Señora Eva de Pera of 1127 Avenida San Martin, San Lorenzo, saw a flying saucer moving at moderate speed across the sky. It was emitting red flashes and flying on an inclined plane as if about to land, with an unsteady wobble. She called her husband and daughters and a neighbor. Señor Victorio Canopreso, and they all saw it.

18. Salta, Argentina. July 2. *La Crónica* (Buenos Aires) for July 4 carried a report from Salta about a strange phenomenon seen by no fewer than fifteen people in the Cófico district, near a mountain known as the "Peak of February 20." After much animated discussion, many residents of Salta had decided that it was all too farfetched to be true when they were jolted by yet another fantastic report. It seems that, at 8:15 on July 2, near the Sporting Club in Salta, a boy named Sola suddenly saw the same bright object that the others had seen, above the same peak. At the same time the boy beheld "at only a few meters distance from him, a strange being about 2:10 meters in height, hanging suspended in the air, his body emitting a strange luminosity."

This being suddenly spun round like a top, his body remaining otherwise quite motionless. Then he began to rise into the air and finally vanished above the Peak of February 20. Young Sola stood there dumbfounded, unable to believe his eyes, and then headed for the nearest police station hoping to find somebody there who would believe him.

Meanwhile fresh reports had reached the Salta police from people who said they had seen either craft or strange beings. In one case the witnesses—three of them—were themselves policemen, who had seen a UFO over the district of El Portezuelo which is on the outskirts of Salta, on the road to Tucumán. Meanwhile, the people of Salta are watching the Andean peaks more closely than ever.

19. Sierra Chica, near Olavarría, Province of Buenos Aires, Argentina, July 2. The Buenos Aires daily *La Razón* reported in its issue for July 4 one of the most fantastic cases of all. The farmer Heriberto Antonio Iriart, aged 51, runs a farm of some 72 hectares near the town of Sierra Chica.

Shortly before 11:30 A.M. on Tuesday, July 2, his 15-year-old son Oscar Heriberto Iriart was out riding his horse. When in the vicinity of a wire fence, he noticed two individuals who were making signs urging him to approach.

Oscar, a bright lad, considered intelligent and serious by his teachers, has already taken a diploma in accountancy.

Thinking the two men might be bird-hunters, he rode over to them. He found that they were more or less about his own height (1 meter 70 centimeters), with white hair, short, or very little of it, and wearing shirts or clothing of a red color. "Apart from the constant unblinking way in which they gazed fixedly at me with their deep-set eyes, they might have been just any ordinary men such as we see every day here in Sierra Chica," the boy told the press.

Apart, too, from one other odd thing. *Their legs were semi-transparent*. The boy noticed that he could see through to the grass behind them.

The following dialogue ensued:

Visitor: "You are going to know the world!"

Boy!! "Yes, of course—when I have money enough."

Visitor: "No. We will take you. We cannot take you now, as we have a big load . . ."

The men showed him a machine standing in the muddy drainage ditch between the wire fence and the road. The boy described it as elliptical in shape, with three landing legs, "one of them behind the other two," the diameter of the whole thing being about 2 meters and its height about 60 centimeters. The length of the legs was about 50 centimeters.

The machine was of a silvery color and had landed near a culvert in the ditch.

After this exchange of conversation, in what the boy thought was Spanish, since he understood them perfectly (though of course telepathy is a possible alternative), one of the two men put a hand into his clothing and extracted what appeared to be an ordinary envelope. This he handed to the boy, saying it was a message for him. He told the boy to dip it into a nearby puddle of water. Oscar, who by now had lost his initial nervousness, went to the puddle and did so, plunging the envelope and both hands into it. When he withdrew them, he found to his great astonishment that hands and envelope were entirely dry.

He now noticed that the envelope contained a message. Written in a crude hand resembling that of a small child that has not yet even commenced primary school, it read, in Spanish: "You are going to know the world. F. Saucer." *(Uste va a conocer el Mundo. P. Volador.)* The spelling was not even correct, for the final *d* was missing from the word *usted* (you).

They then climbed on to the machine, lifted the top and got in, and as soon as it was closed the machine took off vertically at great speed, with flashes of light, and almost instantaneously it was just a tiny spot in the sky and then was gone.

Feeling "as though he had been asleep," Oscar now ran over to his horse. But fear was now to begin flooding into him. For the horse was paralyzed and could not move, and so was his dog. It was some few minutes before the animals could move freely again. Then he mounted and fled in utter terror toward the house, distant no more than half a mile. Some people who saw this ride thought he must have taken leave of his senses, so wild did both rider and steed appear.

The family were profoundly disturbed by the strange bulging and disoriented condition of the boy's eyes, which looked, as one of the papers said, "as though he really were just emerging from a hypnotic state or as though he had been terrified by the vision he had seen."

Accompanied by neighbors, the family ran to the spot where Oscar said the machine had stood and there, to their great astonishment (for the envelope and the message had struck nobody as convincing) they found three holes, each some 12 centimeters deep, and forming a perfect isosceles triangle, the base side measuring 2 meters and the other two sides 1:58 meters each. So perfect were the measurements of the sides and the angles that anybody wishing to fake the story would have had quite a task with stakes and string and setsquare to get such exact results.

In the afternoon, after military personnel from the garrison at Olavarría had called to take away soil samples for analysis, the boy's father went to report to Sergeant Raúl Coronel, the police official in charge at Sierra Chica. Regarding the story as too ridiculous for words, the latter refused to take any notice or to initiate any official action—an attitude that was soon to change sharply, as we shall see.

At the Sierra Chica Social Club that evening, there was much celebration over a recent football triumph over local rivals, but inevitably the story of Oscar Iriart was soon a subject of vigorous argument too. And among the leading local personalities at the club who would not hear of flying saucers, there were, of course, our friend Sergeant Raúl Coronel of the police and a group of fellow skeptics. These were the butcher Carlos Marinángeli, his brother José Luis, an administrative official in the local convict colony. Hugo Rodríguez, a mechanic, and Walter Vaccaro.

At about 11:15 P.M. these five bold and convivial skeptics set out for the landing site, Police-Sergeant Raúl Coronel being careful to take with him a powerful electric torch. Arrived at the site, they quickly concluded that the holes were faked, and they were busily cracking snide jokes about flying saucers when suddenly butcher Marinángeli yelled in alarm: "Look out! A light is coming in our direction!"

Zigzagging very slowly toward them across the meadow, at a height of only a few meters from the ground, was this luminous something, and it was headed right for where they stood, the spot where allegedly a flying saucer had landed almost exactly 12 hours before. In panic the five bold skeptics threw themselves to the ground. As the UFO passed over them, Police-Sergeant Raúl Coronel drew his regulation revolver and was about to shoot, but the butcher Marinángeli prudently and firmly restrained him. The UFO continued its zigzagging course across the field, and then, gathering speed, it climbed straight up and was gone.

Sergeant Raúl Coronel and Butcher Marinángeli and their

friends, all of whom were convinced a few minutes before that all this talk of flying saucers "was just a load of nonsense due to seeing too many queer things on TV," were now miraculously converted into the most enthusiastic of UFO buffs. Questioned by his police superiors at Azul and by reporters, Sergeant Coronel and his friends could only murmur repeatedly: "*Sí sí Señores!* The flying saucers *do* exist!"

Sergeant Coronel was transferred, for his pains, to Azul, where his superiors gave him a wigging for having made statements to the press about UFOs without having submitted any official report on the case to them first. As *La Razón* puts it: "Sergeant Coronel's fervent affirmation, as of now, that *UFOs do exist,* constitutes a ground for some perplexity on the part of his superiors, for he has always been noted for his seriousness and his sense of responsibility."

In the meantime, the fair, blue-eyed lad Oscar Heriberto Iriart sticks to his story, and his mother, Doña Cesaria Donatti de Iriart, cries, between sobs: "He has been threatened, you understand! Those horrible men have said they will come back to get him!" The highly respected Creole family of the Iriarts pass their days in perplexity, and the whole surrounding district of Olavarría and Sierra Chica is in an uproar. Further night vigils by newspapermen and local stalwarts, supported by copious barbecues and powerful alcoholic draughts against the "night air," have failed to draw the UFO back to the spot. The police continue to investigate and to take the case seriously, although everyone is puzzled by the crudely written "message" and the perfectly ordinary terrestrial envelope and notepaper.

Oscar Iriart remains firmly convinced of the reality of his experience and will not budge from his story. Inquiries have revealed that he does not read science fiction and has never displayed the slightest interest whatsoever in anything to do with "flying saucers." He prefers tinkering with the engine of one of his father's old cars.

20. *La Razón*, Buenos Aires, for July 4 had a report that, in a press conference held in Rosario, and devoted principally to other matters, Admiral Benigno Varela, Commander-in-Chief of the Argentine navy, had referred to his service's share in the work of investigating UFOs. He explained that all the navy does is to keep a register of serious reports received. He

concluded: "The Argentine navy reported on one occasion—as did also the Chilean and British bases in Antarctica—that five lights had been seen in Antarctica, all flying in the same direction. This is a phenomenon that so far has not been explained—which does not necessarily mean that they are "flying saucers." There are many, many phenomena that up till now still remain unexplained."

21. Quilmes, Argentina, July 3. *La Crónica* (Buenos Aires) for July 4 reported that a woman claimed to have been abducted by a flying saucer. Señora Alejandra Martínez de Pascucci, of 276 Calle Alvear, Quilmes, told the representative of this paper:

"It was 11:30 last night, and I was just coming home when, reaching the corner of Calle Alvear with Calle Saavedra, I quickened my pace, as I am always afraid of passing that corner which is a big open area that has not been built up. At that precise moment, I felt some invisible force pressing down upon me, absorbing me. Seized with terror, I wanted to shout, but could not. Despite my fear, I did not lose consciousness. Suddenly, I found myself in an enclosed space in which there was nothing else except myself and two men dressed in clothing that looked metallic and that gave off a lot of light, as did their shoes and their helmets, which revealed the part where the hair begins and showed their whole faces.

"One of them, very tall, was over 2 meters. The other one was a bit shorter. They looked at me, talking together the while in an unintelligible language. The heat inside the enclosed space was unbearable. It seemed as though we were in an oven. The shorter of the two men pressed a button, and I felt the machine began to move. The machine was round and had small red and green windows. It could hold four or five people. After a while, in just the same way as I had entered it, I descended from it, it having landed very smoothly. I thought we had landed on Mars, but no! After a few moments I perceived that we were back on our planet, opposite a cemetery. A taxi came by, and he brought me home, free of charge. I'll never forget this experience!"

Comment

From all the foregoing items it should be clear that something very odd is again happening to many people in the southern part of South America. Whether all these reports are fact, or are due to some mysterious form of hypnosis (see case 19) or hallucination or brainwashing, or to some strange new mental disease or poisoning, they are deserving of our most careful attention and study. *Why, for example (see cases* 2, 16, *and* 21), *have alien beings now taken to accosting terrestrials at crossroads?* Is this perhaps why, in myth and legend, a certain aura of danger or of the macabre seems to cling to crossroads?

Note too (cases 10 and 19) the bulging, protuberant, or swollen eyes of the victims of these strange mishaps. Readers will be able to recall other cases in the literature of our subject.

Be it noted too that, in addition to the bizarre encounters at crossroads, the "trips in saucers," and so forth, the accounts of faintings and dizziness and loss of consciousness are on the increase. In a dispatch sent to *The New York Times* on July 13 by their correspondent in Buenos Aires, Malcolm W. Browne, this correspondent naturally had to try to make fun of the whole business, his piece being entitled "UFOs Add Spice to Life of Latins." But he had to admit that a great many people in Argentina and Chile are deeply worried by what is happening, and he even quoted an Argentine government official as having said: "I have no doubt that flying saucers have arrived here. I worry about what they're up to. I just can't understand why they have picked on Argentina." And Browne admitted that, since the news about the Chascomús teleportation leaked out to the press, "young women in Buenos Aires and elsewhere have been declining dinner invitations that would mean going home alone."

As regards the evidence for a northward-moving "wavefront," most readers are no doubt familiar with the theory that the aliens (extraterrestrials on this hypothesis, of course) slip into our earth's atmosphere through the "gaps" above our Poles where, as our scientists are understood to have discovered, the Van Allen radiation belts are either absent altogether or reduced in intensity. On such a hypothesis—and there seem to be strong grounds in favor of it—it is easy to perceive that the vast and remote continent of Antarctica would provide a uniquely useful staging and marshalling area for the interlopers, and also that the Antarctic "gap" in the radiation belts might be thought to be far more attractive to visitors than the corresponding "gap" over the North Pole, which leads to no such vast ice-cap overlying terra firma, and has also the disadvantage that it lies far too near to the main concentrations of the technologically advanced races of Earthlings which are principally upon the land masses of the Northern Hemisphere.

Dr. Jacques Vallée has already drawn attention to the regularity with which these "waves" build up, via South America, from Antarctica, during the months of June and July, and no doubt Australia's and New Zealand's many UFO sightings are also to be explained in this way. It now remains to be seen whether we are in for something different and spectacular—indeed crucial—this year.

A Visit to Valensole

by Aimé Michel and Charles Bowen

Strange things happened in and around a lavender field near Valensole in southeastern France during the last days of June, 1965, and again July 1, the day when the witness, Monsieur Maurice Masse, rushed in a state of shock into a local café and blabbed out his story. He later wished he'd kept quiet, for his privacy was invaded by gendarmes, police, military, hordes of newspaper, radio, and television reporters, and thousands of the curious. Flying Saucer Review *published three consecutive versions of the incident in 1965 and 1966, and then, in August, 1967 the editor went on a vacation in the French Alps, and eventually visited the famous site with his host Aimé Michel, who interviewed the eyewitness.*

Here is an account of that visit, together with a précis version of the original July 1, 1965, incident, as published in Flying Saucer Review, *Volume 14, Number 1 (January–February, 1968).*

On several mornings during June, 1965, M. Maurice Masse and his father, lavender growers of Valensole in the Basses Alpes of France, discovered with growing annoyance that someone had been picking shoots from plants in their field named l'Olivol. On the morning of July 1, 1965, at about 5:45 A.M., Maurice Masse was finishing a cigarette before commencing work on l'Olivol. He was standing near a hillock of pebbles and rakings by the end of a small vineyard alongside the field. Suddenly he heard a whistling noise and glanced round the side of the hillock expecting to see a helicopter; instead, he saw a "machine" shaped like a rugby football, the size of a Dauphine car, standing on six legs with a central pivot stuck into the ground. There were also "two boys of about eight years" near the object, bending down by a lavender plant.

Incensed, Masse approached stealthily through the vineyard and saw that the creatures were not boys at all; he broke cover and advanced toward them. When he was within five meters of them, one turned and pointed a pencil-like instrument at him. Masse was stopped in his tracks, unable to move. (Aimé Michel has suggested that he was immobilized by a form of hypnotic suggestion. If it had been muscular paralysis, Masse would have died.)

According to Masse's testimony the creatures were less than 4 feet tall, and were clad in close-fitting gray-green clothes, but without head covering. They had pumpkinlike heads, high fleshy cheeks, large eyes which slanted away, mouths without lips, and very pointed chins. They made grumbling noises from their middles. Masse will not disclose what happened during the encounter, and says that after a while they returned to their "machine." He could see them looking at him from inside while the legs whirled and retracted. With a thump from the central pivot, the machine took off to float silently away. At 20 meters it just disappeared, although traces of its passage in the direction of Manosque were found on lavender plants for 400 meters.

When he recovered mobility, a confused and frightened M. Masse rushed back to Valensole. There, the proprietor of the Café des Sports saw him and, alarmed by his appearance, questioned him. Masse blurted out part of his story; the proprietor could not contain himself, and the news quickly broke.

The tumult and the shouting had long since died when we contrived to visit the small Provençal town of Valensole. It seemed that the startling event in the lavender field which occurred on the morning of July 1, 1965, had been forgotten, until we reminded ourselves that the official reaction to the Marliens marks[1] had shown otherwise.

Back in 1965, M. Maurice Masse, the witness—or victim, if you prefer it that way—had been left shattered and dazed by his alleged experience with the humanoid occupants of the "saucer," and from the hammering he received from journalists, police, and other official investigators, researchers, and curiosity-seekers. Rumor had it that he had wearied of the case; that he wished he had never blurted out his bizarre story to the proprietor of the Café des Sports.

As far as we are concerned—and if we here sound callous, it is certainly not with deliberate intent—we can only say we are thankful he was so shocked that he was unable to control either his emotions or his tongue for those few brief moments, for we consider the Valensole Affair to be one of the most important cases in the history of the subject.[2] For the benefit of those to whom Valensole is only a name, we have recapitulated brief details of the case: these appear in an adjoining panel.

We have often wondered how M. Masse had fared since his ordeal. When, earlier this year (1967) we learned of other sighting reports from the district, a visit to Valensole was clearly indicated.

AIMÉ MICHEL. What better opportunity than August 1967, some two months and seven weeks after the original landing, when Charles Bowen and his family were visiting France for a holiday?

CHARLES BOWEN. On the morning of August 21, with Aimé Michel at the wheel, an exciting drive over breathtaking Alpine passes and through magnificent gorges, brought us quickly to Digne. There we were joined by Aimé's brother Gustave Michel, who was accompanied by his daughter Sylvane.

South of Digne, a long and sharply winding ascent took the cars up on to the great plateau of Valensole. I confess my imagination boggled when, from afar, I saw this plateau for the first time, for it looks like the base of some enormous mountain, the top of which had been removed by a scything cataclysmic blow. . . .

A.M. I suspect my friend's imagination has been nourished by too much Velikovsky. The Valensole plateau is of *alluvial* origin. It is a huge deposit of alluvium, gashed later by the valleys which form the surrounding country.

C.B. I bow to Aimé Michel's intimate knowledge of the geological origins of his beloved Alps.

This unique tableland stands fully 1,000 feet above the surrounding valleys, and beyond its periphery the Alpine ranges begin to dwindle toward the Mediterranean.

Once up on the plateau, the surface is seen to stretch away as far as the eye can see, and it is covered for the most part with millions of lavender plants which are all arranged in precise rows. The monotony of the landscape is barely broken by the occasional house or hut, a small vineyard here and there, with a few olive trees and an occasional mulberry tree. The sweet smell of lavender pervades the whole of the region.

A.M. The plateau is immense, and although we traveled quickly, there was ample time to discuss many things. In particular I talked of the sighting of an unusual object which had been seen and reported by the astronomers of the St. Michel Observatory. As we approached the village of Valensole, I was on the lookout for a gap in the mountains which we could see at intervals to the west beyond the plateau, for it is beyond these mountains that the observatory is situated. Here is the account which I told Charles.

The St. Michel Observatory Sighting

Toward the end of September, 1965, about three months after the incident at l'Olivol (the name of M. Masse's field), an astronomer friend of mine informed me of the following fact:

At about 3 A.M., local time, in the night of September 17–18, three astronomers who had just finished work stepped out of the cupola to take a breath of fresh air. The night sky was clear and they were able to identify with ease the lights—very familiar to them—of the various villages, far and near. But toward the east-southeast—in a direction that they were able to pinpoint with great precision in relation to the mountains—precisely in the direction of the peak marked 1577 meters lying to the southeast of the village of Aiguine, but much lower down, and on the exact level of the Valensole Plateau, they beheld a large stationary ovoid-shaped, orange-red light. They watched this light for 10–15 minutes without seeing any change in its position or its appearance, nor did it flicker as the flames of a fire would have done. A solid object emitting its own light would have looked no different. The three astronomers wondered what it could be, but none of them dared to suggest that they remain there until something happened and, feeling a bit uneasy, they went off to bed.

I made discreet inquiries of the Valensole Gendarmerie as to whether anything had flown over there that night or any other night before or after the night of September 17 (in case by any chance the astronomers, who had made no notes about it straight away at the time, might have been mistaken by a day or two on the date). I asked the gendarmes whether there had been any fire or nighttime conflagration, or anything similar. There had been nothing, they said, and no marks of any sort had been found or reported anywhere on the plateau.

I then spoke about this matter to a physicist friend of mine who is in charge of certain work at the laboratory which the Ecole Normale Supérieure of Paris maintains at Valensole. This friend drew my attention to the fact that this Valensole laboratory, where certain phenomena of the ionosphere are studied, possesses aerials stretching in a line for a distance of one hundred meters on top of a series of pylons, and that the tops of all these pylons are sometimes illuminated at night by lamps. Perhaps, he suggested, the astronomers might have seen all these lamps bunched together as it were by the perspective? (For the pylons run in an oblique line in relation to the direction in which the St. Michel Observatory lies.) A phone call to the laboratory sufficed to give us the assurance that the lamps on the pylons had never been turned on during the period in question.

However, in order to be able to rule out this possibility absolutely, two experiments were arranged. In the course of a good clear night, the lamps were turned on for five minutes and then turned off for five minutes, this being repeated a number of times. Then, on another night with excellent visibility, the lamps were turned on for half an hour, without break. On neither of these occasions, and even with the help of powerful binoculars, was anything glimpsed of the lamps.

These two experiments proved that the Valensole laboratory of the Ecole Normale Supérieure is invisible from the observatory, which fact it is in any case easy to establish by crossing the Valensole Plateau, from which the observatory's domes (the largest in Europe, and of a silvery-white color) are only visible along a quite narrow strip of terrain between the Volx rocks, on the right bank of the River Durance. *The field called l'Olivol is precisely in the middle of this strip.*

If astronomers with binoculars had looked in this direction on the morning of July 1, 1965, they would have had a perfect view, at a distance of 23 kilometers, of the scene of M. Masse's experience now so familiar to us, and in that case perhaps we should know a good deal more about it all.

C.B. The account of the St. Michel Observatory sighting saw us almost to the end of the long straight road beside the northern edge of the plateau. Suddenly the road dropped in a long curve, and the cars swept into a typical Provençal village. We had arrived at Valensole, and I for one was thankful to see the tree-lined main thoroughfare with its welcome shade from the blazing sunshine.

M. Gustave Michel—a retired warrant officer of police—went straight to the Gendarmerie, where he is well known. We hoped to learn where we could find M. Masse.

It was immediately apparent to me that M. Masse is both well known to the police and respected by them. There were no jokes. We had to appreciate, they said, that M. Masse was a very busy man, especially at this time of the year: we might find him at the lavender water distillery of which he is joint owner with three other farmers.

We drove on for about half a kilometer from the southern edge of the village until we came to the distillery. He was not there, but was expected to return in a few minutes, so we passed the time of day chatting to one of the other joint owners, and to some of the workmen. They entertained no doubts about the sincerity of M. Masse: we also learned one or two other interesting things before his Peugeot was seen coming down from the village.

I confess I found the conversation in the Provençal accent at times difficult to follow, so I gladly leave the account of the ensuing discussion to my friend, who also has a few things to say about his original meetings with the witness in 1965.

A.M. I had not seen M. Masse again since August 8, 1965, although many people, including some Valensole residents, had kept me informed of all he had been doing and saying. I found him again just as he was before, as regards his personality, that is to say calm and patient. But, on the other hand, I was very much struck by the complete change in his attitude toward his strange adventure. In 1965 he had appeared anxious, nervous, and on two occasions even distressed. The first time he was distressed—and I even saw his hands trembling—was when I was moving my compass to and fro near his watch, and he saw the compass needle move. "Then—what about me?" he cried. "Haven't I too been touched by anything? By a ray?"

The second occasion on which he was overcome was at the end of the interrogation by my brother and myself, over an incident which I refrained from publishing at the time but which I communicated to a few people, among them Charles Bowen and Gordon Creighton. Before going to Valensole, on August 8, 1965, I had wished to make a thorough study beforehand of the Socorro case, so I had asked friends to let me have all the data available. Among the documents received, there was a colored picture of a model reconstituted from the description given by Lonnie Zamora of the object that he had seen. When I was absolutely sure that I had obtained from M. Masse all the details that he had decided to give me, I took the photograph of the model out of my briefcase and showed it to him.

The effect produced on him was fantastic. I had the impression that, on seeing that image, M. Masse was at his last gasp, as though he had just looked upon his own death.

At first he thought that somebody had photographed *his* machine. When he learned that this one had been seen in the United States by a policeman, he seemed relieved, and said to me:

"You see then that I wasn't dreaming, and that I am not mad."

In 1965, in a more general sense, M. Masse had an air of anxiety and misgiving about his adventure. He did, it is true, affirm to us that "they were good" and that "they did not wish to do us any harm." But he was not in the least bit easy in his mind as to the possible results of the incident so far as he himself was concerned. Moreover he had been knocked off balance psychologically; the incredible experience clearly could not be fitted in with his simple peasant's way of life.

In 1967, however, we were all struck by his *serenity*, and it is noteworthy that my brother Gustave who is, in his own profession, well used to sounding out people's thoughts and feelings, should have declared that he was far more impressed by this new attitude of M. Masse than by his earlier one. The earlier attitude had been that of a peasant, honest and intelligent, it is true, but in no respect whatever any different from any other honest and intelligent peasant who had been subjected to a psychological test. Now, however, M. Masse is a man in whom there dwells a certainty, a man who no longer displays any curiosity as to what folk who have studied the question at great length, like Charles Bowen or myself, might say to him. Here is a résumé of our conversation with him. By *résumé,* I mean that a desultory conversation is diffuse, repetitious, with lots of expressions like "that's about it" and circumlocutions and so forth, all of which when put into writing can be more condensed without anything at all being lost. I have merely *condensed* what was *diffuse.*

My brother and I had started off by saying we were glad to see him again and by the usual polite remarks, including mention of this year's drought, and the lavender crop, and so on. And then I told him who Charles Bowen was.

Then I said to M. Masse: "I have always had the impression that you did not tell me everything."

"That is true," he replied. "I did not tell all. But I have already said too much. It would have been better if I had kept it all to myself."

"Yes," I said. "But all the same it is very important. Look, there are thousands of people who are seeking to know and to understand. It is necessary to help them. You must go through with it, since you have begun, and not withhold any more of it inside you."

"Yes," he replied. "It's very important, but I can't explain anything. All that I could do would be to say things that would not be understood. You have to have undergone it to understand it."

"How do you know that?" I said. "Just try."

"Monsieur," he replied. "What I have not told you, I have not told anybody, not even my wife, and nobody will make me tell it. Do not insist on it, and let us say no more about it."

As all this had been going on at his lavender distillery, he then added: "Come along if you like, I will show this gentleman [Mr. Bowen] the Olivol field."

So we got into our car and followed him.

The Landing Site

C.B. For one who was very busy, M. Masse was indeed generous to spare us so much of his time. He led the way back through the village and up on to the plateau, where we left the main road, and branched off along a dirt road. At about 1 kilometer from Valensole, we parked the cars beside a small unoccupied house at the edge of the field called l'Olivol.

The immediate impression that one gains is, as always, the vastness of the place. L'Olivol is but a tiny fraction, a tiny corner of the gigantic whole. However, I soon began to discern features that I remembered from past articles and sketches. There, for instance, was the vineyard with the *colline de cayoux*—a large pile of pebbles and other rubbish—just beyond. Frankly I was a little disappointed with the vineyard, for I had always imagined a large plantation with abundant growth through which M. Masse had silently approached his quarry. The plants in the vineyard which I saw, and that includes the few trees, would have afforded a man the size of M. Masse practically no cover. Anyone in that field would have been well aware of his approach.

Which brings me to the next point: the actual site of the landing was more than the length of a cricket pitch (22 yards—a useful standard for measurement) from the nearest point of the vineyard. I would say it is nearer 25 yards away, and if, as M. Masse claims, he got to within 5 meters of the creatures before they stopped him, then he must have covered some 15 to 20 yards in the open.

I can say this with some certainty because the actual landing site is still clear for all to see. It is a circular area of land in the midst of the precise rows of lavender plants, where nothing is growing other than a few sparse weeds. The area is about 3 yards in diameter, and around the perimeter a number of lavender plants are stunted and withered-looking. They are certainly not healthy plants like those in the rest of the field.

There are no longer any signs of the marks left by the object. M. Masse told us that he had replowed the area and replanted it: all the new plants died. The straggling weeds, so Aimé Michel tells me, are *trifolium melilotus*.

The little unoccupied house, beside which we had parked the cars, is another thing which I cannot remember being mentioned in the previous accounts. Again, the hillock of stones and soil, behind which M. Masse was smoking a cigarette beside his tractor on the fateful morning, is very much closer to the end of the vineyard than I had earlier imagined.

When one looks from the landing site toward the little house, one is facing toward the southwest. According to M. Masse, the machine took off toward the west, that is toward Manosque: in that direction there is just a small wooden hut, otherwise the ground is wide open. If the machine had been traveling very, very fast instead of disappearing, according to M. Masse—it could still have been seen going on its way, even if only for a split second or so. British readers who do not know France may not be aware that the fields in that country are rarely enclosed by hedgerows like those so familiar to us. Instead, the boundaries are marked by tracks, or low wire fences. Naturally, this adds to the sense of spaciousness. And up on the Valensole plateau one has unimpeded vision for very great distances.

While I was taking a few photographs for the record, Aimé Michel engaged in another interesting conversation with M. Masse. I had also noticed that he had been more than a little taken aback by the layout and dimensions of the field.

A.M. On arriving at the spot, and looking at the scene, I had the biggest surprise of the whole day. The vineyard was not at all as I had remembered it (or thought I remembered it). It was at least four times farther away from the landing site than I had shown it to be in the sketch with my article in *Flying Saucer Review* for November–December, 1965. It took several weeks of mulling over my notes before I found the origin of this incomprehensible mistake. Here it is and, as will be seen, it is not without importance:

In August, 1965, I had first of all paid a visit to Captain Valnet at the Digne Gendarmerie. There, I had read the report of the first investigation, and with it there was a detailed plan of the site together with photographs. Valnet had warned me that Masse, encouraged by Oliva, had admitted having got very near to the machine and to its occupants.

I made a copy of the plan of the site while I was at Digne, and then I went to Valensole where, without Masse being present, I started off by hearing Oliva's account. After which we went to the lavender distillery where, in the presence of Oliva and of my brother Gustave, Masse gave me the story as we have heard it from him. Then M. Masse's father took me to l'Olivol field, whence I returned, in the afternoon, to the distillery to put a few additional questions to M. Masse.

After I had got back to my own home, which is about three hours' traveling from Valensole, I went to bed and was ill for two days. This brief and intense illness (a high fever) puzzled me, but there are no grounds permitting us to attribute any particular significance to it. When, later on, I began to draw up my account of my investigation, I found to my annoyance that I had lost the little sketch-plan of the site which I had made in Captain Valnet's office, but finding, on reading through my notes, that my memory had not deceived me in any respect, I thought that I could make the sketch-plan again from memory. *Now, as it happens, this plan was wrong.* Why? The explanation is as follows:

M. Masse having told me, most carefully and in the greatest detail, how he had approached the machine and its occupants *across the vineyard,* I unconsciously made the deduction that he would not have been able to approach so close to them in open terrain without their being alerted, and consequently the image of a vineyard reaching to as far as a few meters from the craft had taken root in my mind *without my being aware of it.* Well now, *this implicit reasoning was correct,* as Charles and I were able to establish on the spot. It is in fact totally impossible to emerge from the vineyard and get to as far as a few meters from the landing site without being seen.

But this alters the whole deeper interpretation of the incident. If the two beings remained squatting there without moving throughout the whole of the time that it took for M. Masse to cover about fifteen meters, when they could not have failed to see him coming, *this means that the whole thing was premeditated.* This detail, of capital importance, lends fresh weight to the hypothesis that the depredations perpetrated in the Olivol field during the last few nights of June were in fact designed to arouse the curiosity and the vigilance of M. Masse.[3]

Final Conversation with M. Masse

But now let us return to 1967. At the Olivol field, we asked M. Masse to start telling his story once again. This he did, without producing anything new. Hoping to encourage him to go further, I tell him the story of Barney and Betty Hill, which he does not know. He listens to it, visibly uninterested by it, and makes this comment:

"If those people say that they were forced, it is not true."

"Why?" I asked, somewhat surprised.

"Because they don't force anybody. If those people had said *'No,'* if they had said *'I don't want to,'* *'they'* would have left them in peace."

"Why are you so sure of that?" I asked.

"Because I know."

"How do you know?"

"I have told you that I will say nothing more about what happened to me. I will die without telling anyone. Do not insist. But if I talk like this about those Americans, it is because *I know* that that is how it is."

At this point there occurred an incident which I think will interest all scholars of ufology. When I asked him if he knew "them" sufficiently well to be able to affirm categorically that "they" never forced anybody, this was his reply:

"To say that I know them, no. But there are things of which I am sure. For example, *I know when they are about.*"

"What do you mean?" I said.

"This: that on several occasions something in me has told me: 'they aren't far off,' and then I actually have either seen something in the sky, or I have learned afterward from the newspapers that something had happened. For example, during the famous night of July 17–18 last,[4] I was outdoors and was asleep. Suddenly, I was awakened by the impression that 'they' were going to show themselves, and I began to look up at the sky, and twenty minutes later I saw the thing go over. That has happened to me several times."

Very intrigued by these statements, I tried to get more details from him, but with no useful result. M. Masse takes no notes and makes no effort to remember what does not interest him. And our scientific curiosity does not interest him. The concrete details seem futile to him. What seems essential to him is the mental relationship existing between these beings and men. But in him this relationship is *felt*, rather like a religious concept.

As regards the night of July, 17–18, this (alleged) premonition would have an altogether special interest should it ultimately be established that it was indeed a Vostok. We can engage in various speculations about it, all as fascinating as they are unprovable.

C.B. M. Masse took his leave and returned to his work, and the rest of us pottered around taking photographs. Suddenly Aimé called me and pointed to the west-northwest. In the distance, far beyond the edge of the plateau, there was a range of mountains. These are not very high, being mostly of the order of 4,000–5,000 feet. At one place in the ridge there is a narrow gap, and through this, even without the aid of binoculars, we could see a few white, regularly spaced spots. These are the famed cupolas of the St. Michel Observatory. It was immediately obvious that one would not have to move very far from the field l'Olivol before one could no longer see the cupolas.

I was intrigued by the unoccupied house which can be seen in one of my photographs, and fell to wondering if this was the one connected with an account published by René Fouéré in the GEPA bulletin, *Phénomènes Spatiaux*.[5]

In this article, it was told how one of their members, a M. François Peyregne, had visited Valensole early in 1967. He described the plateau as looking like "an immense platform for interplanetary maneuvers."

By far the most interesting piece of information discovered by M. Peyregne was that at the end of January, 1967, five local people found a little man in an empty room in an old farmhouse that was being repaired. This little creature was reported to be identical with those described by M. Masse, except that he was bearded. The whole party tried to capture the little fellow, and a wild chase ensued. However, it was all in vain, "for something like an invisible force caused him to slip through their hands," and he escaped through the window. Further pursuit across the countryside proved futile.

According to M. Peyregne, the five witnesses desire no publicity whatsoever, and he added that it would not surprise him to learn that other people in the region had had their own incredible experiences but preferred to lie low.

Nobody mentioned this story either to Aimé Michel or to myself while we were visiting Valensole, and we had little time in which to pursue it further. However, there is yet another Valensole case which we feel should be recorded. We first heard about it while we were waiting for M. Masse to turn up at his distillery.

A.M. As Charles Bowen has told you, when he, Gustave, and I arrived at the distillery, M. Masse was not yet there. Five or six men were busy around the machines. We seized the opportunity to talk to them about M. Masse, who, in what they said about him, was described to us once again as a respected man whose good faith is doubted by nobody.

One of the workmen present told us that when he himself was a child he heard an old peasant couple tell how, one night, they had seen a luminous, red, egg-shaped object descend from the sky, settle quietly on the ground, remain there about a quarter of an hour, and then rise up into the sky again and vanish. The two old peasants are long since dead. The thing happened before the First World War (I believe the man said it was—or may have been—1913 . . . C.B.)

The place where it landed was right next to l'Olivol field.

NOTES

1. Rifat, A., "Was It a Landing at Marliens?" *Flying Saucer Review,* Volume 13, Number 5 (September–October, 1967).
2. Bowen, C., "A Significant Report from France," *Flying Saucer Review,* Volume 11, Number 5 (September–October, 1965). Michel, A., "The Valensole Affair"; also GEPA Investigation, "The Significant Report from France," *Flying Saucer Review,* Volume 11, Number 6 (November–December, 1965).
3. In 1967 at Valensole, the spring was cold and dry, and the summer was excessively dry. Vines, which are pruned each year, were consequently very low and thin. In 1965 they were tall and thick, and could easily hide a man (A.M.).
4. The night on which, so some people say, a Vostok satellite disintegrated in the atmosphere over western Europe, which is indeed possible, but does not perhaps explain all that happened (A.M.).
5. *Phéonomènes Spatiaux,* Number 11 (March, 1967).

Postscript
by Charles Bowen

An astronomer, a reader of *Flying Saucer Review* who frequently has occasion to work at the St. Michel Observatory (l'Observatoire de Haute Provence) subsequently photographed from the great main cupola, using a telephoto lens, the disused house at the edge of the Valensole lavender field known as l'Olivol. So here was added confirmation of the observation from St. Michel, which Aimé Michel described in the foregoing article.

More important, however, is that Aimé Michel and his friends and colleagues have "kept watch on Valensole" throughout the years, patiently waiting for news of possible follow-up sightings or of other developments. Our same astronomer friend discovered during his own visits to Valensole that, when the weeds eventually grew right over the landing site where lavender plants no longer grew, someone trimmed them and shaped them to look like lavender plants in their correct positions in the rows! Presumably this was done to conceal the actual position where the "machine" stood and probed the ground with its central pivot. As a safeguard the astronomer took a series of photographs of the field, and arrowed the exact position where the UFO was said to have stood. The photographs were published in *Flying Saucer Review*, Volume 15, Number 4, (July–August, 1969) in an article which appeared under the astronomer's pseudonym "Dr. Jacques Lemaître."

A wise precaution, for before long the vineyard was torn up and, with the field, put to the plow.

UFO over the Mooraduc Road

by Judith M. Magee

Some eyewitnesses claim to be "repeaters." There are many researchers, however, who deny that this is possible, but it may well turn out that such an assumption on their part is untenable. Many of the case histories show that eyewitnesses could be deep-trance subjects, and it may well turn out that there is a high percentage of these. If there is something "out there"—or for that matter "down here"—which exerts a subtle control, then it is possible that the chosen "contactees" could be sensitive to hypnotic control, and on a continuing basis.

It is likely that Mrs. Puddy's case falls into this category. Her case also slots very nicely into another category, as does that of Oscar Iriart, which has already come to the attention of the reader, and that of the two casino workers of Mendoza (page 131) and the Rhodesian couple (page 197). The category is that of the contactee who receives a message. It is true that although she saw the UFO she didn't see the occupants, but according to her testimony she heard them loud and clear, and in her own language. And what she heard is typical of the UFO message. So far, to the best of our knowledge, there have been no further encounters for her.

Mrs. Magee's report was published in Flying Saucer Review, *Volume 18, Number 6 (November–December 1972).*

Here is an account of the remarkable experiences of an eyewitness who falls in the category labeled "repeaters" by some researchers.* The witness is Mrs. Maurene Puddy of Rye, a holiday and residential town on the Mornington Peninsula in the Australian state of Victoria, close to both Port Phillips Bay and the Bass Strait.

It was after her second experience on Tuesday, July 25, 1972, that her story hit the news wires. Soon after her report was made public I was able to speak to her by telephone for an hour, and three weeks later she was guest speaker at a meeting of the Victorian UFO Research Society. For more than an hour she held spellbound an audience of 200, who plied her with questions until we had to rescue her with a cup of tea!

Here is an account of Mrs. Puddy's bizarre experiences, as told to the society.

The witness, aged 27, is certainly no crank, and impressed everyone with her sincerity. She has an invalid husband and two children, a boy of seven and a girl of five. The little boy suffered a bad injury to his leg in an accident at the end of June, and was in hospital at Heidelberg, to the north of Melbourne.

First Encounter: Pursuit

On the evening of July 5, 1972, Mrs. Puddy was driving home along the Mooraduc Road, between Frankston and Dromana, some 35 miles southeast of Melbourne. Her attention was drawn to a blue light which seemed to be coming from above and behind her car, a 1963 Holden. When her little boy had been injured he had been taken to hospital by the Angels of Mercy helicopter ambulance, and it occurred to her that this light might be from the helicopter, flying low. It did not occur to her at the time that had it been the helicopter flying at what was virtually zero feet she would certainly have been able to have heard it and to have seen the effects of the air disturbance which it caused. She stopped the car and got out to take a look: she wasn't prepared for what she saw!

* In his book *The UFO Experience*, Dr. J. Allen Hynek writes that the "repeater" aspect of some UFO reporters is sufficient cause, in his opinion, to exclude their reports from further consideration . . . (p. 30). There are those who will disagree with this view—EDITOR.

A huge object was hovering above and completely overlapping the road at both sides, at an altitude of just over that of two telegraph poles—and there were telegraph poles at the side of the road to enable her to make this comparison. In fact, Mrs. Puddy said that if the UFO had come straight down to land, it would have struck the poles. This made possible an estimate of the size of the object, for the road surface itself is 24 feet wide, to which one must add the width of the nature strips on either side up to the poles. Mrs. Puddy feels that the UFO was at least 100 feet in diameter. (This is a revision of an estimate of 50 feet quoted in earlier reports in the press.)

The UFO was shaped like two huge saucers, one inverted, on top of the other, with a smooth surface, no joins, welds, seams or rivets, no windows, doors, or portholes, and no wheels. And this great object was radiating a brilliant blue light all around, not in beams, but in an intense glow. There was no sign of movement, no wobbling or rotating, but there was a faint humming noise. Her eyes must have registered all these details in the time it takes for idle curiosity to turn into terror: she tumbled back into the car and drove off as fast as she could. The experience became a nightmare when she realized that the object was staying in its position above and behind the car. No matter how fast she drove, the object followed her, maintaining the same position. Then, suddenly, the nightmare passed. Aware that the blue glow was no longer with her, Mrs. Puddy barely had time to see a light streaking away in the opposite direction. The "chase" had lasted about 8 miles.

The witness reported the incident to the police, and then told members of her family about it, and a few friends. Some of them treated it as a joke, and she was subjected to the usual leg-pulling. She said nothing more about it for the best part of three weeks.

Second Encounter: "Auto-Stop" and "Messages"

On Tuesday, July 25, 1972, Maureen Puddy was driving home to Rye after visiting her son in hospital at Heidelberg when, at near enough the same time, and at almost the same place on the Mooraduc Road, she says she became aware of a blue light all around her car. "Oh, hell! Not again!" she thought, and added that, as, after her first experience she desperately wanted to get away from the thing, she bent forward determinedly and put her foot down hard on the accelerator. To her intense alarm this had no effect, for the Holden's engine cut out, and she seemed to lose control of the steering so that the car swung to the verge of the road as it slowed to a halt.

It had been a dark, clear night, yet now the car, the road and verges, and the surrounding trees and bushes, were bathed in a blue light. A terrified Mrs. Puddy sat motionless, bending forward and gripping the steering wheel. She states that she felt as if she was in a vacuum. She peered upward through the windscreen and saw part of the rim of a glowing object hanging in the air above her car.

At this point she suddenly became aware of a "voice"—not audible, but as if in her head, or mind—saying: "All your tests will be negative." Soon this was followed by: "Tell media, do not panic, we mean no harm." Then a short interval, followed by: "You now have control." At that the vacuum effect disappeared and the car engine started up.* Frightened to the verge of panic, Mrs. Puddy drove away as quickly as she could. On arrival at the police station she was still very agitated, but despite her shaky condition her description of the incident was sufficiently lucid to convince the police that something very alarming had occurred. The police informed the Royal Australian Air Force.

Discussing the "messages" she had received, Mrs. Puddy told us she couldn't imagine what was meant by "tests," for she herself had had no medical examinations or tests. As for the second message, the word "media" was not one that she would use, although she had been aware vaguely that it meant instruments of mass communication like broadcasting and newspapers. The implication of the final "message" was obvious enough to her, for from that moment she was able to take control once again of the car.

As for the delivery of the "messages," she supposed it was a kind of telepathy, although she didn't know anything about that subject. She said it was as if the messages were coming to her in a foreign tongue that translated itself into English,

* I hope Mrs. Magee can clear up a point here: did the witness mean that the car restarted of its own accord, or did she operate the starter?—EDITOR.

but of a kind that she, and people like her, would not speak. She also voiced the opinion that the UFO was not occupied by beings, but was, possibly, remotely controlled. "Computerized," she also suggested. Those were the impressions she gained from the absence of windows, portholes, or doors.

She estimated that she was stationary in, the vacuumlike condition, for about five minutes.

Mrs. Puddy told us that she telephoned the RAAF to see if they could offer an explanation as to what it was she saw. This they could not do, but she was told that there were no aircraft in the area at that time, and she was advised to remain quiet about the incident rather than chance causing panic. She declined to take this advice for, in view of the second of the messages, she decided it might be best to "tell the media." She had a strong feeling that if she didn't do this the UFO might come back, and she had no wish to see it again.

She thereupon telephoned Channel 0, where there was some interest as the film *Chariot of the Gods* was due to be shown. She was interviewed about her claims, and a segment of this was put out after the film. Her experience with Channels 7 and 9 was quite different, for they just laughed at her story. After that she did not even consider ringing any others.

Among the questions asked at our meeting were: did she think what she saw was a psychic phenomenon? and, did she suffer any burns or after-effects? To both of these the reply was, no.

On August 24, 1972, the *Australasian Post* published Mrs. Puddy's story, and reported an interview with her. In the article it was pointed out that although the Mornington Peninsula is fairly well populated, stretches of the Mooraduc Road are quite desolate, and there are few people about. Furthermore, although traffic can be considerable, after dusk, the intervals between passing cars can be as long as five or even ten minutes. As for Mrs. Puddy's estimate of five minutes in the "vacuum," readers are reminded that "five minutes" is a figure of speech often used to describe dragging time which could really be a period of much shorter duration.

Another question posed in the *Post* was that if the bright UFO was hovering for a period of time as she said it was, why wasn't it seen from a distance? To which the answer was: "It might have been. It could have been seen by people who wondered what it was without considering it important enough to bother about. If it was there very briefly—and this is a distinct possibility, accepting the idea that Mrs. Puddy's 'five minutes' was a gross over-estimate, although an honest assessment of the situation as she experienced it—there could have been others in the surrounding country who glimpsed the light in the sky and promptly forgot it when it disappeared."

Reporter Ken Collie of the *Australasian Post* then remarked that there are some interesting footnotes to this answer, and this is how he presented them:

> At about 10 o'clock on the night of July 25, which puts it at roughly three quarters of an hour after what Mrs. Puddy says happened on the Mooraduc Road, a young man came out into a street after a dental appointment at Mount Waverly, a southeastern suburb of outer Melbourne.
>
> He was Maris Ezergailis (Australian-born of Latvian parents), 21, a junior engineering executive in a business established by his father.
>
> By training, and outlook, Mr. Ezergailis is a practical man. A realist. As such, he is not in general terms susceptible to irrational happenings. To add to his feet-on-the-ground attitude to what he sees is the fact that he is a qualified air pilot licensed to fly commercially.
>
> And what *did* he see on July 25? Something that didn't quite make sense to him. A flash of blue light from the sky, and when he looked up—a meteor trail, *but an unusually broad one, traveling horizontally!*
>
> Just a streak of light and it was gone, but it left him wondering. It was the horizontal path that bothered him. Told about what Mrs. Puddy says she saw on the Mooraduc Road a short time before, he is interested, but noncommittal. And still wondering.
>
> *(Mrs. Puddy reacted strongly when told about what Mr. Ezergailis saw. "That's the way it looked when it took off the first time I saw it," she said. "A wide streak of light and then nothing.")*
>
> Then there was the experience of Mr. and Mrs. Beel, who live on Main Ridge, Rye. An unusual light in the sky, looking west from their home *(this would have placed it in the direction of the place described by*

Maureen Puddy) caught Mr. Beel's attention and intrigued him to the point of getting some binoculars and dousing the house lights.

It was too far away to identify with certainty, but there was something going on in the sky—"*Something unlike anything we'd seen before*," Mrs. Beel told us. And this on the night of July 25 at some time after nine o'clock.

But the one man Mrs. Puddy has been hoping to catch up with hadn't come forward up to the time this magazine went to press.

As she was approaching the railway crossing, where Mooraduc Road crosses the railway line to Mornington, on that Tuesday night, she saw a man with what she at first thought was a bicycle. It turned out that the man was walking, carrying a flashlight and leading a cow.

She passed him, traveling in the opposite direction, and started up the gentle slope to where the road dips before climbing again.

"Why didn't he come back to see what it was?" she asks. "He must have seen it!"

Perhaps he did; but after all, he was walking away from it and would have been a mile or so from her when Mrs. Puddy says the UFO came down over her car. Chances are he didn't see anything, or anything that caught his attention for long enough to register. Or if he reads this perhaps he'll remember and say so.

Mrs. Puddy says she won't drive along that road again at night unless she has company.

One thing emerges clearly from the whole affair:

Maureen Puddy once scoffed at the idea of flying saucers.

Now she doesn't.

Callery UFO and Occupants

by Robert A. Schmidt

To a certain extent the opening part of this encounter has a parallel to the famous Betty and Barney Hill case which happened while they were motoring from a vacation in Canada to their home in Portsmouth, New Hampshire. An object in the sky, which, at a distance, is keeping pace with the car in which this young Pennsylvania couple are traveling, arouses their interest by its pattern of behavior—much as we have seen in other cases, and quite emphatically so in the Rhodesian case elsewhere in this anthology (page 197). The eyewitnesses become curious and follow the UFO until they find it has landed, but it is at this point that any similarity with the Hills case ends, for there is another instance of strange and frightening exhibitionism which definitely rules out any contact.

Were the Callery eyewitnesses put under sensors during the preliminary maneuvers which preceded the landing? Is it possible that they were then found to be unsuitable subjects for the purpose, whatever it could be, of the controllers of the UFO? Maybe if they were *found to be unsuitable they were lucky!*

Mr. Schmidt is secretary of the UFO Research Institute of Pittsburgh, Suite 311, 508 Grant Street, Pittsburgh, Pa. 15209, and this account was published in Flying Saucer Review, *Volume 17, Number 4 (July–August, 1971).*

This account gives details of a UFO, with "occupants,"

seen near Callery, about seven miles from the scene of the Butler humanoids case[1] on April 14, 1971.

The witnesses are well known to me. They are my wife's cousin, Marion, aged 28, and her fiancé, Dennis,[2] a serious young man, a gentleman in every sense, who lives in Evans City, a small country town between Callery and Butler, and about 37 miles from Pittsburgh, the largest city in southwest Pennsylvania.

That night, when I heard of the affair, I immediately recorded their stories. We all went out to the site next day, and still shaken, they again related their accounts. These I have pieced together in a whole.

The time was 8:00 P.M. E.S.T. Dennis was driving Marion from Evans City to her home in Pittsburgh. They were traveling on a two-lane highway, typical of the unlighted roads through the farmlands of that area, and Dennis was holding the VW to the posted 35 mph limit. They had just passed the Callery Chemical Plant (where the first space fuel was made for NASA's rockets of the Vanguard series), the only plant of any size between Pittsburgh and Butler. The sky was cloudless, and, as the temperature was in the sixties, they had the windows lowered for ventilation. It was Marion who first saw the unusual sky object, through the passenger side window of the VW.

The object was traveling in the same direction as their car and at much the same speed, and it was estimated to have been about 100 yards from them. The witnesses did not feel as though they were being paced by the object, but rather it was just flying along. It was the glowing yellow-white color and low altitude that caught Marion's attention, and she thought she was watching some kind of aircraft. However, even with the window down she could hear no noise. It was obvious that Marion was excited about something outside the car, so Dennis slowed down to about 10 mph and then he too caught sight of the object.

Said Dennis: "It followed the contours of the hills off to our right, staying above them and always equidistant from them, as if using some kind of radar technique."

At no time did the witnesses experience any discomfort or any kind of mechanical or electrical problems with their car.

Dennis continued: "I pulled off and stopped the engine so

that we could listen for any sound coming from the object. It then shot away from its place above the hills, across the road at the same height (about 100 feet) and out into the sky to a point where it became like a small point of light, about the brightness of the planet Jupiter as it now appears in the night sky."

Less than a minute later the object grew in size, as it appeared to be returning to the point where it had last been in motion over the low hills.

The UFO looked like two bowls placed together at the rims, but with the upper section more pronounced than the lower one. The whole object seemed luminescent, and it was this that first attracted Marion's attention. They said it looked the size of a 1½-story bungalow. No odor, sound, or other effects were noticed.

The object then seemed to slew as it went over a larger hill to the right, and about 100 yards distant. As it did so, it appeared to drop behind the hill, and the witnesses thought it may just have continued over and past the hill, becoming lost to sight in the "dead" ground due to its low altitude.

Dennis restarted the car without any problems, and drove down the road to a junction with a dirt road. This narrow track takes off to the right and crosses the railroad tracks of the regular service route of the Pennsylvania RR which runs parallel to the road and past the Callery Chemical Plant.

Marion wasn't too keen to follow something that had just about taken her breath away, but Dennis, an adventurous type, decided to follow the track in the hope of seeing the object in the distance (he assumed it had traveled on). The dirt road twisted and turned for a quarter mile, but they soon arrived at a point where the UFO had gone over the brow of the hill, and there it was again, this time hanging, or hovering, several feet above the ground. It was about 80 yards away over the downslope of a farmer's plowed field.

Dennis drove on up the track which led to a farm house and barn. The house was in darkness, and there was only a small night light beside the barn.

"I was hoping someone would be at home so that we could get others to see this peculiar object, but not a soul was around," said Dennis.

Below the dirt road where they were now parked, the farmland was in the form of a field—freshly plowed—of about 15 to 20 acres. Beyond the plowed field there is an area of wooded land, and the UFO was hovering close up against the woods, in a sort of "cove" flanked by tall maple trees. Dennis was sure it was hovering, because he could see light between the UFO and the ground.

According to Marion the air smelled sweet and clean, much as it does after rain. (When investigating, I found that manure had been spread, but on checking with the farmer, learned that it had been scattered the day following the sighting, in other words the day of our visit. We also checked the field carefully for marks of any sort, but found nothing. This was done by daylight as the area is pitch black at night.)

"We had parked on the road nearby a couple of trees," said Dennis, "and it was while we watched the object with widening eyes that we smelled the unnatural aroma." (Later it was ascertained that there had been no rain within three days of the incident.)

The object was still glowing with a whitish yellow hue, and a mist was seen about it. Next day I attributed this mist to a small marshy area which was located some twenty yards behind the ground over which the UFO hovered, and which would provide a good deal of rising dampness in the gully where the object had settled.

Dennis estimated that the object was about 25-30 feet in diameter and, about 20 feet in height.

The time of this second, hovering sighting of the UFO was about 8:20 P.M., and the sky was not completely dark. The tree outlines could be seen silhouetted against the twilight skyline to the west, in which direction Marion and Dennis were facing. The trees near to the UFO were not illuminated by it; just the misty area immediately adjacent to the object. At this point a shaft of white light shone from the top of the object and went straight up!

"The object had several 'windows' in the upper portion," continued Dennis. "They were the shape of vertical rectangles. The bottom half had three round windows spaced equally across the 'front.' How many vertical ones there were I don't know, but I'm sure at least four. There appeared red lights from within the top windows and the bottom ones: reddish flickering lights from within like those which one sees dancing across computer screens in science fiction movies. That's my impression . . . computer flickers.

"It was Marion who first saw the figures in the windows . . . humanlike forms, two of them. Along with her I took about three seconds to get into the car and beat it out of there.

"They were large figures and, from the distance—which I think was some 80 yards—they must have been about 10 feet high. They stood silhouetted in two of the upper windows, and it was this that turned inquisitiveness into unadulterated fright. The UFO was still in the same position as we went out of sight of it down the dirt road."

Marion and Dennis returned to the site next day (April 15) together with D. Hillman and myself as investigators for the UFO Research Institute, and our observations have been inserted in the report. As I have already indicated, Marion and Dennis are well known to me, and I can confirm that they are straightforward people with respectable positions in the business world. I have no doubts at all that they saw something that alarmed them, for Marion was as white as a sheet, and still shaking, when she told me of the incident on the night of April 14. Neither of them drink or smoke. They consented to the publication of this report as, on reflection, they feel that all who are interested in the careful study of this subject would wish to know of their experience.

NOTES

1. Schmidt, Robert A., "Humanoids Seen at Butler," *Flying Saucer Review*, Volume 14, Number 5 (September–October, 1968).
2. These two young people have agreed to publication of this report on the understanding that their names are withheld. (Full names on file with *Flying Saucer Review*.)

Postscript

Since this article was received and prepared for production, the author has written to say that his wife's cousin and fiancé have agreed to the publication of their names. They are: Marion Lang and Dennis Donaldson—EDITOR.

But I Read It in a Book!

by Gordon Creighton

This article, which is included by way of a pleasant diversion, put to flight some wild speculations concerning alleged landings of "spacemen" in the distant past.

The subject of ufology is littered with such speculations about ancient astronauts and discoveries of evidence among archaeological relics and so on, which seem to point to this. Much of this, however, appears to be based on the flimsiest of evidence and suspect reasoning. This sort of thing only helps to confuse the subject, to smother it in a smokescreen.

This is not to say that all *evidence from the past, from ancient records like the* Bible, *and from the classical epics, is inadmissible; indeed, some of the theories of sky-borne intrusions may carry more than a grain of the truth in them. We must resist the temptation to interpret every depiction of a sun god as being that of an ancient astronaut complete with space helmet. Not every scratch on antediluvian rocks can be declared to be the writings of extraterrestrials among the ancients of Earth.*

In this scholarly piece, Mr. Creighton, a Fellow of the Royal Anthropological Institute and a Fellow of the Royal Geographical Society, dismisses one of these excesses. The work was published in Flying Saucer Review, *Volume 19, Number 1 (January–February, 1973).*

In two Soviet propaganda-publications[1] issued in the English language in 1967, a curious tale was reported by the popular-science writer Vyacheslav Zaitsev.[2] It was to the effect that, according to remarkable revelations made in a German publication called *Das Vegetarische Universum,* Chinese scientists exploring caves high up in the Bayan-Khara Uula (Mountains)[3] in Central Asia in 1938 had found graves with many strange skeletons, rock drawings of beings wearing round helmets, and a total of 716 mysterious 2-centimeter thick granite discs, all with a very high mineral (mainly cobalt) content and all having a central hole, as modern long-playing gramophone records do. These granite discs, so the story went, bore patterns and hieroglyphs, "incised in double-grooved spirals" which represented the "oldest language in the world." This incised script "ran out spirally to the edge of the plates."

After racking their brains for two decades in attempts to decipher the mystery writing, the Chinese scientist Tsum Um Nui[4] and four colleagues had finally been successful, but the results with which they came up were "so shattering that the Peking Academy of Prehistory banned publication." Later, however, the ban was relaxed and the story was finally published in 1963. It related how, about 12,000 years ago, a group of alien beings in a spacecraft had crash-landed on our planet and had lacked sufficient power to take off again. They had come into conflict with the local Earthlings and most of the visitors had been wiped out, though enough of them had survived to leave traces of their stock in two debased local tribes. In the rock drawings and the rows of graves containing weird skeletons the Chinese scientists had found corroboration of ancient Chinese legends that once upon a time small, ugly, big-headed, spindly-legged yellow-skinned beings had descended from the skies and, on account of their revolting appearance, had been liquidated. Even to this day, said the account, the region of the Bayan-Khara Uula was inhabited by the "*Ham*" and "*Dropa*" tribes—"*frail, stunted men, averaging four feet two inches in height*" who "*so far have defied ethnic classification.*"

Since much of my work involves the part of the world in question and seeing that the story was one in which considerable linguistic investigation might be required, involving German, Russian, Chinese, Tibetan, etc., I decided that I would put some effort into following it up to its source, and see where it led me (just as much hard work by Western explorers had to be expended in the selfsame area before the source of the famous Yellow River was finally established). My immediate reason for giving now this résumé of my findings is that a lady correspondent has just taken me to task because I am not a fervent believer in the *Hams* and *Dropas* from Space and their reverberating discs. She explains that the story *must* be true, and the reason she gives: *"Because I read it in a book!"*[5]

While I will yield place to nobody in my enthusiasm for Wang Chieh of China who, on May 11, 868 A.D. issued the oldest surviving example of the printer's art, and for his successor Johann Gutenberg of Mainz, I regret to have to point out that, most unfortunately, the existence of something in print confers no guarantee of its authenticity, and that nowhere is this warning more necessary than in the murky field of "ufology," where we have been regaled during the past quarter-century with some of the most phony, slipshod, and half-baked stuff that has ever found its way on to paper.

My inquiries started with a letter in February, 1968, to the Soviet engineer in Moscow who is my regular correspondent and who, being the unofficial secretary of the Russian group of UFO investigators, performs the function of serving as the link with some of us in the West. I asked him for any information that he could supply about this story. He replied in due course that, although the two English-language Soviet publications where I had seen it were not available to the Russian public, he had been able to ascertain that Vyacheslav Zaitsev had done no original investigation of his own and had simply taken the story as it had appeared in the German publication *Das Vegetarische Universum* (no date given) and in the German publication *UFO-Nachrichten*, Number 95 (of 1964). He also said he thought it had appeared in a "French" [sic] UFO journal described by him as "BUFOI[6]" journal Number 4, of March–April, 1965). My Soviet correspondent confirmed that, according to the original German version, the discovery of the discs had been in 1938, the finder being "the Chinese archaeologist Chi-Pu-Tei."[7]

The next step, in November, 1969, was to make inquiries in Germany about *Das Vegetarische Universum*, and in due course I was informed that it was an obscure vegetarian affair produced by a firm known as the Vegeta-Verlag (in English "Vegeta Press") of 7291 Grüntal b/Freudenstadt. So, hopefully, I wrote off to them too, saying how anxious we were to learn more about the marvelous stone discs. The date of my letter was November 21, 1969, and the result was precisely *nil*. Evidently the Vegeta Press was unwilling to divulge its secrets.

I wrote next to the Soviet Novosti News Agency's London office, and asked to be put in touch with the editor, in Moscow, of *Sputnik*. They replied that the editor was Mr. Oleg Feofanov and that his office was in the headquarters of the Novosti News Agency of Pushkin Square, Moscow.

So I wrote off to Comrade Feofanov, asking for details as to the authenticity of the wonderful tale.

Result: again *nil*.

My next letters went to the Chinese Academy of Sciences in Peking (Red China) and to the Chinese Academy of Sciences at T'ai-Pei, in T'aiwan (Free China). I also buttonholed several visiting Chinese professors and academic types, and received some more than usually astonished glances when I whispered the tale of the spindly-legged spacemen who had dropped in on China all that long time ago.

Results: *nil* again all round. No reply from either Peking or T'aiwan.

It did not look as though the story enjoyed too much credit anywhere.

Meanwhile the years were passing, and we have been favored with a fantastic spate of books by Messrs. von Däniken, Peter Kolosimo, and a shoal of imitators. According to the startling new thesis propagated by these gentlemen, virtually every prehistoric scratch nicked on a rock by our shaggy ancestors or by African or South American primitives, and every portrayal of a big-headed monster, demon, or tribal deity, is in reality a representation of one of our elder brethren from the cosmos, a "spaceman." Likewise, it now turns out that wellnigh every hitherto unexplained mystery, be it archaeological, palaeontological, anthropological, theological, geographical, topographical, or toponymical, simply *has to be* connected with "outer space" and "flying saucers." So, "flying saucers" are at the bottom of the Baalbek Temple of Jupiter; the Great Pyramid; the Piri Re'is map; the Nazca desert images in Peru; Stonehenge; Atlantis; the Old Straight Track, and so on. It looks as though "they" have been responsible for pretty well everything except perhaps Coventry Cathedral and the Pentagon. The agencies at work everywhere—the whole lot of them, Uncle Tom Cobley & All, have been "spacemen." And the only fools have been you and I, who failed to perceive these self-evident truths.

One can imagine no doctrine more likely to bring down upon us the scorn and wrath of all honest investigators in the fields of archaeology and anthropology, and more calculated to put paid for ever to any claim by the "ufological" fraternity that the archaeologists and anthropologists should take them and their crackpot theories seriously.

One of the most enthusiastic propagators of the New Evangelium is of course Herr von Däniken, who tells us in one of his books that in May, 1968, he went to Moscow specially to hear all about the stone discs and the *Hams* and *Dropas* from another Russian popular-science and space-science writer, Aleksandr Kazantsev.[8]

Kazantsev told von Däniken that the plates and all the documentation about the whole story were "preserved in the Peking Academy and the historical archives of Taipeh in Formosa." (Vyacheslav Zaitsev, in his original article, had said, however, that the discs "had been sent to Moscow for study.")

It seems improbable that Comrade Kazantsev knows any more about the matter than does his colleague Zaitsev.

Let us now return to our granite discs and, since we can find nobody anywhere who will vouch for them or show us a photograph or drawing of one of them or of one of the famous spacemen's skeletons, let us examine some of the features of this well-loved, well-parroted tale.

According to Vyacheslav Zaitsev, there was even in existence an age-old Chinese legend[9] to the effect that, thousands of years ago, a horde of "small, gaunt, yellow-faced men came down from the clouds." The locals (presumably the ancestors of the Chinese or of the Tibetans or of the Mongols in the area) took a dislike to the ugly gentry with their huge heads and thin, weak bodies and spindly legs, and there was soon conflict. Evidently the struggle did not end in the total liquidation of the aliens, for, while the graves in the Bayan-Khara Uula contain their skeletons, Zaitsev goes on to tell us that the present inhabitants of precisely that very area of China, who are known as the *Ham* and *Dropa* peoples, evidently contain much of the alien blood still, for they are "*frail, stunted men, averaging four feet, two inches in height,"* who *"so far have defied ethnic classification."*

Well, of course, it is undeniably a humdinger of a story, and how lovely it would be if it were true. Because my own work involves this precise area of Central Asia, I have, most of the time, on my desk in the House of the Royal Geographical Society in London, the maps showing the journeys of all the foreign travelers (including Russians) who have ever been in any part of Tibet or Ch'ing-Hai in general or near the Bayan-Khara Uula in particular, and I am familiar with, and have read, the official accounts of most of them. Not one of them, and not a single Chinese writer of whom I have heard, has a word about any "small, stunted, big-headed, spindly-legged" race or people or tribe known as either *Hams* or *Dropas* and who "defy ethnic classification."

The sad facts of the matter are rather more prosaic and here they are . . .

Let us take first the word *Ham.* This is obviously a garbled rendering of a perfectly ordinary Tibetan word which the Tibetans write *Khams*[10] and pronounce *Kham. And this word is in fact nothing more than the normal, indeed the only, Tibetan name for the eastern portion of their country. So everybody* living there is a *Khams-Pa* (pronounced *Khamba*), meaning "a man of Khams."

The Bayan-Khara Uula (Mountains) lie in what is today the Chinese province of Ch'ing-Hai, or, if one prefers its Mongolian name, Kokonor. Both names mean "blue lake" and derive from a large lake there. The population of the area in past centuries included a few Chinese (it is today being flooded with them), and sparse tribes of Tibetans and Mongols. The region is not nowadays counted as part of Khams or of Tibet at all, since Tibetan influence is now in retreat there. But the region does lie on the immediate northern side of Khams, and in past times was usually considered by the Tibetans to be part of their country. The whole area is a melting-pot of Chinese, Mongols, and Tibetans, plus a few tiny minority peoples like the Muslim Salars. Since the region adjoins Khams on the north, it is not surprising that many of the ordinary Tibetans found today in Ch'ing-Hai are identical with those of Khams. They are all *Khams-Pas (Khambas).*

Then what about the *Ham* and *Dropa* runts, frail, stunted

creatures averaging four feet two inches in height, who so far have defied ethnic classification? (To quote Zaitsev.)

The people of eastern Tibet, Khams, far from being miserable spindly-legged little folk, are great strapping robust fellows, who make marvelous soldiers. They have long been dreaded by all their neighbors, Chinese, Mongols, and western Tibetans alike, for their martial prowess, particularly displayed as marauding bandits, robbers, and highwaymen lying in ambush on the mountain passes. In the great lamaseries around Hla-Sa, vast beehives where hordes of monks had to be ruled with a rod of iron, none were more turbulent than the men of Khams, the *Khambas.* None more loyal either to the Dalai Lama and to his theocratic government in Hla-Sa, and it is therefore not surprising that, when the moment came for His Holiness to escape into India after the rape and pillage of his country by the Chinese Communists, the bodyguard chosen to ride with him on circuitous and dangerous mountain paths through southeastern Tibet were also some of the barrel-chested men of Khams.

There remain now the *Dropas.* "Well, at least *they* must have been spacemen!" someone will perhaps hopefully argue.

I am sorry to have to be a wet blanket again, or to disappoint anybody, but, once more, the sad fact is that, just as the word *Ham* or *Kham* does not signify any species or tribe or *kind* of men but simply a whole vast area of Central Asia, so the Tibetan word *Dropa* (correctly rendered into English under the Gould-Richardson system of transliteration for Tibetan as *Drok-Pa*)[11] means simply *an inhabitant of the high pasture lands or high solitudes of Tibet. In other words, what we might call, in Scotland, a "highland herdsman," or a crofter.* The primary meaning of the word is *solitude.*

Again, should anyone suffer from the misapprehension that perhaps these *Drok-Pas* may be more promising candidates than the *Khambas* for the description of "stunted," "frail," "spindly-legged" and so on, I hasten to add that not one of the European travelers (often terrified) who have encountered these upland nomads, in their black tents, guarded by their fierce and positively gigantic mastiffs, has ever described them, so far as I know, in such terms. They are in fact, like their southeastern neighbors the *Khambas,* some of the most impressive and robust-looking ruffians and robbers on our planet.

I hope it may now be clear that a *Khams-Pa* (pronounced *Khamba)* is a man of eastern Tibet, and a *Drok-Pa* or *Dok-Pa* is a Tibetan Highlander, that is to say a person from the even higher region of northern Tibet which is known as the *Chang-Thang* (written *Byang-Thang*),[12] meaning the "northern expanse." Neither term has, or has ever had, any sort of "tribal" or alien or exotic meaning, and certainly no "spaceman" meaning!

All Khambas and Drokpas are Tibetans, pure and simple. To say that they are two exotic, different species is like saying that Yorkshiremen or Scottish crofters are not British but are "spacemen."

It looks, alas, as though our spindly-legged *Ham* and *Dropa* "spacemen" of the Bayan-Khara Uula are beginning to recede into the murky realms of speculation and fantasy where they were no doubt begotten. It has been undeniably most enjoyable to hear all about them and their cobalt discs inscribed in a language from out of this world, and I have no doubt that their saga will go on being repeated parrot-fashion, without checking, and without the least comprehension, by "ufologist" after "ufologist" for many years to come, and will feature in book after book. *The Condon Report* (Section V, Chapter 1) poked fun at this weakness of the UFO buffery, and the criticism was well merited.

I am gratified that, at any rate until today, the *Hams* and the *Dropas* do not seem to have got into the pages of *Flying Saucer Review,* and I can only express the fervent hope that the present article will suffice for them.

If, of course, somebody *(and somebody a little nearer to China than a Black Forest vegetarian journal)* can come up with any *real information*—and any photographs—relating to caves high up in the Bayan-Khara Uula containing evidence that Central Asia received a visitation from elsewhere 12,000 years ago, *FSR* will be very glad to print it. Meanwhile, I hope I have given some idea of how a nice story can get around.

NOTES

1. *Soviet Weekly,* London, February 11, 1967, and *Sputnik,* No. 1, 1967, London. The first-named is still being issued by the Soviet embassy. The second, an ambitious and interesting

glossy competitor for the capitalistic *Reader's Digest,* seems to to have petered out after a few numbers. During its brief existence, it had several good factual articles on the UFO problem. Did it fall foul of the authorities on this account? Soviet suppression of discussion of UFOs coincided with the Condon kiss-of-death. The timing cannot have been a matter of chance.

2. By June, 1969, poor Vyacheslav Zaitsev was in the dog house good and proper with the Red authorities for having suggested that Jesus Christ and His disciples were "cosmonauts" and "spacemen," and that the Star of Bethlehem was a "spaceship." Jesus, he said, was the representative of "a higher civilization from another planet." Zaitsev's ideas were disseminated in a series of articles (I hope to find time one day to translate them for *FSR*) and in letters. This was during the years 1967 and 1968. Such ideas were naturally found to be dangerously close to the hated doctrines of Christianity, and the series of articles about the bringer of salvation from Space was terminated most summarily, halfway through, and without a word of explanation. Since then, Russia has experienced a powerful swing back to Stalinism and atheism, an intensified suppression of all religions, *and, among other things, a total blackout on the subject of UFOs which, as stated above, was timed to coincide with the Condon liquidation of the subject in the U.S.A. There is far, far more in this than meets the eye, as the saying goes.*
3. At Lat. 34°.00 N., Long. 98°.00 E. The name is Mongolian, meaning "the good black mountains," and more correctly rendered into English as *Bayan Har Uula.* The Chinese name is *Ba-Yen K'a-La Shan.*
4. As it stands, this name is corrupt and quite unidentifiable. Neither *Tsum, Um,* nor *Nui* are monosyllables used in the transliteration of standard Chinese (Mandarin) of Peking, though they might perhaps be understandable in one of the more outlandish minor dialects.
5. For the benefit of the critic who will perhaps point out that the same doubt can be cast upon anything that we publish in *FSR, I aim to show that at least we try!* My investigation of this story has gone on for five years.
6. Not identified. (It is *not* BUFORA journal for March–April 1965.)
7. As it stands, this name is also corrupt and unidentifiable. *Tei* is not one of the standard Chinese monosyllables.
8. Herr von Däniken gives the name, incorrectly, as *Kassanzev.*
9. Chinese literature is vast, and to comb the whole of it for possible UFO-inspired material will be a mind-boggling job if anyone ever tries it, which I greatly doubt. I have managed to to turn up (and one of these days will offer for publication in *FSR*) a few interesting old Chinese accounts that do seem to

refer to real experiences and involve alleged meetings or fights with some decidedly odd creatures that sound rather familiar and could possibly be our old friends the Humanoids. But I have not, so far, come across any Chinese legend about creatures landing from another world or descending from the skies in a "spaceship."

10. A Chinese name formerly in use for the same region, eastern Tibet, was *Hsi-K'ang*.
11. In Tibetan written *Hbrog-Pa*. There is no such thing yet in Tibet as a standardized national pronunciation, and this word is pronounced variously as "Drok-Pa," or "Dok-Pa," or "Do'-Pa."
12. In Tibetan written *Byang-Thang*. The Tibetan written language is full of irregular or "lazy," silent letters, *Hbrog-Pa* and *Byang-Thang* are good examples. Likewise, the Tibetan word for "English" is pronounced simply as *"In,"* but it is actually written *Dbyin*, so that it has two pronounced letters and *three* silent ones! I give these examples, so that it may be understood how *"Hbrog-Pa"* is read *"Dropa"* or *"Drok-Pa."*

Close Encounter of the Third Kind in Italy

by Renzo Cabassi

By their own admission, the eyewitnesses in this account had enjoyed a convivial evening—and how the detractors do love to produce that hoary old veteran of an explanation that the witnesses only "saw things" because they'd had one too many. To have seen the sort of thing that Signor Bellingeri and his wife saw—and if the drinks were responsible for them seeing what they saw—then they must have had far more than was good for them. Which, of course, doesn't make sense, for it is quite clear that they drove home quickly and carefully, and that they conversed happily en route. Furthermore, they were able to give objective accounts of their experience, which included a view of strangely garbed occupants.

This case is particularly interesting in view of the fact that it took place at the end of the big European UFO-wave of 1973–1974 and in the same area as the Caselle Airport radar-visual UFO event which had such a prominent part in the earlier days of the wave, and which had important repercussions. The Caselle incident took place on November 30, 1973 when a Piper Navajo descending toward the runway received a warning from ground control that there was an unknown object hovering some 400 meters above the runway. The pilot of the Navajo decided to have a closer look at the object, and as he approached, he saw it make off, shining brightly and emitting changing colors, and following an erratic course including "fantastic lateral deviations, and sud-

den vast jumps to and fro . . ." The Piper pilot gave up the chase as the UFO zoomed off toward Genova at some 900 kilometers per hour. There were other witnesses, professional pilots skippering two Alitalia DC9 jets, one on its way to Rome, the other coming in from Paris. At the same time the commandant of the Caselle military airfield saw the object and tracked it on the radar.

It was news of this incident that prompted Jean-Claude Bourret to launch his 39-program series on UFOs over French radio early in 1974, in which the broadcast interview on February 21 with the French Minister of Defense, M. Robert Galley, was the highlight. M. Galley had also been impressed by the report from Caselle.

On April 20, 1974, four days after the event, the Santa Maria del Tempio case was investigated by Signor Cabassi and colleagues of the Comitato Nazionale Independente per lo Studio dei Fenomeni Aerei Anomali (CNIFAA). The report published in* Flying Saucer Review, *Volume 22, Number 5 (1976 series) was prepared from a translation by Francisco Izzo of CNIFAA.*

On the night of April 15–16, 1974 Carla and Mauro Bellingeri, husband and wife, each aged 26, were driving home after a happy evening spent in the nearby village Cascina dei Rossi where there had been a festival in homage to the local patron saint. It had been a very pleasant evening in every sense; folk had eaten, drunk (normally), and danced.

It was 0:50 hours (local time) and therefore April 16 when, about 400 meters from his home in the village of Santa Maria del Tempio (strada Frassineto 15/A), Mauro Bellingeri checked his watch; it had been only three or four minutes since they left Cascina dei Rossi and, in a minute or so, they should reach their house.

The Bellingeris were talking of this and that when Mauro's attention was drawn to a bright object moving through the sky to the left. "Look at that!" he said to Carla.

The "thing" was high in the sky and possessed of such an unusual motion that it forced itself upon their attention, so

* For address, see Appendix.

much so that Mauro found it difficult to concentrate on the road in front of him, especially when the object lost height in a rapid dive, seemingly vertically, to stop, without wavering, some 12–13 meters directly above their house.

Mauro ran the car straight into the entrance gate and drew up in the little square in front of their house. He got out to open up the garage door, while Carla remained seated in the car. Mauro next returned to the car and Carla got out to join him; together they watched the strange object, Carla standing at the right and her husband to the left, respectively, of the car. As will be seen from the report they made after the event, their attention was entirely concentrated on that very prominent part of the object which they described as the "cockpit," a feature that was bright, but not particularly so.

The object hung motionless in the air as they stared at it, at approximately 12–13 meters above the ground, soundless . . . It consisted of two clear-cut portions: the first a sort of dome (the Bellingeris' "cockpit"), bright inside and completely transparent, roughly hemispherical in shape (see Figure 1); the second, a diametrical disc-shaped ring surrounding the "cockpit" at its base. The ring did not seem to be in one part with the "cockpit." Indeed it appeared detached from it, and carried lights like "electric bulbs" of red, yellow, and green which rotated clockwise and slowly in a horizontal plane (one circuit, it seems, in every 20 seconds). The colored lights were arranged in alternate groupings, red—yellow—green—red—yellow—green, and so on, and Mauro, who has a good knowledge of electrical lighting, describes them as being anomalous, but he cannot specify if

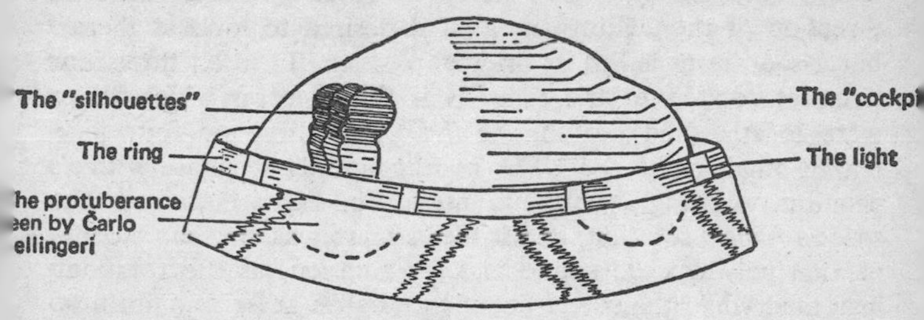

FIGURE 1: Diagramatic sketch of the object based on a drawing by the witnesses with additional details supplied by them.

they were either part of the ring, or sources of light on which the ring (by way of a screen) was sliding. To him those lights recalled, both in power and effect, the strobe lights of police vehicles, giving the illusion of intermittence while in realty they revolve.

Under the ring Carla said she could see two "protuberances" just beneath the "cockpit," but Mauro could neither confirm nor deny this.

The UFO reflected the light of some flood-lamps switched on at night in the nearby Torno building yard, which faces Bellingeri's house. On that holiday evening such illumination was more powerful than on other evenings, and it lit up the Bellingeri house too. Indeed it was Carla's personal view that this illumination could have attracted the object.

The Bellingeris stated that they could see three seemingly human shapes (they called them "people" in the "cockpit") arranged in a horizontal row in what was assumed to be the front of the dome. A highly shaded zone surrounded the three darker silhouettes which seemed to make slight movements. The outermost [*not clear what is meant by that*—C.B.] silhouette, which seemed similar to the other two, was nearest to the witnesses. Accordingly it was very useful for a general description of the morphology of all three entities.

The entities appeared to have big grayish round helmets, completely opaque and, near the base (that is, at the point where one would expect the head to end, and the shoulders to begin) and corresponding with the presumed front of the head, there was a protuberance similar to a sort of valve with a nozzle such as that used by frogmen (see Figure 2).

Suddenly the outermost silhouette rotated its head in the direction of the Bellingeris, as if it desired to look at them, but it soon returned to its original position. Then all three silhouettes rotated to the right as if the base on which they were located had turned. At this point three or four jets blazed out beneath the UFO, and apparently in phase with a peculiar pulsating, "whizzing" noise. The lights increased the speed of their rotation, and it seems there was also some connection between the sound and the rotation, as the rotation increased when the sound commenced. The noise was not unlike that made by a whirling sling; a kind of "sound pulsation."

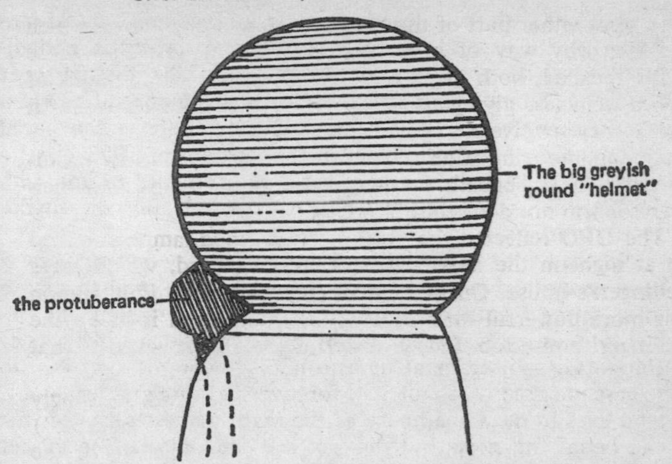

FIGURE 2: The general form of one of the entities observed by Carla and Mauro Bellingeri. Besides the big, grayish round helmet, we see a sort of exhaling device as employed by frogmen, appearing as a protuberance near the base of the head.

Finally the object departed at the same altitude in a northeasterly direction, with the "cockpit" lightly rotating "rightward" [*presumably anti-clockwise?*—C.B.] As it went, the UFO passed low over the pebbly shore of the River Po, going in the direction of Valenza-Milan (Lombardy).

As the UFO began to depart, namely when the jets blazed and the strange sound was heard, Carla ran in a panic into the house, while Mauro remained where he was. He recalls: "I was forced to remain near the car by a great rush of air."

Mauro Bellingeri is an industrialist in a small way, in association with four other people in the SILCAM industry s.a.s., packing in wood. With an average education, he is polite, well bred, and rather shy. Before associating with SILCAM he worked as an electrician. He has no eyesight defects, or defects in his other sensory organs, and he seems to be a well-balanced individual. Carla Bellingeri, housewife, is the same age (26) as her husband, and is of similar character. Her maiden name was Fare. She seems to have been the most frightened witness of the close encounter, and she passed a sleepless and troubled night after the event.

The scene of the alleged event is in Piedmont, 51 kilometers from Alessandria. It is a rather prosperous agricultural-industrial zone. Casale Monferrato, the district near which lies Santa Maria del Tempio, is an important garrison area. About 30 kilometers from Casale there is the aerial command on Mortara which, in the autumn of 1973 was involved in a radar-UFO/radar-case. Mortara lies in line with the direction of the UFO when it departed after the Bellingeris' observation.

According to information reported in the newspapers *Il Monferrato* and *La Stampa* of April 20, 1974, and thanks to information I gathered during my field investigation, the object in question was seen also by other individuals like Signor Enrico Giaroli, an amateur astronomer, who did not want to release statements about it. Moreover, Mauro's sister-in-law, who lives in the same house as the main witnesses, stated that she heard the noise but did not see the object. One of her sons, a child of three, looked out of the window at about 10:00 P.M. (April 15) and immediately drew back in, shouting: "The ogre, the ogre!"

Of course, when the story of the Bellingeri sighting had been publicized in the press, many people stated they had seen something, but the reliability of these individuals was not probed.

The Bellingeris have not experienced any remarkable physiological or psychological effects, other than understandable excitement before going to bed on the night of the incident. Carla had been scared by, and experienced a persistence of, the high-pitched noise emitted by the object on its departure but, on the other hand, she was not frightened by the unusual sight itself.

One of their dogs, normally very sensitive to the passing of jet aircraft, evinced no symptoms of nervousness during the sighting.

It is difficult to state clearly the duration of the incident. Signor Bellingeri spoke during the interview of about two or three minutes in all.

A screening with the Geiger-Muller counter revealed no anomalous radioactivity, (1) on the ground in front of the house; (2) on the Bellingeris' car; (3) on the trees and the grass of the square [*front garden*—C.B.]; (4) on the clothes worn by both witnesses that evening. Two or three days after the event Mauro saw a number of spots and small bubbles on his car which he hadn't noticed at first. I suspect that these—especially those visible on the windscreen and the side windows—to be due to splashes of mud and so on, dried out under the hot sun.

Mauro Bellingeri's opinion about their strange experience is as follows: "I cannot pretend to understand it. It was certainly a 'disc' but I don't know who might have made it. If I had known more about this subject (UFOs), I would have gone into my house to fetch my camera. As it happened, however, I preferred to remain out there."

Said Carla: "I don't know what to say. There is a lot of talk about it in the village, but I don't know what to think." Under pressure from his colleagues in the firm, Signor Bellingeri informed the press. Now he says: "If I had known previously about the resultant bother and harassment (inquisitive persons, ridicule, and so on) I would certainly have kept quiet."

My experience as an investigator is that the witnesses were very polite and concise in the telling of their unusual experience. They have not over-dramatized it in any way, particularly where they might have overdone the sensational aspect, for example, of the UFO's departure. Not surprisingly they give some importance to their experience, but that importance seemingly has no ulterior or personal motive. Instead there is only the wish to make the experience useful to others in the hope that the enigma of their observation may be clarified; note, for example, Mauro's statement ". . . but I don't know who might have made it."

My feeling as field investigator was much as that expressed by Dr. J.A. Hynek in his book *The UFO Experience* (Chicago: Regnery, 1972, see page 15): ". . . I realized at length that the reporters were telling because they wanted me to *explain* their experience to them."

To close, I have to emphasize that for ten days after the Bellingeri sighting there were other sightings in the same area, but less interesting than the first. As a result of these, according to an agency dispatch: "An investigation to ascertain, if possible, the nature of some of the unidentified flying objects sighted in the last few days in the suburbs of the town (Casale Monferrato) has been undertaken on behalf of the Carabinieri [*an Italian military corps*—C.B.] with the assistance of skilled personnel."

The Vilvorde Humanoid

by Jean-Luc Vertongen

Whenever humanoid creatures or entities are reported it seems they have usually displayed some very odd tricks. None more odd than the little game revealed in this delightful account which, like all the others of its kind, gives one cause to stop and think. *What* are *the controllers (for surely these unidentified flying objects must be controlled) and the occupants,* if they are not controllers, *up to? Quite recently, for example, we have had an account of FSR of "occupants" parading mechanically around a landed craft which was described as looking like an Italian coffee pot. In their hands the entities held "fishing rods"! Elsewhere they've been observed collecting stones, soil, and manure, and they've been caught picking shoots off plants, which are relatively reasonable occupations. Elsewhere the absurdities abound.*

This Belgian report was researched and investigated by Monsieur Vertongen for SOBEPS (Société Belge d'Etude des Phenomenes Spatiaux) and was reported in their journal Inforespace, *Number 18.* The translation, by Gordon Creighton, was published in* Flying Saucer Review, *Volume 20, Number 6, November–December, 1974.)*

This Belgian case, which has been very thoroughly investigated, occurred at Vilvorde, an industrial town in Flanders, some 12 kilometers to the north-northeast of Brussels.

The eyewitness made the sighting from the ground floor of

* For address, see Appendix.

his home, a modest house facing on to the street and surrounded by dividing walls. Behind the house lies a small garden measuring about 72 square meters and with three, high, whitewashed walls. Beyond the back wall there is a large property owned by a convent of the Ursuline Sisters. The witness has asked that his identity be kept confidential.

The sighting was in mid-December of 1973 and has been under thorough investigation by SOBEPS since that date. The happening came only a few days after an interesting near-landing case at Boondael already reported in *Inforespace*, Number 14 (pp. 43–46).[1] The weather was very cold at the time, though there was no longer any snow, and a strong wind was blowing over the region.

The witness, Monsieur "V.M." was aged 28 at the time. He and his wife were in bed and asleep. At 2:00 A.M. he arose to go to the toilet, which is in a small outer yard adjoining the kitchen. In order not to disturb his wife he made his way in the dark, using a hand-torch. Reaching the kitchen, he heard, coming from the outside, a sound like that of a shovel striking the ground, and filtering in through the gap at the left-hand side of the kitchen window curtain, he perceived a greenish light. He compares it with the diffused glow of an aquarium light. Knowing that his garden would normally be plunged in total darkness at such an hour, and puzzled by the noise, he went to the window and parted the curtain, to behold an astonishing sight. At the other end of the little garden there was a small being about 1 meter 10 centimeters in height and wearing a shining one-piece suit emitting a greenish luminosity. The entity's back was toward him in three-quarter profile. He was of medium build, and his head, arms, and legs normal in appearance. His green uniform was very bright and sparkling and the witness compared it with the material of the upholstery of certain "buggy" types of cars (polyester tinged with metallic particles). The entity's head was protected by a transparent globular helmet, and from the rear of it a tube led down to join a sort of rectangular "haversack" on his back. The "haversack" covered his back roughly from the waist upward to the level of the shoulderblades—should indeed a humanoid possess such things as shoulderblades. All this apparatus was of exactly the same appearance as the rest of the uniform.

The clothing appeared to be entirely without stitching, with

FIGURE 3: The "Detector."

no buttons, no fasteners, or pockets. The witness noticed a belt, and when the entity moved about, he was able to see that, on his abdomen, at waist level, he had a small bright red "square box," luminous and sparkling. The belt was about 3–4 centimeters wide and the small "box" was about 8 meters long and some 3 or 4 centimeters wide (we must emphasize that these measurements are very approximate). The box emitted a red light of constant intensity. The entity's trousers, the lower parts of which were slightly baggy, were thrust into small, close-fitting boots which had the same appearance as the rest of the uniform. No detailed features of the entity were visible. His hands were of the same shape as ours, but with smaller proportions. They were gloved and the sleeves of his suit were tight-fitting at the wrists and, like the bottoms of the trousers, slightly puffed out. Seen from the rear, the head looked round and black, and V.M. thought the entity must have short hair. A luminous halo surrounded him from head to foot, and also partly illuminated the ground and the wall on his left. No sound was emitted by the entity and the witness could detect no respiratory movement in him.

In his hands he was holding an instrument closely resembling a vacuum cleaner, or a mine detector, which he was slowly passing to and fro over a heap of brick-bats that the witness had gathered together at the bottom of the garden a few days previously. The instrument had a long shaft bent at one end to form a handle, with a small rectangular box below the handle. The "detector"' itself consisted of a thick rectangular plate with the frontal edge leveled. The other side, to the rear, consisted of a cylinder with about the same diameter

FIGURE 4: Sketch of the humanoid by the witness.

as the thickness of the plate. The shaft was connected to the instrument between these two areas. In color the instrument was identical with the humanoid's uniform. Witness detected no sound or light emission from it.

The witness noticed that the small personage seemed to have difficulty in getting about. He moved slowly, with a waddle, and bending his knees slightly. His gait seemed particularly heavy. It was at this point that V.M. made use of his torch, flashing it twice toward the end of the garden. Thereupon the humanoid turned round, and it seemed as though his neck must not be movable, for he did not simply turn his head but slewed the whole body around. Then, for the first time, the witness caught sight of the dark face of the strange visitor. Neither nose nor mouth was visible. All that he could distinguish was a pair of somewhat pointed ears. The eyes, oval and yellow in color, were particularly large, very bright, and surrounded by a green rim. Upon the iris part of the eyes the witness noticed small black and red veinlets. The pupil was black, and slightly oval. At times lids came down

FIGURE 5: Artist's reconstruction of the scene when the humanoid was in the garden.

over the eyes and simultaneously the face became completely dark for a few moments. When the eyes were open, these two upper lids were invisible. One might liken them to a kind of black blinds or shutters, which progressively masked the eyes as they descended.

As he now stood there, eyeing the witness face-to-face and holding his "detector" in his left hand, the ufonaut seemed to answer the luminous signals from the flashlight by raising his hand and giving the "V" sign with the index and second fingers, after which he turned away again and, with his characteristic gait and gently swinging his arms, walked off toward the back wall.

Arrived at the wall, the creature placed one foot flat against it and then, without any hesitation, did likewise with the second foot and walked straight up the wall with no change of gait except that now he was holding his legs stiff. During this astonishing progression the personage still continued with the same arm movements and continued to hold his instrument in the same position as when he was on the ground. Reaching the top of the wall, which was about 3 meters high, he executed a complete arc of a circle as he became erect again and then swung down and forward to descend the other face of the wall in this same surprising fashion.

FIGURE 6: Artist's impression of the entity going over the wall.

Four minutes or so after this unwonted exploit a, vivid halo of white light appeared beyond the wall and the witness heard a faintly perceptible chirring sound somewhat muffled by the wind. (Let us also bear in mind that throughout the sighting the witness was behind a closed window.) Then, rising very slowly, a round object began to appear, hardly a few meters distant beyond the wall.

After rising a short way, the "machine" halted and remained there stationary for about four minutes, still emitting the same chirring noise comparable to the noise of a cricket rubbing its wingcases together, and with about the same degree of loudness. The diameter of the object might have been about 5 meters (this estimate being based on the width of the witness's garden). Its upper half was orange-colored, phosphorescent, and surmounted in the center by a transparent cupola emitting a greenish light. The color of the lower half was a dark claret and on this darker area, showing up very sharply, were three lights disposed horizontally, the one on the left as seen by the witness being blue, the middle one yellow, and the right-hand-side one red. These three lights flashed on three times in sequence.

On the periphery of the machine, the witness noticed what looked like showers of sparks resembling the sparks of a cigarette lighter. They were located at the juncture between the dark underpart and the bright upper-part of the machine, that is to say, at the part where the craft's circumference was greatest. The sparks seemed to be thrown outward by a rotary movement, although the object did not seem to be rotating on its own axis.

Beneath the transparent dome, V.M. could see the humanoid, bathed in a bluey-green light. No other detail in the cabin was visible to him.

Immediately below the cupola, the witness noticed moreover an emblem outlined upon the orange portion of the craft. It consisted of a black circle traversed diagonally by a yellow lightning flash of a brighter shade than the phosphorescent orange area. (See witness's sketch, Figure 7.)

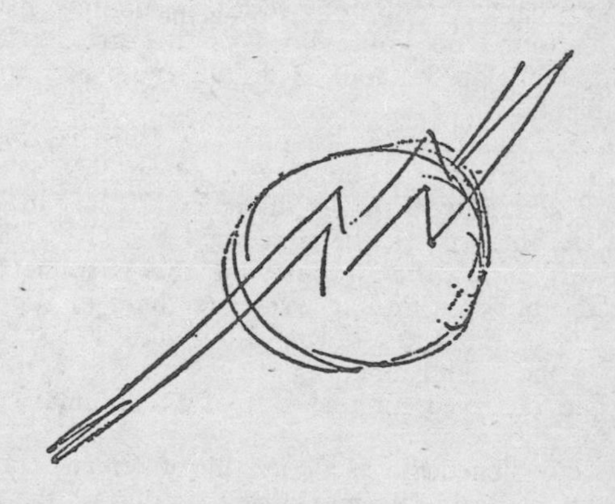

FIGURE 7: Sketch of the emblem, by the witness.

The UFO now rose again vertically about 20 meters, still retaining its horizontal position, and began to rock gently to and fro. The showers of sparks were still coming out all around it. Then the chirring sound grew louder and became a sort of hiss, and the craft gathered speed and shot straight up into the sky, leaving behind it a luminous trail. In a few seconds it was no more than a tiny point of light lost among the stars.

At no time during this extraordinary encounter does the witness claim to have felt any fear and he says he experienced no hostile reaction against the humanoid. It must likewise be mentioned that throughout the whole close encounter V.M. received no verbal or "telepathic" message. After the machine had vanished he does not seem to have been greatly shaken by all that he had seen, for he sat down at the kitchen table and prepared himself a light snack, after which he very normally returned to bed and peacefully went off to sleep again. In addition to his wife, a cousin of his was also living in the apartment. During the sighting he thought of calling the cousin, but in the end, we don't know why, he did not do so.

Next morning he arose, as on every other day, without any complaints about headache or any sort of malaise, and in the course of the morning he went out to inspect his garden. He found nothing particular there: seemingly nothing had vanished and he found no impressions on the ground and no marks or scratches on the wall. The humanoid had not even left his footprints.

This sighting was reported to us by a SOBEPS member, but not immediately, and so our investigation did not get under way until several weeks after the episode. Only in March, 1974, were we able to visit the presumed site of the landing. When we went on to the property of the Ursuline Sisters' convent in the hope of finding evidence there in support of the statements of the witness, the sister who was serving as gate porter to the establishment said she knew of nothing unusual and had observed nothing out of the ordinary on the convent premises.

When we questioned the gardener, his statement confirmed what the sister had said. No marks were found on the ground and the vegetation at the site presented no anomalies apart from a few dying fruit trees—but these, we were told, were the result of the all-too-frequent atmospheric pollution caused by the neighboring factories. We have examined the surrounding wall of the witness's garden and when we inspected the face of the wall on the convent side we likewise found no suspicious marks. One thing we were able to establish was that the vegetable garden of the convent was sufficiently isolated for a machine coming from the air to land there; a helicopter, for example, could very well have landed there without difficulty.

With a view to discovering further witnesses in the case, 500 circular letters in both French and Flemish were distributed to all the letter boxes of the vicinity, inviting the residents to inform SOBEPS of any unusual occurrence that they might have observed during that period. However this effort produced no results.

To round off and complete our account, we must mention that this was in fact not the first UFO sighting that V.M. had had. Several months previously, he and his wifc were on vacation at Westende, on the coast of Belgium. While walking with their cousin and V.M.'s sister-in-law on the beach one evening in the last week of August, they saw a strange object flying over the sea. The time was around midnight, the weather was fine, and the sea calm. The party were walking along beside the water (it was high tide) when they heard a peculiar noise coming from out at sea, somewhat resembling a medium-powered ship's siren.

It was V.M.'s cousin who was the first to see, moving along above the surface of the water and very near to the beach a very flat, red, rectangular object about 5 or 6 meters long, more or less hidden in the darkness and the faint mist. As the object passed in front of them, they were able to make out four very faintly lit, square "portholes" set horizontally beneath the object. They also heard the splashing noise caused by it as it flew over the sea. It had come from the direction of Nieuw Poort to the northeast and was traveling very slowly, parallel with the shore, toward Ostende to the southwest.

V.M. shone his torch at it and at once the lights in the four "portholes" went out, only the "red hull" remaining visible. Ahead of it lay a breakwater against which the "craft" was bound to crash. But, quite to the contrary, when it came to the breakwater, the object rose, still maintaining its horizontal position, crossed the breakwater, and then went down to water level again and continued on its way. One further curious detail: when the object was passing over the breakwater they still heard the water splashing below.

When we visited the witness again in July, 1974, he said he had had yet another sighting between Vilvorde and Brussels. He does not recall the precise date but thinks it was an evening in April. He was driving in his car (Ford Escort), with his wife and his cousin, when, on an open plateau near Koningslo, they noticed that there was a "second moon" quite low in the sky. They were traveling in third gear at about 60 km./p.h., and the engine began to sputter and finally failed completely, and the lights went out. He tried to restart the engine, but without success.

After a minute or so, the luminous object in the sky moved away and then, as is now becoming fairly frequent in incidents of this kind, the engine started up again by itself without any action by the driver. Being still in third gear, the car ran on for a while, but then, unlike what happened in a similar case, at Aische-en-Refail,[2] it failed once more, because the road was now uphill and third gear was therefore insufficient to take it. It is a pity that the witness, who was acquainted with SOBEPS, did not inform us immediately of this fresh incident so that we could have investigated immediately rather than several months later.

Comment

Returning now to our primary sighting (the Vilvorde humanoid), we find that, if we consult Jader U. Pereira's study of the humanoid types,[3] we can classify the Vilvorde entity under his category T8XI, i.e., "diver-type of entity varying between 90 centimeters and 1 meter 20 in height, wearing a one-piece suit, opaque or transparent, carrying lamp(s) and wearing a transparent globular helmet." This description calls to mind, in particular, the humanoids seen at Quarouble[4] on September 10, 1954.

On the other hand, the witness states that at more or less regular intervals eyelids of a sort came down simultaneously over the eyes of his ufonaut. Without wishing to establish a direct correlation here, we would nevertheless point out that this description might be considered comparable to the so-called *nictitating membranes* or eyelids of certain of the *Raptores* species of nocturnal and predatory birds. This supplementary eyelid passes at regular intervals across the eye (without the central nervous system being involved) for the purpose of eliminating the environmental impurities which adhere to the iris and for accustoming the iris to over-bright light. Cats too have a similar eyelid. Unlike the movement of the eyelids of the ufonaut, however, the nictitating membranes of these few species of creatures, *Raptores* and cats, move across horizontally from the inner part of the eye toward the outer side of it. (Indeed, man himself presents this same organ, but in a degenerated form, for it is the little red blob in the inner corner of the eye.)

Finally, some readers may feel astonished that the witness should have been able to describe such tiny details as the "small veinlets" when giving his account of the eyes of the entity. During our investigation he drew the eye for us to full scale, and subsequently we made tests, holding up his drawing at a distance of about 10 meters from him (which was the distance of the humanoid from him) and we have to admit that, provided the drawing is well lit, it is in fact quite possible to make out such small details in the eyes at that distance. Moreover, we must not forget that the eyes of the ufonaut were *luminous*, a fact that would have made it possible to see them correspondingly more clearly.

As regards the emblem on the machine, we feel, without having made a systematic search on this point, that there is no record of such an emblem having been seen previously. Our information on this comes principally from Monsieur Franck Boitte. Monsieur Yves Vezant who also took part in this inquiry, undertook to find out for us whether the witness might have got some of the material of his story from a book lent to him by a friend whom he had told about his nocturnal encounter. And indeed, although the witness, V.M., maintains that he is not well informed on the UFO phenomenon, it is a fact that he has read the French translation of Frank Edwards's book *Flying Saucers, Serious Business. But he read it after his sighting, and before our inquiry had got underway.*

In this particular book by Frank Edwards we find the following references:

p. 96. (French edition.) The case of Marius Dewilde; man-like creatures wearing shiny helmets like divers. Height between 1 meter and 1 meter 20.

p. 144. Small beings of around 1 meter, moving about like automata and having to move their feet first, in order to change direction.

p. 148. Creatures that were phosphorescent, like the dial of a watch.

p. 152. Small "human" beings of about 1 meter in height; shining one-piece suits and, on their chests, a box the size of three cigarette packs stacked together.

p. 158. Shining eyes, like the yellow eyes of cats.

p. 163. Entities wearing transparent helmets with tubes linking the helmets to a device on the back.
p. 166. A strange insignia on the side of the machine.
p. 252. A machine with lights that were red, blue, white (flashing on intermittently) and red, blue, white, again, in the same order.

All these details appeared in varying degree in the account of our witness V.M., but they alone are insufficient for the construction of the whole of his story, which indeed does contain plenty of other features that are *not* mentioned in Frank Edwards's book.

Apart from this one book on UFOs, V.M. (who is a great reader) claims that he had never gone into the subject of UFOs, his interests lying rather in the direction of works on early history, and the enigmas presented by vanished civilizations of the past.

Being of the younger generation, V.M. had participated in the meetings of a group where people of different religions debated on religious themes, and these discussions, which were at times lively, indeed impassioned, could fleetingly have exercised a powerful impression upon his still malleable personality. We would add, furthermore, that he has a great liking for modern music and owns a big collection of records.

Despite all our efforts, all the same, we have been quite unable to find any other testimony from any other people who might have been able to confirm this unusual sighting which thus, alas, has only the one witness.

Consequently, we must remain very cautious in our evaluation of it, and give only a relative rating to this account which is, nevertheless, "all-of-apiece" and entirely coherent from start to finish, the witness's descriptions often being very precise.

(On the Poher Scale, we give it a rating of *credibility:* 3, *strangeness:* 5.)

We would emphasize the fact that the witness stated that the strange being left no traces on the ground or on the wall. This factor could be taken as evidence in support of the argument that his story is authentic. For, had this been a well-staged hoax, it would seem highly probable that V.M. would, for example, have presented us with some scratches on the whitewashed brickwork of the wall in order to lend more weight to his story.

When we visited him a second time, he still stuck to all the details of his statement, and the fresh sketch of his humanoid which he did for us proved to match up entirely with the one he had drawn for us in our first interview several months earlier.

Some folk may perhaps be surprised at the great number of UFO sightings that this witness claims to have had. It is indeed astonishing that one individual should witness so many happenings within so short a period—this being against all the calculations of reasonable probability.

Nevertheless, we are obliged to recognize that over the period of three years in which our SOBEPS investigatory teams have been in action, it has been shown to be a fact that there are other persons too who are equally privileged in this respect and who have had several sightings without their credibility being thereby abated. Consequently, while it may have its weak points, we feel that the account of V.M. may contain sufficient information that is quite original for it to merit a place in our pages.

NOTES BY GORDON CREIGHTON

1. Not translated.
2. Not translated. Original report in *Inforespace*, Numbers 16 and 17.
3. This very useful catalogue of entity types, by our Brazilian friend Jader U. Pereira of Pôrto Alegre, has appeared in a French translation in *Phénomènes Spatiaux*, Numbers 24, 25, 27, 28, and 29. I regret that I have not yet had time to tackle the job of making an English translation of it.
4. This is the famous case of the steelworker Marius Dewilde, which happened, incidently, in the France–Belgian frontier area and consequently not so very far from Vilvorde. It is Case Number 9 of Jacques Vallée's *"The Pattern Behind the UFO Landings,"* in *Flying Saucer Review*'s compilation *The Humanoids,* edited by Charles Bowen, and now available in a new paperback edition issued by Futura Publications Ltd., 49 Poland Street, London, W1A 2LG.

The Robots at Warneton

by J. M. Bigorne et al.

This is a puzzling, even alarming case—although productive of uneasy amusement—which was part of the great European wave of UFO reports which spread over France, Belgium, and Italy in 1973 and early 1974, during which year it also spilled into Spain. The beginnings of this wave were concurrent with that in the United States in 1973.

It is the descriptions of the entities, their ludicrous garb and their queer mechanical gait, which provoke the uneasy amusement; there is nothing amusing about the description of the death's head "faces" under the weird headgear. Indeed there is a distinct ring of truth in the story as told by the witness, and one must speculate that if he had possibly concocted this story as a hoax then surely he would have put together something a little more "comfortable," even rational, and with a more conclusive ending. For here, as in so many other close encounter cases, the reported behavior of the entities seems pointless and the testimony dreamlike or, perhaps, one should say nightmarish.

The investigation of this report was carried out in meticulous detail by Monsieur Bigorne, with the able assistance of Messrs. Bazin, senior and junior, and Monsieur Boidin, all of the Lumières dans la Nuit *team in France.* The report appeared in the* LDLN *journal, Number 139 of November, 1974. The version that was published in* Flying Saucer Re-

* For address, see Appendix.

view, *Volume 20, Number 5, of 1974, was translated from the French by Gordon Creighton.*

The date was Monday, January 7, 1974, and the witness, Monsieur "X," Belgian, aged 31, was driving in his Ami 6 from Comines toward Warneton, on the Franco-Belgian frontier. It was about 8:40 P.M., and he had nearly reached Warneton. The road surface was wet, for it had rained recently. The sky was clear, with stars, and there was virtually no wind. There was a fine moon (it would be full moon on the following night, January 8). His Schneider car-radio cassette player was playing. He was doing a moderate speed: 60-70 km. p.h.

Suddenly his headlights go out and practically simultaneously the car's engine cuts out after a few misfires. The car radio goes dead too. Surprised, Monsieur "X" puts the gear into neutral and the car goes on running for 100 meters or so (the gradient at this point of the road is around 1:20). Then he uses the hand brake to pull up. A good car mechanic himself, he thinks a fuse has gone, and as soon as the vehicle is stationary he gets ready to step out and see to the trouble. He has his left hand on the door handle on the driver's side and with his right hand he presses down lightly on the passenger seat to aid himself in getting out.

But he gets no further, for, turning his head slightly to the right, he sees, through the front door-window, something about 150 meters distant in the field bordering the road at this spot. He thinks at first that it is a load of hay, but then he notices areas of orangish white light on the object, and finally he perceives that it is standing on three legs. A few further moments of inspection bring him to the realization that he is not looking at a cartload of hay but at an unknown object, the shape of which, slightly silhouetted against the horizon, is reminiscent of the type of "tin hat" worn by the British "Tommies"—the soldiers of World War I.

And then his attention is caught by something else. . . .

He sees, through the windscreen, two figures about thirty meters from his car, in the field. A farmer and his son, he thinks. But very soon he realizes that these two peculiar customers have nothing whatsoever to do with agriculture. They are approaching his car, walking in a rigid, slow fashion, and they come to a halt at fifteen meters from him and then, after a few seconds, come on again toward the car. Now he is able to see them in far better detail: one of them, the smaller, has the appearance of the man in the French "Michelin" advert, but with the rings scarcely delineated, and with a round helmet on his head, with quite a large "window" in it, allowing the witness to see a considerable part of the face. In his right hand this being holds a strange object (quite short, like a short, thick ruler with a pointed, pyramidal tip). He holds it somewhat in the fashion that one carries a revolver, and he points it at the car.

The second character, slightly taller than his companion (who is about 1 meter 20–1 meter 30) is walking slightly in front of the other. The silhouette of this second one is different. On his head he has a cube-shaped helmet, the sides of which are opaque except for the front, which is transparent like glass and reveals a weird face (their faces are identical, like twins). The shape of his head is like a pear, of a uniform faintly grayish shade, with two perfectly round eyes like agate "marbles" which are slightly sunken, in relation to the rest of the face, in what might be reminiscent of the eye sockets of a human face, and with a scarcely detectable arch to the eyebrows. The nose is small and shows up but faintly against the face, the mouth is simply a horizontal slit with no lips to be seen, and when, at one particular moment, the being opens its mouth, the witness sees in it neither tongue nor teeth.

In the cube-shaped helmet, beneath his chin, the being has a black rectangular "box." The overall suit is a dull metallic gray and seems to be made in one piece from the helmet down to the fingertips and down to the footwear too.

The two beings continue to approach, and the witness can now establish all these details and also take in others—in particular that the boots are heavy and pointed. Above the cube-shaped helmet there is a sort of tube which suggests the existence of a breathing device (?) or which perhaps is a handle of some kind.

The silhouette of the humanoid in the cubic helmet is very different from that of his companion. Slightly taller than entity No. 1, he also has an athletic sort of build, broad shoulders, narrow hips in the fashion of a toreador, and a black belt at the waist with a luminous, or rather phosphorescent, oval—almost round—at the spot where the buckle of a belt lies. A sort of oblique black "Sam Browne" runs from the belt to the left shoulder. Starting from the base of his helmet, a row of buttons—at least this is what the witness supposes them to be—runs down on each side.

The two "ufonauts" have very long arms, their hands reaching down to just slightly below the knees.

Monsieur "X" was enabled to observe the faces of the two beings in such precise detail because there was a soft, uniform light inside each of their helmets, which did not seem to radiate at all to the exterior. The witness likens this light to the light on the belt.

Shortly after the two creatures had started walking toward the witness again, and when they had halted again very near to the ditch, Monsieur "X" felt a faint shock in the back part of the cranium, at the level of the cerebellum. Then straight away after the "shock" he heard, but, he explains, not with his ears (all the doors of the car were closed), a low-pitched, modulated sound, growing detectably louder and louder.

We emphasize once more that the two beings had stopped at a point about four meters from the car of the witness who was just sitting there rooted to his seat with fear and amazement. Just before he felt the shock on the back of the head and heard this sound, the entity in the cube-shaped helmet had opened its mouth as though about to speak: but he had heard no sound from it at that moment. A few seconds later came the shock at the back of the head and the modulated sound, but by then the being had his mouth closed again.

Right from the outset of the encounter Monsieur "X" had also sight of a third being, identical in appearance to entity No. 1 (the "Michelin man") but this one remained all the time close to the UFO and never left his "sentry post."

Let us now return to the two "ufonauts" standing on the edge of the field. The duration of their "*tête-à-tête*" with the witness is difficult to estimate for in such times the seconds tend to seem pretty long! At one particular moment during the confrontation a sort of small object, oval in shape and luminous, fell from the left side and from the level of the black belt of the entity in the cube-shaped helmet, who did not appear to notice it or to worry about it. It has not been possible to recover this "object"—if indeed it was a material object—for over two and a half months elasped between the sighting and the making known of this happening—the witness remaining silent out of fear of ridicule and other annoyances. In the meantime, the field had been plowed up by the farmer, who knows nothing about these events.

But the *tête-à-tête* is to be brusquely disturbed. Suddenly the two beings turn their heads, in a perfectly synchronized movement, toward their left, and look away behind the witness's car. The low-pitched modulated sound terminates—without any shock in the back of the witness's head—as, in a still perfectly synchronized movement, the two entities execute a half-turn to their left, seeming to pivot on one leg (in military fashion), turn their backs to the witness (who notes nothing further regarding the details of their appearance except for the black "Sam Browne" shoulder-belt on one of them, running down the back and joining the waist-belt) and set off again at a brisk pace toward the UFO. Their movement is almost human, their knees bending and their legs moving normally, except for one feature—they seem not in the slightest degree hampered by the wet, sticky soil of the field, as though they were in fact walking with the utmost ease across hard ground in their big, pointed boots.

The witness no longer recalls in what manner the beings reentered their "craft." What he does remember is that the tripod legs vanished, and then the machine rose about 50 centimeters or so off the ground and then, after remaining there stationary for three or four seconds, began to climb horizontally, following a trajectory at an angle of 60° or 70°, and finally vanished from his sight. Just as the machine was about to take off, after retracting its tripod legs, the witness had noticed in his rear-view mirror the lights of a car approaching from behind. Overcome by the thoroughly understandable sudden release from nervous tension the witness flopped for a few minutes over the wheel in an indescribable sensation of relief, at the same time wondering whether he had not perhaps just been dreaming or been the victim of some private hallucination.

Meanwhile the approaching car (it was driven by a Belgian) was getting nearer and nearer, and finally drew up, with all its lights blazing, right in front of his own car. The Belgian got out and came over and opened the door, to find the witness slumped there over his wheel, still convulsively clutching the door handle.

The witness recovers himself, and the Belgian motorist asks: "Have they hurt you?"

To which the witness replied: "Did you see them too?"

Yes, said the Belgian. He had seen them, and his engine had faltered a few times, but his lights had not failed.

The Belgian took his leave and drove on. The witness, whose headlights and radio were now working again, was able to get his engine going after a certain amount of work on his starter. He made for home. As fast as he could go.

Be it noted that the Belgian driver said to the witness (who is French) that he, the Belgian, would return with some friends to look for any traces of the landing which might remain. If they found any, he said, the matter would be given full publicity. If not, they would pursue the matter no further and drop it.

The Belgian took the witness's address. Having heard no more on the matter, our witness assumes that the Belgians found nothing.

Here are a few details regarding the behavior of the UFO throughout all phases of this sighting, from start to finish:

Estimated Size of UFO: Height: 2.5–3 meters, calculating from the ground. Width: 7–10 meters.

Structural Details: No structural details apparent apart from the bulge on the upper side. No change of shape observed.

Color Sequence:
(a) "Orangish white."
(b) Blue (blowpipe dart).
(c) Reddish (dirty garnet).
(d) Electric blue finally, until takeoff.

From the moment that the ufonauts started walking rapidly back to the UFO, the blue began to pulsate like the revolving strobe light of a police car. All these color changes took place on surfaces that were an orange-tinged white at the start of the observation. These variable luminosities did not diffuse themselves outward toward the exterior. The only one of the lights that actually furnished illumination was located beneath the UFO and seemed to come from its interior, and lit up an area lying between the three legs of the tripod landing-gear. This white light vanished at the moment of takeoff.

Throughout the whole duration of the sighting, the UFO did not move and underwent no change of shape: only changes of color. The total duration of the sighting is estimated by the witness at about 20 minutes. He had no watch but was able to estimate the duration from the amount of time by which he was late in arriving home that night.

Despite the fact that there are certain houses in the vicinity, it seems that nothing was noticed by the occupants. Those persons who have been interviewed have replied that they were watching TV at the time, but they no longer recall whether or not there was any disturbance on their TV screens.

The radio/casette in the witness's car remained defective after this experience.

Witness and his wife found that it was working badly thereafter. It was new, and up till then had worked impeccably. But after this experience with the UFO entities, he had to turn the volume up higher when he started the car again to drive on, and the programs all came out distorted by disturbances and interference and background noise.

The player has been examined by experts and these have given their findings.*

Almost precisely five months later, the second contact occurred, and quite peculiarly too, being also at the very same spot as on Monday, January 7, 1974; at the very same time and in the very same circumstances, that is to say, while the witness was on his way home from a business refresher course. *And, be it noted, Thursday, June 6, was the very first day on which he had resumed attendance at this course since having an accident at his work during February.*

This time, at this season of the year (summer), it was still

* Translator's Note: The report of the experts, occupying half a page of *LDLN*, is incorporated in the original text of the report. But I shall need a bit of help with some of the technical terms, in all likelihood, and this will cause delay. I have thought it better therefore to present this extraordinarily interesting story straight away. We can give the technical report when I have got it ready. Once again, our thanks to *LDLN* for a fine report on an astonishing case.

broad daylight. Sitting in his car and driving along, everything normal, the witness perceives the two beings (seemingly the same two as in January) standing right on the edge of the road just like a couple of hitchhikers! As on the first occasion, the engine sputters a few times, but there is no effect on the lights since these are not on, it being daylight. The cassette player, which he has had turned on, also falls silent. The witness stops the car himself, pulling up level with the two beings, which are now so near that they can touch the bodywork of the car. But he does not budge from his seat: prudence and emotions dictate. . . .

Once more he feels a slight shock at the back of the head, and a modulated sound, which then ceases. . . . It has lasted scarcely two or three minutes, and the beings vanish instantly, suddenly, as though disintegrated, without sound, and without any other reaction!

A few seconds after this instantaneous disappearance of the two beings, his cassette player begins to function again, just as before, without his touching it. He has no difficulty in restarting his engine, and he drives on home, pretty shaken by this second encounter, though a good deal less so than by the first.

Shortly before this second contact, he had been overtaken by a Ford car with a Belgian registration number, which was by now about a kilometer ahead of him, and which apparently did not experience any disturbance, its occupants seemingly not observing the two "ufonauts" standing beside the road. Did the driver not see them, *or were they perhaps invisible for him?*

On the other hand it is to be noted that, as soon as this second experience started, the witness looked around over the fields to see if he could detect any object in the vicinity, but this time without result. He saw no object or flying craft, whether on the ground or near to it.

We think it right to add that we have made the closest and most thorough investigation of the witness: his good faith cannot be doubted.

Consequently we can conclude that the Warneton region has been the scene of happenings that are out of the ordinary, and that are outside the scope of our normal conceptions.

We shall not attempt to interpret them. We confine ourselves to *verifying them strictly and objectively* and reporting them.

In our view the affair is something very important, which we are going to follow up as closely as possible. Other developments can be expected. . . .

The Little "Electric" Man

by George M. Eberhart

Here, from the days of the North American wave of 1973, is a charming tale of a weird encounter which produced UFO entities seemingly elevated into the realms of psychic experience. A UFO bobbed about nearly out of reach of the eyewitnesses, and for a few fleeting moments a spectral figure appeared which is vaguely reminiscent of the one in the Winterfold encounter in England in 1967.

Note, too, the second little figure which the young lady could almost "see through" if she looked hard enough. Shades of Oscar Iriart's contact, which Gordon Creighton described in his "South American 'Wave'" (see page 40). Was something, somewhere— in *the UFO, say, or even by way of it—testing out the reactions of a couple of human beings, and itself coming under some pretty cool and calm scrutiny?*

Mr. Eberhart's contribution appeared in Flying Saucer Review, *Volume 20, Number 5 (1974).*

The principal witness of the following, rather unusual UFO case was Mary Geddis, aged 21, who was living with a friend, Joe Ben-Israel, in a house trailer near Albany, Ohio, at the time. She stated that she was a businesswoman, about to open a store, and that she was wearing glasses when she had her experience (she always wears them). Her friend was working for a masters degree in the School of Communications, College of Radio and TV, at Ohio University in Athens. Neither of the two had been drinking that evening.

On October 16, 1973, at 7:30 P.M., Mary Geddis was returning home from an evening class. The first thing she noticed when she pulled into the driveway was a tall "thing" of ghostlike appearance, about 1,000 feet away, standing or floating about 50 feet from the ground. It was like "a person with a close-fitting sheet draped over," and was about four feet tall and thin. A head and body shape could be distinguished, but the body was straight, without any limbs. She watched it for a few seconds, and then, on looking out of the open window on the passenger side of the car, toward the road, she saw a bright white light. It appeared to be "jotting around. . . ."

"It was like it was looking. It would look here and then it would look over here, over here—like that. But then when it came over here it came straight, like I drew it. When it saw me, it kind of wanted to see what I was all about . . . it was just like it was staring at me, and it kept coming closer and closer, then hovering and coming closer . . . and I got scared and kind of turned away and tried not to pay any attention to it, and it moved back.

"It went away back over the field . . . it went directly to the side and then directly back. It went behind a telephone pole that blocked off some of its lights, and from there it just went back across the field, away from me. Then it faded a little and then it was gone." At closest approach, the light came within 200 feet of Miss Geddis. The ghostlike object was seen only for a few seconds, but the second object was sighted over a period of three to four minutes. She estimated its diameter as 20 feet, and it was only 25–30 feet from the ground when seen at closest proximity.

When she got out of the car, Mary Geddis says she had a weird feeling of a "presence," as if something were near, invisible. In fact she was scared of walking over to the trailer. She was still standing by the car when Joe Ben-Israel returned later. While they were preparing supper, their neighbors, Chuck and Rhonda, came home and said they had seen something strange in the sky. Joe went outside to talk with the neighbors, leaving the trailer door open. Just then, what Mary called a little "aqua-ish" thing looked around the corner of the door.

"It was like the electric man they have on the Co-op signs. It just looked at me. It didn't try to say anything to me. It just stared for a few seconds, probably ten seconds. . . . It sort of had a face. It had what looked like spiky things at the top and sides of the head." The creature was about two and a half feet tall, with stumpy arms, but no legs were distinguished. . . . "You couldn't see through it, but I felt I could almost see through it if I looked at it more." Mary later described him as an "energy form."

"He had eyes and mouth. I'm not sure about the nose, but I think he had a nose, because he didn't look that strange to me in his face—except for the spikes and the color." (She picked a blue-green on a color chart.) "This looks like a monster, the way I've drawn it. But it didn't look like a monster, it looked like a friendly little thing. Only it had these spikes all over it. It didn't try to hurt me or anything. It was just looking, like it was peeking around the corner at first, and then it was just kind of standing there looking at me. It didn't move clear in front of the door. It must have had a hand at or behind the door . . . I got the distinct impression that he wasn't sure about whether he should be there or not. He was kind of timid . . . Its eyes didn't blink. Nothing moved. It just kind of disappeared back behind the door. I went after it and looked behind the door and didn't see anything any more. It was gone."

Mary Geddis was asked if she had received any psychic impressions, and what she thought when she saw the creature. What did she think it was?

"I don't know. I was just shocked that it was there. It just looked at me and I didn't think about it very much until afterwards. Then I went outside and said, 'Ohh! Something looked at me!' But I didn't feel anything while it was looking at me. It just looked at me like it was seeing what I was. And I was just looking at it the same way, seeing what it was."

Afterwards she thought about the white "creature" and the UFO she had seen. She thought also about the other UFOs that were seen that night—things hovering, but never coming close, although in the distance they could be seen coming down to earth.

"I thought at first it might be some kind of philanthropic society from outer space, to bring some sense of civilization here. But then the more I thought about it . . . the reason I got scared was, that I realized that these people would be super in comparison to us and I didn't think that they'd probably be helping people so much as they'd probably need some kind of power source. And they really seemed to scare the cows, and it was the time of the beef shortage, and we were talking about how they were coming down to get the cows."

The sky was clear during the evening that Mary Geddis had her strange experiences. Joe Ben-Israel related what he saw that night.

"We saw in a couple of places in the sky objects that didn't seem to make any noise. They were close enough so that if they were planes, you could hear them. They seemed to be going at a faster rate than planes usually travel (but not faster than jet planes)."

"Did you see more than one object in the sky at a time?"

"Not in the same spot, but in different parts of the sky. There aren't any jets around here, I don't think. . . . There were intermittent red and green flashes, although they weren't consecutive—they weren't equal intervals. They would flash, then flash-flash."

"About how high off the ground? Can you estimate?"

"Around here they were slightly higher than the horizon. This is on top of a mountain . . . it would be approximately 30 degrees."

"Could you say these objects were less than a mile away?"

"If you compare the same light as a plane, they would be just about a mile, I guess."

"And how long did you have these objects in sight this particular time?"

"Well [giving a particular example] as it was traveling across the sky it must have been about five or six minutes. And then at one particular point it stopped—stopped in the middle—and then it just went back again. And it stopped there and went back again to its original spot. And then it sort of flashed a bit. It got brighter and then dimmer. And then sort of changed between blue and red coloring. That was the same kind of object as the one we saw standing there in one spot and doing this."

The couple claimed to have seen unusual lights many times subsequent to that first night, though generally they were rather distant and small in size. In fact, throughout the week following Mary's experiences a number of UFOs were reported in the Athens area, according to the local newspaper, *The*

Post, of October 22. The week ended with the inevitable anticlimax in the form of a hoax UFO constructed of two kite sticks bearing birthday candles, covered with a plastic bag. This floated through the air and then crashed into trees lining a street, causing a small fire. Nevertheless, such a hoax could not account for the sighting made by several Athens policemen the night after the Geddis sighting.

At 12:55 A.M., Patrolman B. S——— and Detective T. ——— observed a white light hovering over the old airport on State Street. Patrolman L. G.———* joined them and observed it through 7 × 50 binoculars. The UFO hovered over East Hill to the southwest, then slowly headed south. The object was positioned vertically and shaped like a cone or a "flame." It was brighter than anything else in the sky. The object drifted south and disappeared behind some hills at 1:05 A.M.

Patrolman B———, on Stimson Avenue, saw a UFO through binoculars. He said at 1:05 A.M. another object appeared above him, brighter than any star. The other patrolmen saw it from their position also. The object was cylinder-shaped and had a round ball at one end. This was higher than the first UFO. It seemed to turn, and bright lights blinked on and off from it. At 1:20 A.M. it moved north and then stopped again. The police resumed patroling, but kept watching it. The sky clouded over at 1:40 A.M. and they lost sight of it.

Patrolman G——— said in the police report: "Ordinarily we could pass the sightings of these objects off as airplanes or balloons, but not after seeing them with binoculars. I have a slight night blindness problem, but to the best of my knowledge, Ptl. S———, Ptl. B——— and T——— S——— all have 20/20 vision."

The police have requested that none of the witnesses' names be mentioned, but details of the sighting and mention of the Athens police in general is permitted.

* The only patrolman interviewed by M. Eberhart—EDITOR

Postscript to "The Little Electric Man"
by Charles Bowen

So, in the midst of an intense local "flap" of strange, soundless lights seen cavorting in the skies by many eyewitnesses—among them Mary Geddis, her friend Joe, and their neighbors—police officers make a spectacular corroborating observation and report. While all this goes on, Mary encounters her ghostlike image outside the gate and then, at home, the nearly transparent little "electric" man. Could these have been projections of the kind I have discussed elsewhere (particularly in our book, *The Humanoids*) when the images were induced in her mind's eye? Induced by what? By whatever controls the UFOs?

Mr. Eberhart is a member of Dr. J. Allen Hynek's Center for UFO Studies, 924 Chicago Avenue, Evanston, Illinois 60202.

One Day in Mendoza

by Charles Bowen

A UFO landing, one of many reported in Argentina, an encounter with strange entities who vandalized a car, delivered an illustrated lecture to, and performed a blood sampling on, the astonished witnesses. (We have many other recorded instances of blood tests, the most famous being that carried out on Antônio Villas Boas, whose sexual encounter case was first reported in Flying Saucer Review *in January, 1965, and in complete detail in our book* The Humanoids *(Chicago: Henry Regnery Company; London: Neville Spearman Ltd., 1969). After the initial furor and widespread publicity, the two young casino workers recanted and "confessed" that their story was a hoax. It seemed, however, that they had been under some pressure, and their volte-face should be taken with a liberal "pinch of salt."*

This is the point made by the writer in an article "Softly, Softly in Mendoza," in Flying Saucer Review, *Volume 15, Number 3 (May–June, 1968). Soon after the news of the Peccinetti–Villegas encounter had broken, notices appeared in the press to the effect that ". . . the authorities have issued a communiqué that the spreading of saucer rumors is an offense penalized by law." The communiqué added that ". . . the penal code contemplates prison terms for those people indulging in spreading unwarranted fear, and legal action will be taken against those who break this rule."*

Quite sinister, that, and small wonder that the witnesses, having become involved with the police (who had impounded their car), decided that discretion was the better part of valor. However, our speculation that the witnesses had been frightened into their recantation received some support when a letter arrived from an Argentinian reader of Flying Saucer Review *in which there was some valuable follow-up information. The reader asked that her name be withheld. It seems that a builder who had been working on the house of this lady's niece had been staying in Mendoza and learned from a nurse at the hospital where Peccinetti and Villegas had been admitted that the doctors and psychiatrists had found the two casino workers to be completely sane and rational. The builder went out of curiosity to see the landing site. He said: "There was a foreign car there, with foreign-speaking people measuring the place, and nobody was allowed to get close." Police were everywhere, and he believed the foreigners were Americans.*

"One Day in Mendoza" appeared in Flying Saucer Review, *Volume 14, Number 6 (November–December, 1968).*

Mendoza lies among rugged foothills heaped high against the lofty Andean wall, the natural frontier between the republics of Argentina and Chile. Like most towns in Argentina, it has featured sporadic bursts of UFO reports, and Rodolfo Braceli, writing in *Gente y la Actualidad* for September 5, 1968, tells how nineteenth-century records reveal that glowing objects passed through Mendozan skies for several days before a disastrous earthquake destroyed the place. Reports of similar objects in July this year were followed, fortunately, by nothing more than a strong tremor. *FSR* too has had its accounts of strange affairs in the district particularly the "much ado about very little" that happened nearly four years ago.[1]

Now, even the recent case of the nurse at the Mendozan Neuropsychiatric Hospital of El Sauce[2] pales beside the alleged events of September 1, 1968.

Around about 4:00 A.M. that morning, the soldiers on duty in the guard room at the General Espejo Military College were surprised by the sudden appearance of two young men, casino workers, obviously in a state of shock, and babbling that their car had suddenly stopped, and that when they got out to investigate the cause they had seen a flying saucer close to the ground and five small beings who communicated with them in a strange manner, took blood samples from their fingers, left inscriptions all over the car, and disappeared up a beam of light into the object which accelerated away vertically.

The startled guardsmen, no doubt feeling singularly unqualified to deal with people who saw things like that, suggested that the men should go at once to the Lagomagiore Hospital. This, according to the *Gente y la Actualidad* investigator, they did, and we learn that the police came into the picture soon afterwards. An earlier report carried in *Los Principios* of Córdoba (September 2) stated that the two men went from the college to the police, and then on to the hospital.

Whatever the correct sequence of their visits, possible corroborating events—unknown at the time to the witnesses, to the Military College guards and to the hospital staff—had taken place. One was that the staff at the Mendoza station of the Belgrano Railway Line had reported a sudden and total blackout of the lighting system at the precise time that the witnesses stated that their car had stopped. Another was that at 3:45 A.M., three minutes after the reported "auto-stop," a Senora Maria Spinelli telephoned the police from her home on the calle Luzuriaga in the Dorrego suburb some 6 kilometers from the scene of the encounter, and reported that a strange, luminous object was flying around very low overhead.

Before I proceed with details of the case, I feel it is necessary for me to restate my position with regard to UFO/humanoid reports of this kind. I take the line that it is essential that researchers should not overlook *anything* that is claimed or reported, however ludicrous it may seem. Furthermore, it is incumbent upon the editor of a serious journal to ensure that everything possible is examined objectively and put into the record. This is a very different kettle of fish from "believing," about which I have already expressed my views quite clearly,[8] and I never hesitate to recommend Aimé Michel's advice that we should see and hear everything, but believe nothing.

So let us return to the events that were supposed to have taken place at Mendoza in the early hours of September 1.

The Alleged Encounter

The witnesses who claimed the remarkable experience were Juan Carlos Peccinetti (married, aged 26) and Fernando José Villegas (married, aged 29). They are employed at a Mendoza casino and, when they finished work at 3:30 A.M., they set off for home in Villegas's vintage 1929 Chevrolet, number plate 2999.

When they reached a dark part of the calle Nequén, near the calle Laprida, the car stopped and the lights went out. Villegas got out to look under the bonnet.

Later, in an interview at the *La Crónica* offices in Buenos Aires—reported in the edition for September 9—Peccinetti confirmed that his watch stopped at 3:42 A.M., and added that despite earlier reports to the contrary, only *he* had a watch. As he was getting out of the car he heard Villegas shout: "Look, Skinny," and thereupon they found themselves unable to move (the word "paralyzed" was used) and face to face with three "humanoid" beings. Two more of the creatures, so we are told, were standing near an "enormous" circular or oval-shaped "machine," some 4 meters across and 1.50 meters high. This object was "floating" in the air 1.20 meters above a piece of wasteland at 2333 calle Nequén. A powerful beam of light was directed from the object toward the ground at an angle of about 45°.

The beings, about 1.50 meters in height, appeared to be of human shape except that their heads were "strikingly" larger than normal. The heads were also hairless. The creatures wore overalls like those of attendants at a petrol filling station. Their movements were "gentle and quiet," and as they approached the two witnesses they crossed a ditch. Peccinetti observed that they crossed "as though by a bridge."

Both Peccinetti and Villegas said that when the entities had come close they could hear a foreign-sounding voice saying repeatedly: "Do not fear, do not fear." Said Peccinetti: "It was as though they had put into our ears the tiny ear-plug 'speakers' used with transistor radios."

Villegas gave details of a message that was passed to them in this way, with, all the time, the persuasive backing of "Do not fear. . . ." The gist of the message was: "We have just made three journeys around the sun, studying customs and languages of the inhabitants of the system. The sun benignly nurtures the system; were it not so then the solar system would not exist."

The alleged message then ended with the statement: "Mathematics is the universal language."

While this lecture was going on, another of the little humanoids was busily tracing inscriptions on the doors, windscreen, and running-boards of the vintage car. He used a small device which, we are told, was not unlike a soldering-iron, and which gave off dazzling sparks. (When during subsequent investigations a blow-lamp was used on a panel of a door, the paintwork was badly burned, as would be expected, but there were no burn marks whatsoever in the vicinity of the inscriptions.)

There next appeared, close to the hovering object, a circular screen, not unlike that of a television set. On this there appeared a series of images. The first was a scene of a waterfall in lush country; the second a mushroom-shaped cloud; the third the waterfall scene again, but no water. (The moral of the story is . . . ?)

Peccinetti and Villegas assert that after this the entities took hold of their left hands—the creatures' hands felt no different from human hands, we are told—and pricked their fingers three times. Then they turned toward the hovering "machine" and ascended to it along the light beam. Swiftly there followed an explosive effect, and the object is said to have risen into the sky surrounded by a vast radiance, and then to have disappeared into "Space."

Investigation

An earlier report (*Los Principios*) stated that "when the UFO crew were returning to their machine, one of them fell down, but was quickly picked up by his companions." A few days later, during a reconstruction of the case by a judge in Mendoza, there was talk of discrepancies is the various accounts, to which Peccinetti replied in *La Crónica:* ". . . the celebrated bit about them falling over . . . that's all wrong. When the dwarfs seemed to be climbing up the light beam . . . and we heard the explosion, I heard Villegas shout: 'Run, Skinny!' and we bolted for the Military College. It was Villegas who fell over . . . and I picked him up."

It also transpired that the soldier on duty at the college said he heard an explosion and saw a glow in the distance, but afterward denied what he had said. However, the two witnesses told *La Crónica* that several other people in the district had testified as to what they had seen and heard.

From the college guard room Peccinetti and Villegas went to Lagomagiore Hospital. There they received attention, and the report on them indicated: "Picture of psychomotor excitation, and three small punctures on the fleshy parts of the index and middle fingers of the left hand. Identical in both of them."

The examination then continued at the Central Hospital with blood tests, the results being negative. It was also revealed that for two days the witnesses were kept apart, and it is understood that during that time their stories tallied one with the other.

It was at this stage that the police intervened. Police Commissioner Miguel Montoza of the Sixth Police Section impounded the car that had been abandoned by the witnesses. Radioactivity tests on the vehicle at the site, and at the Neuropsychical Hospital, revealed nothing abnormal.

Peccinetti and Villegas assert that they are Catholics, not belonging to any spiritualistic organization, or having any links with societies or sects.

Attempts have been made to interpret the inscriptions on the car—Gordon Creighton with his vast knowledge of languages and scripts tells me they seem to be childishly unsystematic—and we read that the Mendoza Center for Space Research proposed this hypothesis to the *Gente y la Actualidad* reporters:

> The sketch done by the humanoids represents two solar systems, the Earth's system, consisting of Mercury, Venus, and Earth, and the Jupiter system, containing the planets Io, Europa, and Ganymede. Between Ganymede and Earth there are two parallel lines, as though to indicate a two-way trip, and establishing that the source of these beings is Ganymede, a sphere that is 776 million kilometers from Earth.

It surprises me to learn that they could deduce all that

from the squiggles shown in the sketch, but I'm no expert in these matters. I did read in *Gente*, however, that the hypothesis was based on concepts contained in a book by Manuel Sáenz and Willy Wolf. I think I'll side with Mr. Creighton—it's safer!

Comments

That, for the time being, is the best I can do with the material available. There was obviously an initial scramble by newspapers to get this sensational case into print—and if it *is* true, then it is indeed sensational. Later investigations, like those by *Gente* and *La Crónica*, seem to have been carried out reasonably carefully. A correspondent of mine in Buenos Aires tells me that when he saw Peccinetti and Villegas on television: "They did not appear to be the 'mythomaniacs' or 'publicity seekers' that the Mendoza authorities say they are. The two men looked very ordinary, and I doubt if they are publicity-seeking, for they would lose their jobs. I doubt if a casino would entrust the job of cashier to anyone about whom they were not sure. In my opinion," concludes my correspondent, "theirs is a down-to-earth job, which leaves little time for 'fancies'."

Speculation

If true, this is an amazing case calling for further rigorous investigation. It is also a case with ingredients to suit adherents to both the extraterrestrial hypothesis, and those who are convinced we are being contacted by entities who only wish us well. (On the other hand, for those who see only the gloomy side of things, it could just as easily be that they were "unpleasant" types—having a good laugh at the expense of a couple of credulous humans.)

Joking aside, could this case fit in with ideas I expressed in my last article?[4] I would suggest it could. It is conceivable that the witnesses' car could have been stopped by the presence of a "solid" object—the UFO—and that the rest of the story could have been implanted in the witnesses' minds by hypnosis, radiation, or some other form of induction. It is equally conceivable that the sighting of the object as well as of the creatures, and of all that transpired, could have been induced from afar, or from one of those enigmatic "other levels." Induced, too, with such intensity that the witnesses could be forced to inflict minor injuries on themselves, to damage their (prized?) vintage car, and to imagine the touch of the entities.

This, I insist, is *not* a "belief"; merely an idea, a suggestion for the direction of researchers more qualified than I to investigate these things. As far as I am concerned, it makes better sense than many of the other speculations to which I have listened for the past twenty years.

NOTES

1. Bowen, C., "Crash-Landed UFO near Mendoza?" *Flying Saucer Review,* Volume 11, Number 3 (May–June, 1965).
2. See "World Round-Up," *Flying Saucer Review,* Volume 14, Number 6 (November–December, 1968).
3. Editorial "Beliefs," *Flying Saucer Review,* Volume 11, Number 6 (November–December, 1966); also see Editorial "The Other Phenomenon," *Flying Saucer Review,* Volume 14, Number 2 (March–April, 1968).
4. Bowen, C., "Strangers about the House," *Flying Saucer Review,* Volume 14, Number 5 (September–October, 1968).

SOURCES

Los Principios (Cordoba), September 2, 1968.
La Cronica (Buenos Aires), September 9, 1968.
Gente y la Actualidad (People and Events), Buenos Aires, September 5, 1968.
Our thanks are due to *FSR*'s associate in Buenos Aires, Señor Guillermo J. Gainza Paz, for sending the above newspapers.
Ya (Madrid, Spain), September 3, 1968.
Credit for sending the above account to Señor Ignacio Darnaude of Sevilla.

"Forced Feeding" by UFO Entities

by J. Bigorne et al.

A strange and, for the witness, a very frightening affair, once again with a new twist to it: what on earth was it that they forced him to eat? Again, there was nothing about the entities whom the unfortunate motorcyclist encountered that relegated them to the class of semi-transparent "projections," for, according to his testimony, they apprehended him physically.

Once more, a story that appears to have little point to it, apart from the possibility that some obscure experimentation was being carried out.

Excellently investigated by members of one of the experienced and highly competent Lumières dans la Nuit *local teams, led by Monsieur Bigorne, and on this occasion aided in the field by Messrs. Chappat and Fourtouil. Impeccably written, the report was first published by* LDLN *in their issue Number 139 (November, 1974)*, and Gordon Creighton's translation appearing in* Flying Saucer Review, *Volume 21, Number 6 (December, 1975).*

At 5:35 A.M. on Thursday, February 28, 1974, the witness (whose name we are not at liberty to divulge) was riding as usual to work, on his Moped, along French Departmental Highway 38 and then along RN (Route Nationale) 363. He is a very simple man, in the broadest sense of the term, aged 59, but aged prematurely by the very hard and arduous nature of his employment, which is as a forge worker at Hirson.

* For address, see Appendix.

He is a close, uncommunicative sort of person, speaking very little. His environment is essentially the proletarian, working-class milieu, with all the features and the mentality that are quite special to small villages. Before his sighting he had no credence whatever "in all that twaddle about 'flying saucers,'" and knew nothing whatever about the UFO phenomenon. No importance is attached in his family to the subject of UFOs, and proof of this is to be seen in the fact that, even after he had experienced the extraordinary adventure which is related below, his wife and his two sons did not so much as take the trouble to go to the spot and see for themselves the marks on the ground.

Nevertheless, despite such bleak indifference, the whole family has been marked by this unwonted event and, above all, every one of them fears a repetition of it. The witness himself has been left in a state of shock by his experience. On the day on which it took place he did nothing about it; he did not even report it in official quarters (and he never will). When he arrived at his place of work his colleagues—observing his strange and abnormal behavior—questioned him, and he, innocent that he is, revealed the facts to them. The consequences of this disclosure were very unfortunate indeed for him: he was mocked, ridiculed, the butt of the nastiest sort of scoffery. Whereupon he fell into a deeply depressed state.

Because of this, our task in conducting our investigation was very difficult, particularly at the beginning, with him refusing to speak to our investigators and even fleeing from us. It was only after an exchange of correspondence and after we had come to an arrangement with his wife and his son, that we were able to have a meeting with him. He struck us on that occasion as very disturbed, totally disoriented, not only by the experience he had undergone but also, and indeed more particularly, by the general reactions with which his disclosures had been received.

We would point out that he has little talent for observation, which explains the paucity of the details noted by him during his strange encounter.

The Facts of the Case

It is 5:30 in the early morning. The witness has set out from home and is driving along the Departmental Highway which will bring him to Origny-en-Thierache.[1] He has just passed the last houses of the village of Les Routières and he is coming round the bend just before the bridge over the river Thon (a tributary of the Oise, which it joins at Etreaupont). So far, he has no idea of what awaits him, for he has seen nothing, observed nothing.

Suddenly, as soon as he is over the bridge, he finds himself pulled up short, face to face with two "cosmonauts" (his own term!). He is dumbfounded, unable to grasp what is happening to him, and wonders how it is that he has been able to pull up, seeing that, as he claims, he had neither slowed down nor applied his brakes. Above all, what he finds most amazing is this sudden meeting with the two beings, for he had seen nothing whatever, right up to the last moment!

And then he catches sight of a large, dark, circular mass at 35 meters on his left in the field below (one meter below the level of the road). At once he thinks that this must be "their machine." He notices nothing else; no light, nothing flashing, no sound, absolutely nothing, except for that dark, circular mass.

The witness emphasized that the night was dark, very dark. We asked him whether this degree of darkness was abnormal, but he was unable to give us an answer. Maybe this, in fact, is the reason why he has given us so few details. . . .

So there he was, on the road above the level of the field, and he had put one foot down to the ground to keep his balance. Immediately on his left was the gate leading into the field, but he was unable to see whether it was open or shut. Meanwhile the two ufonauts are there, standing facing him, one on each side, grasping his handlebars, and they seem to be peering at him. And he is very frightened.

He estimated the height of the machine at around 1 meter 80 to 2 meters, and said it was as big as two cars. Dark, completely circular, it gave out no sound. It had no legs and seemed to be standing directly on the ground. It had no antennae or protuberances, no portholes, no luminosity as far as he could observe.

The two "cosmonauts" before him now began to make gestures, very expressive, "quasi-human" we might even say, indicating to him that he should eat something. He was panic-stricken. The two beings no doubt exchanged a glance, for the two helmets turned to face each other, and maybe they communicated with each other in some fashion, for then the one on the left gave a sign to the one on the right, and the witness saw the latter put his hand behind his back and grope about in something (a pocket?—a bag?) which he could not see. Then, forthwith, the entity produced a piece of some substance, about one square centimeter or so in size, on the tips of the fingers of his right hand, and once more made signs to him with the left hand, seemingly to intimate that he should eat this substance he was offering.

Completely terrified, our witness took the substance ("this piece of chocolate"), to use his own words, raised it to his mouth and ate it . . . ! It was a substance which seemed to be of the brown color of chocolate, with no detectable taste, and of a consistency somewhat softer than chocolate. He insists on the fact that the two beings patiently waited until he had quite finished eating the substance before they let him go. In fact, as soon as he had eaten the substance, they moved away from his Moped and so permitted him to depart, which he did with the utmost speed, terrified, without waiting for anything else to happen.

May we emphasize that the poor fellow was not even able to tell us whether or not his engine had stopped during this extraordinary encounter. Nor does he recall whether or not he had to pedal in order to start it up again for his departure. He says he noticed no misfire from his engine and no effect on his headlamps. He was so scared that he did not look back again to see what his two "interceptors" were doing, and so we have no details on that score.

The Sequel

We conducted our investigation two months after the episode, during which period certain details may have dropped out of the witness's memory.

He noticed no abnormal effects on his organism as a result of his incredible "limited diet" meal—no headache, no stomachache or diarrhea, etc. As regards his mental and emotional state, there was no detectable change, if we are to believe those around him, except that, nevertheless, his experience has marked him profoundly.

The notable fact is that he is now even more uncommunicative than before, speaking less and less. As he fled from the scene of his encounter and continued on his way to Hirson, his only thought was "I'm well out of *that*!" At the plant he had a disturbed day and was unable to work normally.

He did not consult his doctor after his dubious meal. We have ascertained that the family doctor was informed of the facts and was indeed himself interested in the UFO phenomenon. However he paid no visit to his unusual patient. Was this due to apathy, or to the desire to conform with the routine of ordinary daily life. As a result, it has been impossible to do any serious investigation in the medical domain such as might have enabled us to grasp what the unknown beings did to him, and to know whether the affair was physical, or purely psychic, or maybe again something else?

Two months later, at the time when we made our investigation, the marks had disappeared. The witness and his family did not even go to look at them. It was neighbors and colleagues who, without believing greatly in the story, went out of pure curiosity to the spot in the field where the circular mass had stood at a distance of 35 meters from the road, and who found the marks and confirmed that they were there. Those of them with whom we spoke were honest, reliable people, who said the marks were precisely where the witness had said the object stood, "near the fourth apple tree from the road." They said there was a whole circular area there, with the grass all squashed and flattened—details which put us in mind of the case at Les Nourradons given in *LDLN*, Number 118.[2]

Here once again, in the case at Origny-en-Thierache, we were informed of the affair too late, and no samples could be taken for analysis.

The Beings

They measured about 1 meter 70 in height and were dressed in a dark one-piece suit, like astronauts. They were wearing a sort of square[3] helmet over the area where the head would be, with an opening where the face would be, but the witness could see nothing whatsoever in this opening apart from an even darker veiled area, their faces seeming to be, as it were, "masked." Their movements were normal, without anything particular such as hopping, etc., etc. Their one-piece suits were quite lusterless and did not shine. He noticed no pockets, etc., on the suits. One single detail struck him, however: the beings were wearing five-fingered gloves, and these gloves came up very high indeed on the arms: to use his own expression, "like the gloves worn for the artificial insemination of cattle." He said these gloves were not an integral part of the suit but seemed to terminate at the shoulder.

The Site and the Surroundings

The landing took place in a field through which the river Thon flows (some 4–5 meters wide here). The dark mass standing 35 meters from the road was in line with the entrance to the field and was 45 meters from the river Thon. There are a lot of apple trees there and, some 50 meters before the bridge, there are a calvary and a chapel. The nearest farms lie at a distance of some 120 meters. As far as we are aware, there were no other witnesses, owing to the hour at which the incident happened (5:35 A.M.) and also owing to the fact that the object in the field was totally dark and gave out no light.

As far as the geology of the area is concerned, no fault is known to exist in the vicinity. Within a radius of one kilometer of the spot there are four or five power lines to be noted and there is the TV relay transmitter at Landouzy-la-Ville. Then another feature to be noted is the Saint-Alexandre spring, known as "the fever spring," near the Abbey of Foigny (founded in 1121) in the valley of the river Thon. An incredible number of people come there to fill their bottles with the mineral water. This water has the power to expel fevers.

The region consists of a deep, narrow valley a little over one kilometer wide and seven or eight kilometers long. The subsoil is limestone and marl. There are lots of inaccessible subterranean springs. It is the region of the river Thierache, with its verdant pastures, its forests, and its pools. The area forms the first outlines of the foothills of the Ardennes.

We might mention also that the area has already had its UFO visitations, with cases at Fouronines, Macquenoise, Hirson, etc.

Other Sightings

1. Les Routières, February, 1974

Over a period of 1½ weeks which included the date of this remarkable case, three other people in the hamlet of Les Routières claimed to have seen luminous red balls which appeared on the top of the slope opposite their house and then shot down at great speed toward the valley, rose up over the slope opposite, and disappeared finally behind the woods.

2. Foigny and Les Routières, March 5, 1974

Monsieur Theeten and his wife (a professor) were driving in their car along Departmental Highway 38 and were just approaching the last turn before entering the hamlet of Les Routières, when they perceived, on their right-hand side, at a distance of some 50 meters and below them, a sort of yellowish orange cigar flying at a height of about 50 meters above the meadow. The time was 8:25 P.M., and the sighting lasted a few seconds. The driver pulled up. Twenty seconds later they saw the cigar again, this time in a different position. It was now inclined at an angle of 45° whereas, just before, it had been completely horizontal. This second sighting also lasted about ten seconds. They estimated that the cigar was some 15 meters or so in length and about 1 meter 80 thick. They heard no sound from it, detected no odor, and detected no effect from the machine upon them or their car. They reported the matter to the Gendarmerie, who came and conducted an investigation on the spot.

A week later, Monsieur Theeten had a second sighting. At 6 kilometers from Etreaupont he watched, for a duration of 15 minutes, a big red light, flashing very regularly, in a field beside the road. He went toward the light several times, retreating again, and each time that he tried to get near it, it stopped flashing. After that, the witness drove on.

Conclusions

A cigar is seen. Then it disappears and reappears at the same spot. Did it go away and come back again, or did it become temporarily invisible to the eyes of the witness?

We understand from the newspapers that a "cigar" identical with the one seen by the Theetens had been seen ten minutes earlier, on the same evening in the nearby Ardennes.[4]

After making a thoroughgoing investigation of him and of those around him, we have reached the conclusion that our motorcyclist, the forge worker who encountered the entities at Origny-en-Thierarche, is telling the truth. In the first place it is clear that this man is incapable of making up such a story. And secondly, we have found him, when we interviewed him, in too deeply depressed a state for hoax to be possible. Furthermore we must bear in mind the other sightings in the same area during the same week.

What strikes us as a very serious matter is this desperate eagerness to ridicule the witness. The explanations for it may lie in the fact that mankind likes to employ this oldest and most simple of all forms of escape, namely to *laugh at what he cannot comprehend!* Our witness in this case is the very image of the typical ordinary man of simple tastes, the everyday man, who is born and lives and dies without seeking to know the great human mysteries—the enigma of why he exists. And then, suddenly, after a lifetime spent without knowing that there are fantastic phenomena occuring on earth, he experiences this sort of thing, at the age of 59.

Comment
by F. Lagarde,
Editor of *Lumières dans la Nuit*

This is a fascinating and well-written account by our friends in the north, who seem to have overlooked nothing. The only addition one might suggest could perhaps be to say that the site in question (if this fact be of any importance) lies 7 kilometers to the northeast of the Southend—Po di Gnocca orthotenic line.

Another point might also be noted (and this is also a geological fault-zone effect)—namely, the recurrence of phenomena on several successive days. It is probable that, had there been informants already in the area, alert for all that was being whispered to and fro, our investigators would have received reports of further sightings.

The compulsory mastication of the mystery substance presents a problem. Whenever I hear of mastication or teeth in UFO reports I am reminded of the case of Betty and Barney Hill (see Dr. Hynek's *The UFO Experience*). In the course of one "amusing" episode in that case, the entities removed Barney Hill's false teeth. A similar attempt was made by them on Betty's teeth, which failed lamentably, her dentures owing nothing to artifice. If we place ourselves in the shoes of our visitors, maybe we shall find that, to the latter, human mastication is a mystery and so they wanted to know, by actually seeing it, how it is performed![5] As will be noted, there are two stages. First the witness is invited to eat. Then, as he does not perform for them, the "others" think that maybe the witness lacks the necessary foodstuff so then (stage 2) they supply him with it and then watch the operation. As an explanation, this is perhaps a little simple, but at any rate it fits the story as related.

NOTES

1. Origny is at 49° 50 N, 3° 30 E, in the Department of Aisne, and to the northeast of Paris.
2. See my translation, "A French Repeater Case: Events at Les Nourradons," in *Flying Saucer Review*, Volume 19, Number 3 (May–June, 1973).
3. Reports of "square" helmets are very rare. Compare, however, the similar case at Warneton, on the Franco-Belgian border and not so far distant from Origny, in which a Belgian motorist twice encountered creatures about the same period (January 8, 1974, and June 6, 1974). One of the creatures was described as wearing a "cubic" helmet. (This case appeared in *Flying Saucer Review*, Volume 20, Number 5.)*
4. The Ardennes, scene of the "Battle of the Bulge" in World War II, lie due east of Origny.
5. This may indeed be possible, but is it not far more probable that the "piece of chocolate" may have been intended to produce some kinds of results in the witness, perhaps long after? If the *LDLN* investigators watch him carefully, they may one day have something extraordinary to report!

* See page 116 of the present anthology.

A Humanoid Was Seen at Imjärvi

by Sven-Olof Fredrikson

Some UFO encounters are decidedly unpleasant; others have unpleasant after-effects or consequences. Two preliminary reports of a mid-winter encounter in the snow and ice of Finland had already been recounted by Mr. Fredrikson of the Swedish investigating group GICOFF (Göteborgs Informations Center för Oidentifierade Flygande Föremål). However, he felt that reinvestigation was called for in view of the unpleasant after-effects suffered by one of the witnesses, and the reticence on his part, which was a natural outcome of the experience. The report of this appeared in* Flying Saucer Review, *Volume 16 , Number 5 (September–October, 1970).*

Since the appearance of my first two reports in *Flying Saucer Review,* "on-the-spot" investigations in Finland have shown that in their letters to us Messrs. Heinonen and Viljo did not tell us the whole story. There were two reasons for this. First, Heinonen, who gave us most of the information, appears to have been suffering from a partial loss of memory. This means that, until recently, he had recalled only parts of the incident. Now that personal interviews have taken place, we believe that most of the story has been told. Secondly, Viljo and Heinonen have not spoken to each other about the incident, at least not, in any detail.† As a result, Heinonen

* For address, see Appendix.

† In "Finnish Encounter in the Snow," *Flying Saucer Review* for July–August, 1970, Heinonen's growing fear of Viljo, and how he hadn't the courage to visit him, was described—EDITOR.

thought he had seen a grotesquely distorted image of Viljo when he looked through the mist, whereas Viljo considered he had seen something "that does not exist," and did not speak about it as he did not wish to have people laughing at him about it.

Early in June this year, a Swedish reporter from a weekly magazine went to Finland to investigate the case and to write an article. We have been in contact with him for about six months, during which time he has become very interested in the subject. Together with a photographer, he met an interpreter when he was in Finland. The two witnesses were located and interviewed (we have a tape of this). Photographs were taken at the scene, the doctor was interviewed, and a discussion was had with a professor of electrophysics. The two men also signed a drawing of the object.

It was not until Heinonen and Viljo were confronted with the reporter's questions that they began to tell the whole story, not only to the reporter, but for the first time to each other.

After comparing the material we obtained from the reporter with the contents of our letters from the two Finns, and after studying reports of the physiological effects which were claimed to have resulted from the encounter, we compiled a case report in Swedish. A translation of this now follows.

The Case Report

The incident occurred on Wednesday, January 7, 1970, at 4:45 P.M., in a forest outside the village of Imjärvi, 16 kilometers north-northeast of the town of Heinola in southern Finland. Heinola is 130 kilometers northeast of Helsinki. The two witnesses, forester Aarno Heinonen, 36 years of age, and farmer Esko Viljo, 38, were out skiing. Both men have been active ski-runners, and also runners in athletics, and they still take part in smaller competitions. They are both total abstainers and nonsmokers.

They were descending from a little hill, and halted in a glade where they usually take a pause. It was sunset, and a few stars were visible. It was very cold, −17° Celsius, with no wind.

They had been standing in the glade for about five minutes when they heard a buzzing sound. They looked up and caught sight of a very strong light moving through the sky. . . . It approached from the north, made a vast curve, and came toward them from the south. At the same time it descended. The weak buzzing sound became louder. The light halted, and then they could see that a luminous cloud rotated around it. It was like a red-gray mist pulsating with a strange light. At the same time puffs of smoke were thrown up from the top of the cloud. The two men were standing still, staring upward. Neither of them uttered a word.

The cloud was soon as low as 15 meters, and it was then that they could see, inside it, a round object, flat at the bottom, and metallic-like. They estimate that it was about three meters in diameter. On its underside there were three hemispheres, and in the center a tube, some 25 centimeters in diameter, which extended about 20 centimeters.

The object hung in the air a short while, the buzzing sound continued. Then the sound became louder, and the object descended slowly. At the same time the red-gray mist slowly disappeared. The object stopped moving when it was 3 or 4 meters above the ground, and the buzzing also ceased. Heinonen said it was so close that he could have touched it with his ski stick.

A bright light beam was suddenly emitted by the tube. This beam moved around a couple of times before stopping, creating a bright illuminated circle over the snow. This circle was about one meter in diameter, while around it there was a black edge, about 1 centimeter wide. The two men were standing quite still while a red-gray mist descended over the place.

Said Heinonen: "Suddenly I felt as if somebody had seized my waist from behind and pulled me backward. I think I took a step backward, and in the same second I caught sight of the creature. It was standing in the middle of the light beam with a black box in its hands. Out of a round opening in the box there came a yellow light, which was pulsating. The creature was about 90 centimeters tall, with very thin arms and legs. Its face was pale like wax. I didn't notice the eyes, but the nose was very strange. It was a hook rather than a nose. The ears were very small, and narrowed toward the head. The creature wore some kind of overall in a light green material. On its feet were boots of a darker green color, which stretched above the knees. There were also white gauntlets going up to the elbows, and the fingers were bent like claws around the black box."

Esko Viljo describes the creature like this: "I saw it too. The creature stood in the middle of the bright light and was luminous like phosphorous, but its face was very pale. Its shoulders were very thin and slanting, with thin arms like those of a child. I did not think of the clothes, only noticing that they were greenish in color. On its head was a conical helmet shining like metal. The creature was less than 1 meter tall, and very thin."

While the two men were standing there, staring at the creature, it turned a little and put the opening in the box toward Heinonen. The pulsating light was very bright, almost blinding. While the creature was standing in the light beam a thick red-gray mist descended from the object and big sparks came from the illuminated circle above the snow. The sparks were large, about 10 centimeters in length. They were red, green, and purple in color. They were floating out in long curves, and rather slowly. The sparks hit the two men, but they did not feel them. The mist became thicker and thicker, and Heinonen and Viljo could not see one another. At last it became so thick that they could not see the creature in the light beam. By then, they think they had seen the creature for about 15 to 20 seconds.

Said Esko Viljo: "Suddenly the circle above the snow decreased, the light beam floated upward like a trembling flame and went into the tube of the object. Then it was as if the mist was 'thrown apart,' and above us the air was empty."

They were standing still at the place for maybe 3 minutes. Said Heinonen: "We were not afraid and we did not talk; we did nothing."

Aarno Heinonen. Two minutes after the mist had dispersed, Heinonen felt that his right side had become insensitive, and when taking a step forward with his ski, he fell to the ground.

"I had had my right side toward the light: my right leg hurt and I could not feel anything from my right foot upward. I could not raise myself although I tried several times."

He had to leave his skis at the place, and Viljo helped him. It took an hour for them to move 2 kilometers. When they reached their village and the cottage belonging to Heinonen's parents, he did not feel at all well. He had pains in his back and in all his limbs. He had a headache and after a while he vomited. When he later passed water, his urine was black like coffee. (This symptom continued for a couple of months.) He also had problems with his breathing.

At 8:00 P.M. the same day, he went to Dr. Pauli Kajanoja in Heinola. The doctor took his blood pressure and found it to be much lower than normal, which indicated shock. Heinonen was given some sleeping pills. On January 8 he visited the same doctor who then prescribed a sedative. The symptoms continued, his limbs were sore, and he had problems with his balance. He felt cold but had no fever.

On January 14 he went to the doctor for the third time and was given medicine for the blood circulation. The symptoms continued and he could not work. In the middle of May he told us in a letter: "I am still sick. I have a headache and I have pains in the back of my neck, as well as in my stomach and my back. My right hand feels very heavy. I cannot work. I have not improved much since winter. The doctors in Heinola cannot help me. Is the government so poor that it cannot help us? I have tried to get contributions from the authorities but have received nothing. I think they ought to pay me, because I do not know why I am sick. I have been to the place where we saw the object, and after this became even more sick."

Heinonen has had bouts of loss of memory. He did not remember the occurrence in full until some time after the incident. In the beginning of June he was still very weak. He has eaten very little since January. Before January 7 his physical condition was excellent, but now he becomes tired when he is doing even the easiest work.

Esko Viljo. Viljo did not feel anything abnormal immediately after the occurrence, but one hour later his face became swollen and reddish in color, and he walked in an unbalanced way. Doctor Kajanoja prescribed and provided 2 sleeping pills. The next morning Viljo had difficulties with his balance, with a feeling of lightness, particularly in his legs. His hands and chest became red. On January 9, 1970, he went to the doctor and got a sedative. He suffered from a headache for a couple of days.

On January 12, he visited an eye specialist in Lahtis, because he had a pain in his eyes. They were swollen. He obtained eyedrops.

On January 14 he went to the doctor in Heinola and got medicine for the blood circulation.

On January 17 he went to the same doctor who could find nothing wrong with him. When having his sauna, his body became reddish in color.

In a letter to us in the middle of May he wrote: "Some people visited the site of the occurrence, and they were sick a couple of days later. Could it be some kind of infection?"

Dr. Kajanoja who examined the two men says: "I think the men have suffered a great shock. Esko Viljo was very red in the face, and seemed to be a little swollen. They both seemed to be absent-minded. They talked quickly and incoherently. I could not find anything clinically wrong with Heinonen. He did not feel well, but that could have been his stomach reacting to the shock. The symptoms he described are like those after being exposed to radio-activity. Unfortunately I had no instrument to measure that. As to the black urine, it seems inexplicable. Possibly it could have been blood in it, but this cannot go on for several months. It was impossible to diagnose. Therefore I could not prescribe any particular medicine."

When a friend of ours, who is a reporter for a weekly magazine in Sweden, visited the place with a photographer in the beginning of June—together with Viljo and Heinonen—the following happened: after standing a short while at the place, the hands of Viljo, Heinonen, and an interpreter became red in color. Heinonen had to leave the place because of a headache.

On the day of the incident, January 7, and at the same time, two other witnesses saw a strange, strong light in the sky. One of them was Elna Siitari, in Paistjärvi village, about 15 kilometers from Imjärvi. The wife of a farmer, she was on her way to the cow house when she saw the strange light toward Imjärvi.

The same happened in the village Paaso, 10 kilometers north of Imjärvi, where a man saw the light phenomenon. The time was then 4:45 P.M.

Matti Haapaniemi, 46 years old, is a farmer and a close neighbor of the Heinonens. He is a member of the communal council in Heinola rural commune. He says: "Several persons in the neighborhood have laughed at this story, but I do not think they should do that. I have known both Aarno and Esko since they were boys. I trust them. They are both calm persons, and they are also total abstainers. I am sure their story is true."

A year ago, a 16-year-old-boy, Matti Kontulainen from Imjärvi, saw a strange light only a hundred meters from the glade where Viljo and Heinonen saw the object. He says: "It was about 11:00 P.M. in the evening. It was in February, and no stars were visible. I came skiing through the forest after having been to a friend's. I was on my way home. It was dark, but suddenly the forest was lit up by a very bright light going above the tree-tops. It was like a gigantic welding flame. It disappeared very fast. I have never before seen such a strong light. It came from the south and went to the north. I did not hear any sound, so it could not have been an airplane."

Matti Tuuri, professor of electrophysics at the University of Helsinki, is interested in this case. He says: "The two men say the light was blinding, and white or yellow. This means that it could not have been ultraviolet radiation, which does not go through the clothes. It ought to have been radiation with a higher frequency, for instance X-rays." Professor Tuuri believes that the flying saucers are traveling along the magnetic power lines around the earth. "There is a lot more to learn in electrophysics. For instance about the fireball. According to all physical laws it ought to explode at once, but it does not."

Stig Lundquist, professor at the Institute for Research in High Tension, University of Uppsala, Sweden, has studied some of the accounts. He says in a letter to us: "As far as I can say the phenomenon does not have any connection with any known thunder or electricity. Although I have a great interest in fireballs, I do not think I can explain the phenomenon as being one."

We at GICOFF have had an earth sample, together with melted snow, and branches from the place. At the Chalmers Institute of Technology in Gothenburg they have done an analysis of the earth sample to see if there was any radioactivity. The result: negative.

I and my colleagues are impressed with the authenticity of this case. Of course one cannot ignore the possibility of a hoax, or even of a delusion, but when one considers the way of writing of the two witnesses, their background in society, the opinion of the reporter who interviewed them, the opinion of the photographer, the doctor and the close neighbor, hoax seems to be ruled out. Then, of course there is the persisting evidence of their post-incident illness. There are also many details in the descriptions given by them that are commonly known to many UFO researchers, and I feel these could not have been known to the two witnesses. Among other things I refer to the sound, the descriptions of the object and of the black box; also the manner of disappearance of the object.

Among details which I consider of importance in this report are (1) the rotation of the cloud when the object descended, (2) the fact that the black box was stated to have been pointing at Heinonen who, subsequently, was far more ill than Viljo, (3) the description of the creature, (4) the mode of disappearance of the object, and (5) among the physiological effects, the black urine.

Berserk: A UFO-Creature Encounter

by Berthold Eric Schwarz, M.D.

We now see the UFO phenomenon more and more as it overlaps other dimensions, for it seems quite clear that not only could it be part of what is covered generally by the blanket term "psychic phenomena," but also that whatever controls UFO manifestations may well control a whole gamut of psychic events.

Dr. Schwarz is a psychiatrist with a busy practice, whose own vital energy somehow permits him to find time for considerable interest both in parapsychology and in UFO and peripherally aligned phenomena. He is also a consultant at the Brain Wave Laboratory, Essex County Overbrook Hospital, Cedar Grove, New Jersey. We at Flying Saucer Review *first learned of him when an article of his on studies of UFO witnesses appeared in the* Medical Times *of October, 1968 (Volume 96, Number 10). Entitled "UFOs: Delusion or Dilemma," it was the first contribution on UFOs ever to appear in a medical journal, and* FSR *reprinted it in its Special Issue Number 2,* Beyond Condon, *now unhappily out of print.*

Berthold Schwarz joined the panel of FSR *Consultants in 1969, and has made thought-provoking and challenging contributions to our pages. "Berserk" appeared in* Flying Saucer Review, *Volume 20, Number 1 (January–February, 1974).*

One September Sunday afternoon I received an unusual phone call from Allen Noe,[1] Trustee of SITU,* and Stan

* Society for the Investigation of the Unexplained, founded by the late Ivan T. Sanderson.

Gordon, Director of the Westmoreland County UFO Study Group (WCUFOSG). They told me of an exciting and bizarre UFO-creature epidemic that included 79 documented creature cases and two dozen more in process of analysis, then raging in a six-county area of western Pennsylvania. My curiosity was thoroughly aroused and I made plans to visit Greensburg in November.

Matters were advanced on October 27, 1973, when during a UFO field trip to Mrs. Stella Lansing's[2,3,4] in Massachusetts, I received a telephone call from my office in New Jersey to contact Stan Gordon immediately. It concerned a multiple-witness landing-creature case with dangerous overtones.

From Gordon's telephone description of the details I learned that much of the data, including an episode of a presumed fugue for the possible contactee, was taped out in the field. I gave first-aid advice and made arrangements for my visit the following week (November 1-3, 1973). At that time, thanks to Gordon and his group's generosity and cooperation, I listened to all their tapes in connection with this episode and conducted a psychiatric interview of the leading figure as well as interviews with members of the study group and others, including direct contact with ten-year-old fraternal male twins and their siblings, telephone interrogation of a state trooper, and the farmer-contactee's parents. I also read Gordon's excellent written collations.

(The local newspaper carried an article on this case, but in this report pseudonyms will be used for the farmer, the witnesses, the police official, and place names.)

At approximately 10:30 P.M., Thursday, October 25, 1973, Stan Gordon received a call from Trooper Byrne of the state police. Something unusual had happened on a farm not far from Greensburg. The UFO Study Group field team left shortly to investigate the situation. At police headquarters the initial witness, farmer Stephen Pulaski,† stated that Trooper Byrne had also heard something in the woods and that Byrne saw a glowing area at the location where a UFO was reputed to have landed.

Stephen was questioned by the Study Group on the telephone about what had happened, and arrangements were

† Referred to as Stephen hereafter.

made to meet him and his father at the shopping mall, from where the group could go to the scene of the sighting. The group arrived at the mall at approximately 12:45 A.M., on Friday, October 26, 1973. In the team was David Smith, a physics teacher and a radiation expert in civil defense; Dennis Smeltzer, who majored in sociology; George Lutz, Jr., a former Air Force officer, and the co-director of WCUFOSG; David Baker, a photographer, and Stan Gordon. When they arrived, Stephen related the entire experience.

Landing and Creatures

At approximately 9:00 P.M., Stephen and at least fifteen other witnesses, including relatives and neighbors, noticed a bright red ball hovering over the field at a fairly high level. Stephen and two neighbor boys (ten-year-old fraternal twins) decided to go up toward the field. Stephen took along a 30.06 rifle. As they were approaching closer, Stephen mentioned that his auto headlights became dim. They could see the object slowly descending toward the field. The three of them walked up over the crest of the hill and saw the object sitting directly on, or hovering just above, the field. As the object was approaching, Stephen's male German shepherd (third generation inbred), at the house, became very disturbed. The object was now bright white and was illuminating the area. The witnesses estimated the object to be about 100 feet in diameter: "It was dome-shaped, just like a big bubble. It was making a sound like a lawn mower."

As they were observing the object, one of the twins yelled that there was something walking along, silhouetted by the fence. Stephen could not see them well (he wears glasses for myopia). Since the first rifle slug was a tracer, he fired directly over the heads of the two figures that he thought at first were bears. As soon as he fired and was able to see clearly, he knew that the creatures were something strange.

Both creatures were similar in appearance, but one was about 7 feet tall and the other a little over 8 feet. They were observed to be higher than the fence posts which were over 6 feet high. The larger creature's left hand touched and followed along the fence posts. Both creatures were completely covered with long, dark grayish hair[5] and they had greenish yellow eyes.[6] Their arms hung down almost to the ground.

The smaller creature seemed to be taking long strides, as if trying to keep up with the larger one. The creatures were making whining sounds, almost like that of a baby crying. They seemed to be whining back and forth to each other. A strong odor was also present—something like burning rubber.

Stephen then fired a second bullet over their heads, realizing that they were different from anything that he had ever seen and also that they were slowly walking toward the trio. He finally fired three rounds directly into the larger one. One of the boys, now quite scared, ran back toward the house. When the creature was hit, it made a whining sound and moved its right hand up toward the other creature, almost touching it, at which time the glowing lighted object just disappeared in the field and the noise from it also stopped.

The creatures, after having been shot at, slowly turned around and walked back toward the woods. Stephen and the remaining twin noticed that on the field, where the object had been, there was a glowing white area, so bright that you could read a newspaper by it. About this time Stephen's eyes (and those of one of the twins) began to bother him. The bull and the horses would not go near the area after the incident.

Stephen was reluctant to go to the police to report the incident, but then thought he had better. After the officer heard about the experience (and came to the farm), and at about 9:45 P.M., Trooper Byrne and Stephen got in the patrol car and drove up the dirt road about 100 yards from where the UFO landing was and stopped just below the corn field, near the woods.

The headlights of the trooper's car were shining toward the field and Stephen said the glowing ring was still visible. At first the trooper thought it was from the headlights, but when he moved his car the ring was still visible. The trooper also shone his flashlight into the bright ring and the beam could hardly be seen. They walked down to a double-stranded electric fence, where the trooper noted that the bottom wire was broken. He asked Stephen about it, who stated that to his knowledge it was not broken before.

Then, about 50 yards to the right they heard a loud walking noise in the woods. The sound of something large appeared to be coming toward them. They could hear trees being torn and breaking. When they moved, the noise would follow, and when they stopped it would continue a few seconds and then stop. The trooper saw a small saddle in the field and about 100 yards to the left there was an illuminated area about 150 feet in diameter. The house was about 250 yards away from the craft and a mercury lamp was in the area, but neither could reflect into that locale. According to Stephen, the trooper was already in the car and they were both quite scared.

The trooper said he wanted to walk up toward the lighted area. But, as he and the trooper got within about 200 yards of it, Stephen stopped and told the trooper: "I don't get paid for being brave. I'm not going any further." The trooper started ahead on his own and then decided it was better for him to go back since Stephen was very excited and might mistake him for something else. He then told Stephen that he would go back to the barracks and call Stan Gordon, who would come up if there was something to it.

At this point, when they started back toward the car, they again heard the movements in the woods. By this time they had been in the area about half an hour. The trooper said that when they got back in the car he was going to turn off his headlights to see if the glowing area would disappear. The trooper got into the car. Stephen then noticed a brown object coming toward them and he wanted to shoot his last round to see if anything would happen. The trooper said it was okay to do so. Stephen then fired his one remaining bullet.

While the trooper was standing at the patrol car door, he noted how Stephen was very upset, perspiring, and pale. Stephen's actions and appearance began to get the trooper worked up. Stephen suddenly yelled that something was coming out of the woods toward them. They both jumped into the car and the trooper drove about 50 yards out of the field when he came to his senses and realized that he was in the safety of the car. He turned the car around and shone the high beam of the headlights into the woods. No sound could be detected at this point.

Later, the trooper described a soft glowing area about 150 feet in diameter. In the glow he could make out small plants. The glow extended about a foot up from the ground and the trooper guessed that if you bent down you could probably read a newspaper by the light. The trooper would not say definitely that it was a circular area, since they were on a slanted strip of land. He said that he did not know for certain if the light was from his headlights or not. He felt that when they were in the area of the glow, the temperature might have been a little warmer than the surrounding area, but he couldn't be sure of this because of the excitement. He also said that the dogs around the farm were kicking up a fuss and that no animals would go near the area where the glow was, even though they were moving around it. However, Stephen stated that when the trooper turned the car around, the glowing area disappeared. When the trooper looked around, he couldn't see the glowing area any longer. (The next morning when he went out to check over the area, he couldn't find anything unusual.)

It was about 1:30 A.M. when the Study Group arrived at the secluded farm and made their way up the long dirt road which went into the field. Two boys stayed behind in Stephen's truck. The team started to move up the field where Stephen told them the object and the ring had been. There was no ring apparent when they arrived. First they checked the area for radiation. Stephen had been checked at the shopping mall before they left for the scene. No unusual level was observed in either case.

While the team was looking over the field, at approximately 1:45 A.M., both of the Pulaskis (father and son) yelled to them. The group ran down to the truck where they were standing and they related how they had seen the entire farm-house area light up with a glow. The glow had disappeared when the group arrived, but George Lutz and Mr. Pulaski, Sr., went down to the house to look around. They radioed that nothing was found.

The team and the two Pulaskis walked up from the truck toward the area where the creatures were observed. It was about 2:00 A.M. Suddenly the bull (in a nearby field) was scared by something. Stephen's dog also became alarmed and started tracking something. The dog kept looking at a certain spot by the edge of the woods, but the group didn't see anything. George Lutz was asking Stephen some questions when all of a sudden Stephen began rubbing his head and face. George Lutz asked him if he was okay, and Stephen then began shaking back and forth as if he were going to faint. George Lutz and Mr. Pulaski, Sr., grabbed Stephen. Stephen, aged 22, is over 6 feet 2 inches tall and weighs around 250

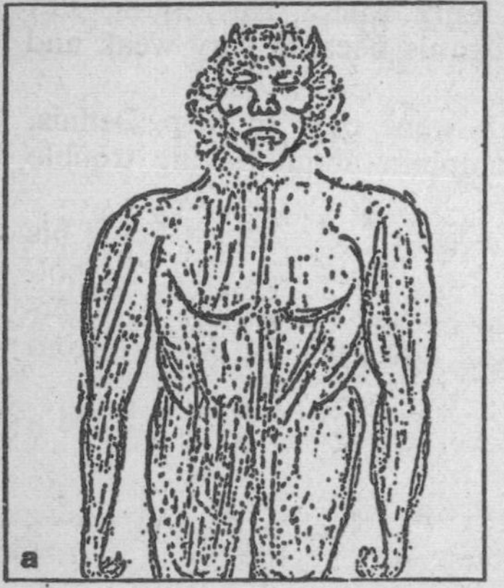

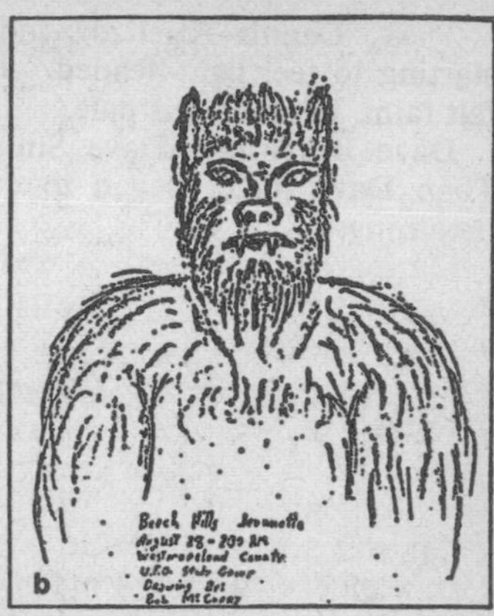

FIGURE 8: Study Group artist Bob McCurry's reconstruction of creatures sighted in nearby communities: (a) above left, Latrobe, Pa., August, 1973; (b) above right, Beech Hills, August 23, 1973, 2:30 a.m.; (c) below left, Luscon, August 26, 1973, 5:00 p.m.

pounds. He then began breathing very heavily and started growling like an animal. He flailed his arms and threw his father and George Lutz to the ground. His dog then ran toward him as if to attack, and Stephen went after the dog. The dog started crying. George Lutz and Mr. Pulaski were calling to Stephen to come back, that it was all right, and that they were returning to the car.

Then, Dennis Smeltzer suddenly said, "Hey, Stan, I'm starting to feel light-headed." Dennis became very weak and felt faint. His face was pale.

Dave Baker and Dave Smith went over to help Dennis. Then Dave Baker began to complain about having trouble breathing.

During all this, Stephen was running around, swinging his arms, and loudly growling like an animal. Suddenly he collapsed on his face into a heavily manured area. Shortly afterward he started to come out of it and said, "Get away from me. It's here. Get back."

Just then Stephen and Stan, as well as the others, smelled a very strong sulfur, or chemical-like odor.[7]

George Lutz said, "Let's get out of here." Then he and Mr. Pulaski, Sr., were helping Stephen along when, suddenly on the way down the hill, Stephen pointed and yelled: "Keep away from the corner! It's in the corner!"

Stephen kept mumbling that he would protect the group. He also mumbled that he saw a man "in a black hat and cloak, carrying a sickle." He told Stephen, "If Man doesn't straighten up, the end will come soon." He also said, "There is a man here now who can save the world." Stephen said that he could hear his name—"Stephen. Stephen"—being called from inside the woods. When he collapsed, Stephen's glasses fell off.

On the way down, as Stephen was coming out of his confused state, his father handed him the glasses and Stephen asked whose they were. Stan asked Stephen if he could see okay, and he said, "Just fine."

The group asked Mr. Pulaski if his son had ever acted like this before and he said never. He told them that Stephen had been taking nerve pills[8] since an accident about three years ago.

The group felt that Stephen was part of a contactee syndrome that was involved with future predictions, etc., and they were concerned that Stephen could physically harm himself or others and that professional help was needed.

More Information and Discussion

How can the presumed UFO-and-associated-creatures sighting be related to Stephen's fugue? Although such a brief study as this is not comparable to data derived over an extended period, the uniqueness of Stephen's experience and what we did learn about him from psychiatric study warrants speculation. What might apply to him might also hold for others and provide clues for future studies of such examples.

The unusual circumstances, and the fact that the various segments of events at different times were witnessed by thirteen people, indicate the reality of the experience. In all instances it seemed that Stephen and the others were truthful. There was no evidence for dishonesty, lying, sociopathic behavior, use of hallucinogenic drugs or alcohol, in connection with this experience or previously. The reports of the various witnesses, family members, and neighbors were compatible. Part of the action was tape-recorded as it was happening. Specifically, it would seem in "reality" that there were lights which were first low in the sky and which then descended to nearby land, or hovered closely above the ground, and which had an associated lawn mower sound; that the UFO might have dimmed the truck's lights; that the brightness of the UFO's lights inflamed the eyes of two witnesses; and that the action and the stench associated with the creatures caused presumed behavioral reactions for the people involved and for dogs, horses, a bull, and cattle. Stephen's story was essentially the same whether given to the UFO Study Group, the trooper, or to me (BES). It was fully corroborated by independent interviews of the other witnesses by the Study Group and by me.

Because Stephen is an experienced hunter, and presumably a good shot, it would seem likely that he did fire three rounds into one of the creatures with the apparent effect of the creature's moaning, lifting its upper extremity, and walking back into the woods with its companion. This happening is confirmed by one of the twin boys who was with Stephen at the time. As in other alleged creature situations,[9] it is amazing that after all the action there is such an overall paucity or even a total absence of tangible evidence for the events. In this case there are only broken branches, possibly a strand of interrupted wire, and five rifle shells found on the ground at the site. Although the search was not exhaustive, there were no "bigfoot" prints, blood, hair, scorched earth, or other evidences—unlike some other cases studied. What happened to the creatures? Did they just disappear? How could the source of light, which appeared to be on, or just above the ground, have disappeared without any trace or any indication of its source? Where do these things come from and where do they go?

Stephen's acute fugue with furor is apparently out of context for him. A study of his past life revealed no evidence of any previous similar dissociative, disoriented behavior, nor any character traits like sleepwalking, sleep-talking, fainting, amnesia, trance-like states, etc. Furthermore, there is no past history for convulsive disorder, brain injury, or disease that could cause temporal lobe seizure or automatism analogues to Stephen's reaction to the creatures. The information derived from Stephen, his parents, neighbors, and several physicians indicates that the fugue was a specific reaction to the UFO-creatures experience—a solitary, outstanding event in Stephen's life. During the interviews Stephen had no memory of what happened during the fugue.

Farming and coal mining are hazardous occupations. While working in the mines, Stephen had had injuries, including a recent alleged trauma to his right eye, fractures and sprains of the left ankle. Three years ago he had a serious back injury. He had no permanent disability, however, and was never diagnosed "accident prone." Stephen recalled how, following his back injury, his physician allegedly told him that he would not live beyond young adulthood. This gloomy prognosis must have disturbed Stephen and, coupled with other events in his past life, made him a good candidate for being (as one physician wrote) "scared to death." Nevertheless, he worked hard and was a "going concern" without any history of fugues or psychosis.

It can be assumed that the trauma and terror, precipitated by the UFO landing and the creatures—by the fact that one of the creatures failed to be killed by the shots fired at close range—nearly unhinged Stephen. The fugue was precipitated when the Study Group was with Stephen on the scene, and about the time of the sudden appearance of the stench. The stench might possibly have been subliminally detected by Stephen and the others just before the fugue, but it was during and after his going berserk that it was noticed. At that point, all the cascading aspects of the dangers were suddenly realized and he was overwhelmed with anxiety. He lapsed into the fugue, and acted out violently until he collapsed face down upon the manure-strewn ground.

During this part of the psychiatric interview Stephen dangerously tottered between varying planes of entrancement and frequently had to be brought back to consciousness as he supplied more details. "Was it a dream? I heard a crying noise. I could see a man in a black robe, carrying a scythe. Behind this man was fire and in front of him was a force, and in this force were the creatures. They were calling. 'Stephen, Stephen!' One was laughing. It was a tantalizing laugh, and was making me mad. My hands were clenched tight. Behind us was a big light. In this light something was telling me to go forward. 'Go forward. Come on!' It was edging me. I could see myself as crazy, as a man so powerful that I wasn't scared of anything. The creatures kept calling me and the light kept saying: 'Go, my son, you can't be hurt.' I think of a mother sheep calling her little lambs. As I walked to the edge of the woods, the creatures kept wailing. I looked at them and all I could think of was death and the faceless form in the black robe who was commanding these things to kill me—it was hate . . . a hatred for everything. I knew that these things came from this force and if they got to the light they would be destroyed. The tension was so terrific that I passed out. Then I heard, 'He is here—He is here.' But who is He? Somebody was putting a puzzle in my head. My hands and ankles were hurting. Somebody was telling me that these people are going to destroy themselves. I kept seeing the date 1976—1976. It popped out of my mouth: 'If these people don't straighten out, the whole world will burn.' "

When Stephen was asked his opinion about what happened, and why he, a Pennsylvania farmer and coal miner, was chosen for this experience, he answered: "I'm living in hell now. What I'm telling you happened before. This is how the earth was destroyed. It will be very soon, and this world will be gone. Somebody better find out before long or the world will end. We're destroying the world. What's the fire? What's going to happen in burning. Is there someone smarter than us that is playing upon us, laying a picture or puzzle out for us? It seems stupid but it seems like I *have* to tell the President of the United States, because somebody else has to know. It seems that somebody else is also being told at the same time, but they're not going to do it. They're scared. I don't know what happened in the field, or what these guys told you, but I felt like an animal. If you could find the one who would believe me—1976 is not far off. I don't believe America is going to live to be 200 years free, because that's been getting to me too. And the world will go. Man will destroy himself."

Might the truest explanation for Stephen's fugue be found in the psychodynamics of his past life? Stephen is the oldest of three siblings, the youngest being ten. Life has always meant intense struggle to survive. He claims that since the age of ten he has practically run the farm himself (his father was away from home, driving a truck). In addition to all the chores, Stephen had his school work. He was also involved in frequent fights. He recalled once beating up a bully so badly that the youngster could not return to school for three weeks. One of his few pleasures in high school was being a first-string tackle on the football team; at the time he was 6 feet 2½ inches tall, and weighed 250 pounds.

Stephen related his story in a serious and somber way. There was little fun in his life. For example, his first memory of his mother was when he was at puberty and she was pregnant with his youngest sibling. In commenting about his desire to be a veterinarian, he said it was only because of the money he might earn, and had nothing to do with humanitarian aspects. He described his father as a rather brutal man given to sudden outbursts of temper. The father nicknamed Stephen "Pooch." Stephen was frequently punished when the father was angry at the younger children, and the punishment was swift and severe: punching in the mouth and beatings. The mother never intervened. Stephen also recalled his father telling how the grandfather was banged and cut up by the Mafia and had to go into hiding for fear of his life. Violence became an important part of Stephen's life. He recalled the time he was driving through a town and saw a street fight. He stopped his car, jumped out, started punching. He said that the combatants were amazed that he, a stranger, would subject himself to such risk. He then recalled an episode, with some relish, where an older neighbor made remarks about Stephen's girlfriend (and later wife). When the man entered the house, did $1,700 damage, and it was known that it would be some time until the police arrived, Stephen, as a last resort, grabbed a rifle and made elaborate plans to shoot the man in the leg and finally to kill him. Tragedy was narrowly averted by the timely arrival of the state police. His life ambition to enter the military forces was thwarted by an injury to his right leg. Stephen summed up his life by saying: "Everything I tried never ended right."

Stephen appeared intelligent. Although he was not well read and seldom went beyond the Pennsylvania *Farm Journal*, he could clearly describe various life experiences, and his accounts were well thought through and hung together. He had no previous all-consuming interest in UFOs, supposed monster lore, horror films, or such. He was a Roman Catholic but apparently not very devout. His wife is Protestant. His father is of Polish descent and his mother half English-Scottish-Irish and half French. Stephen had no previous interest in religion, prophecy, werewolves, the occult, or any esoteric philosophies. Life meant a grindstone and reality.

One enigmatic experience happened approximately five to six weeks before the alleged UFO-creature episode, shortly after Stephen and his wife moved to their apartment and had a telephone installed with a private, unlisted number. They received a mysterious phone call in which a man's voice told Stephen that he would be killed if he didn't get out of town in one week. This threat was not taken lightly. Also, shortly after this incident he claimed that the starter wires were pulled on his car. He could account for neither of these experiences. They are mentioned in this report because of the recurring motif of violence through so much of his life and, of course, because of the violent episode under study.

Perhaps these various background factors gave Stephen ample permission for violent acting out as a means of coping with otherwise overwhelming situations. Thus, it was no wonder that Stephen, who could usually succeed by brawn if nothing else, was terrorized by the creatures when they failed to succumb to his shots. It is not unusual under such circumstances for mechanisms of psychic containment—suppression and repressions—to break down completely, and for the patient to lose contact with reality, and for psychosis or fugue to ensue. Furthermore, it is not unusual at such time for the patient to regress via a mechanism of hostile identification with the aggressor—and to take on the posture and characteristics of the aggressor. In this way, the one who was terror-stricken by the trauma (or what associatively reminded him of it, or what precipitated the original trauma) defends himself from his own anxiety and fears, and perhaps in Stephen's case, of being unable to kill or *lex talionis*, his fear of being killed in return: "I'm going into those woods to kill them or they'll kill me." This might have accounted for his fugue-like state, when the appearance of the approaching creatures was imminent—either real or otherwise. Stephen lost control and was carried away by his unconscious, and mimicked what he observed the creatures to be: he growled, clawed with his outstretched hands, and made violently flailing movements, which decked one of the investigators, and his father, and culminated in Stephen's collapse. The excitement of what had happened, which was then being relived when the Study Group arrived, was pressed to the breaking point by the appearance of the stench which might have heralded the possible reentry of the creatures. This was more than Stephen could handle.

In the minds of the Study Group members, the fugue (and as it sounds from the tapes) might have conformed to Stephen's transfiguration or possession by the creatures. That possibility is highly speculative; it can neither be proved nor disproved. His vivid "possession" by the creatures was also similar to some spectacular séance situations in which the entranced medium assumes the alleged personality, expression, voice, etc., of the deceased. However, in those situations other elements are operative, such as histrionics derived from subliminal clues or possibly telepathy from the living, or for that matter, disembodied entities. It is of interest that these creatures, as well as the study group's and artist's reconstructed drawings of other creature cases studied by the UFO group (see Figure 8 for Study Group artist Bob McGurry's reconstructions of creatures sighted in a nearby community) might have some resemblance to medieval paintings of werewolves.[10] Could the myth of the werewolf[11] as it survives today in dreams and associated alleged psi phenomena have a germ of truth in past and forgotten UFO-creature cases? If the clock were turned back four centuries, would Stephen be diagnosed as suffering from lycanthropy.[12]

There is an element of psi in many UFO sightings. Stephen's experience has so many bizarre aspects, such as the UFO lights coming and going without any clearly discernible source; strange appearances and disappearances of the creatures with minimal evidence for their continuing existence, that one wonders if the common force in all these events was a UFO-induced psi-effect, and if this influence could in some way, either independently or in conjunction with the psychopathology, have effected the changes in Stephen and accounted for his fugue. Could the UFO and the creatures have materialized or dematerialized into another dimension? How does one prove this? What explanations are there? If materialization were possible, then this could account for many strange happenings and it would not be unusual to anticipate many wild and unheard-of science-fiction-like yet "real" effects.

For example, Pierre van Paassen[18] (the newspaperman) wrote how his German shepherd dogs savagely fought with a poltergeist black hound, until one shepherd dropped dead. If this was so, then why couldn't this be possible with the UFO-associated creatures? As a matter of fact, Stan Gordon and the Study Group have in their files instances where creatures may have killed chickens, ripped off the hindquarters of a St. Bernard dog, and torn the throat of a pet deer. If these experiences are projected (materialized?) by such an unknown force—invasions from another reality—the appearance of the creatures with the UFO could not have been better designed to inspire terror, nor could they have chosen a more suitable subject than Stephen as their Frankenstein to produce a more predictable result. Although one of the creatures was shot, it didn't collapse and there was no tangible evidence of its existence or wounds. Unlike the relatively infrequent examples of the creatures maiming other animals, the Study Group has no evidence of injuries to human beings. Perhaps this inexplicable fact is similar to the weird events where under favorable conditions and trained observers the entranced Polish medium Kluski allegedly materialized a large bird of prey, a lion, and an anthropoid ape. Like the UFO creatures, these experiences also had associated stenches and in no instance did they harm any present at the séances.[14]

The sensational, bizarre, and potentially dangerous significance of the UFO-creature cases, as in this instance, makes it mandatory that the greatest care and responsibility be exercised in collecting and reporting the data.

Careful analysis of each such encounter as Stephen's would seem essential in order to determine whether there is a tenable cause-and-effect relationship or whether it is coincidence, a hitherto unrecognized expression of florid psychopathology, or some intention from the "UFO force" that one is unaware of and incapable of understanding at this time.

The ideational contents of the warning in the fugue are similar to many reported contactee prophecies and, in Stephen's case at least, might be viewed as part of his psychodynamic makeup. It is more likely that the ideas which were ostensibly from the Man in Black with the sickle actually came from Stephen himself, when confronted with the major life-death threat, rather than that they were implanted from elsewhere (UFO, etc.). In this case there is evidence for the former and not much for the latter, other than a similarity to the oft-repeated gloomy prophecies of contactees, as noted by Keel.[15] All these cases of supposed prophecy and other psi phenomena might be profitably studied by the psychiatrist for psi and psychopathology.

The fugue prophecy might be a caricature or projection of Stephen's ambivalence toward his father and of his ready involvement in many fights with victory or defeat, life or death at stake. The portrayal of good and evil was dramatically highlighted in this cruel exchange. It was what Stephen saw and heard—no one else. The group contended with, shared, and suffered the reactions to the horror; therefore, it is likely that Stephen's cosmic prophecy of doom and salvation was a projection of his own horror of the moment and of past emotional experiences. This is more likely than the unprovable assumption that it was directly related to some unknown force associated with the UFOs and creatures. But who knows? The latter possibility cannot be completely disavowed when considered with the many documented UFO-psi cases in the worldwide literature.

Perhaps the acceptance of this assumption is similar to the reasoning that favors the ET hypothesis, viz., because the phenomenon is not explainable by any known technology of Planet Earth, it must come from a different planet. This approach seems to leave out of consideration the vast and impenetrable possibilities of psi. It is analogous to the specious, misinformed reasoning that the psychiatrist sometimes deals with in his consultations, e.g., it is erroneously assumed that because there is no "organic" cause, such as physical signs implicating the patient's cardiovascular system, etc., that the cause must be emotional. The psychiatrist does not make a diagnosis on negatives or absence of evidence. He must have a plausible series of facts, experiences, pattern of reactions, etc. ET versus UT—who knows?

This case is but one of many that Stan Gordon and the Westmoreland County Study Group have documented. More might be speculated about various intriguing aspects, but suffice it to say that this case demonstrates (1) the here-and-now implicit danger to those witnesses who are involved in such an experience, (2) perhaps more so, the dangers to those who study such people, (3) the challenging need for collateral, psychiatric investigations, and (4) the urgent need for a bold but responsible stance in finding out all we can about the UFO-creature relationship.

NOTES

1. Noé, Allen, V., "ABSMAL Affairs in Pennsylvania and Elsewhere," *Pursuit,* Volume 6, Number 4, pp. 84-89, (October, 1973).
2. Schwarz, B. E., "Stella Lansing's UFO Motion Pictures," *Flying Saucer Review,* Volume 18, Number 1, pp. 3-12, (January–February, 1972).
3. Schwarz, B. E., "Stella Lansing's Movies of Four Entities and Possible UFO," *Flying Saucer Review,* Special Issue Number 5, *UFO Encounters.*
4. Schwarz, B. E., "Stella Lansing's Clocklike Possible UFO Formations," *Flying Saucer Review,* Volume 20, Number 4 (July–August, 1974) through Volume 21, Number 1 (January–February, 1975).
5. Most of the members of the Study Group, and the witnesses, are thoroughly familiar with the appearance of bears, which are most infrequently seen in the area.
6. The creature's eye colors seem to be a distinctive feature of many reports. The greenish cast may be due to the possible existence of a *tapetum lucidum,* which is found in dogs and some nocturnal animals. For example, cats' eyes glow in a beam of light because of this special tissue, which reflects the light forward and improves the night vision. When the eyes are red, it might be due to the retinal reflex. Whatever the origin of the creatures: e.g., if they are materialized, or have existed in dark caves, completely undetected, etc., it is amazing that witness accounts seem to be consistent on these points, which conform to an anatomical reality that most witnesses would not ordinarily know about.

7. At approximately this time George Lutz was using his carbide lamp which emits the familiar odor of acetylene ($CaC_2 + 2H_2O \rightarrow Ca(OH)_2 + C_2H_2$) which was not confused with the presumed creature stench.
8. In my telephone interview with him, the father did not know the name of Stephen's drugs. At the time of the incident, Stephen said he was not taking any medication. Emergency room visits to his local hospital were for sprain of the left ankle (February 19, 1973) which was recently fractured; for a piece of glass in his eye from an exploding light bulb (April 25, 1973); and situational anxiety in the coal mine where he injured his eye (May 29, 1973). He was given a prescription for a mild tranquilizer (Vistaril, 25 mg.), and referred to a neurologist. But, first, on his own, he saw an opthalmologist (May 25, 1973) for the alleged eye injury and the physician found no evidence for ocular injury. "The one abnormal finding was a best corrected visual acuity of the right eye of 20/50." The neurologist saw Stephen on July 11, 1973, because of "severe orbital headaches and right temporal pain." The neurologist noted that the patient had previously seen four or five physicians about glass in his right eye. All except one could not find anything. The neurologist's examination revealed the central nervous system to be objectively intact; and an ophthalmological exam, aside from conjunctivitis of the right eye, to be within normal limits. He made the diagnosis of severe anxiety neurosis with pain in the right eye. The patient was treated over a period of time with "sedation, analgesics and reassurance." He improved considerably and returned to work. Here, again, is data that might have contributed to Stephen's fugue. He was very vulnerable to any injury or, in particular, ocular disturbance (UFO-induced "eye burn"?).
9. Noé, *op. cit.*, Keel, J. A., *Strange Creatures from Time and Space*, a Fawcett Gold Medal Book, Greenwich, Conn., 1970, 288 pp.; Clark, J., and Coleman, L., "Anthropoids, Monsters, and UFOs," *Flying Saucer Review*, Volume 19, Number 1, pp. 18-24 (January–February, 1973).
10. Hill, D., "Werewolf," in *Man, Myth, and Magic: An Illustrated Encyclopaedia of the Supernatural*, Marshall Cavendish Corp., New York, 1970, Vol. 22:3008-3012.
11. A fascinating account of the werewolf as it survives in modern man's dreams, with similarities to the data in this report, can be found in pioneer psychoanalyst-parapsychologist Nandor Fodor's *New Approaches to Dream Interpretation*, Citadel, New York, 1951, Chapter 4, "Lycanthropy as a Psychic Mechanism," pp. 146-159.
12. Superficially considered, hypnotic studies, including an attempt at regression (or a sodium pentothal interview), might seem

attractive but they were contraindicated because during his interview with the Study Group, as well as with me, Stephen frequently gave indications of becoming entranced while recalling certain aspects of the creature-MIB sequence. He had to be forcefully called back to consciousness and there was a clear-cut danger of violence under the prevailing conditions and without any opportunity for follow-up treatment, etc. Although of no statistical significance, it is an odd fact that five outstanding male contactees whom I have studied or known about were all liners, or "touch-me-nots." They all seemed to be in excellent physical condition and the kind who would not be trifled with. They all seemed to have good mechanical ability (e.g., could repair motors, etc.) and they were adept in the use of firearms; and, with one exception, they had had past experiences with what might be considered excessive violence (see *Flying Saucer Review* Special Issue Number 2, *Beyond Condon,* pp. 46-52 (June, 1969); the *Journal of the Medical Society of New Jersey,* Volume 66, Number 8, pp. 460-464 (August, 1969); *Flying Saucer Review* Special Issue Number 3, *UFO Percipients,* pp. 20-27 (September, 1969); *Flying Saucer Review,* Volume 18, Number 18, Number 4 (July–August, 1972).

13. van Paassen, Pierre, *Days of Our Years,* Hillman-Curl, Inc., New York, 1936, pp. 248-251. For additional allied phenomena and references see Schwarz, B. E., "Human-Animal Paranormal Events," *Journal of the American Society of Psychosomatic Dentistry and Medicine,* Volume 20, Number 2, pp. 39-53, 1973.
14. Fodor, Nandon, *The Unaccountable,* Award Books, New York, 1968, pp. 121–125.
15. Keel, J. A., *Operation Trojan Horse,* G. P. Putnam Sons, New York, 1970.

Abduction at Bebedouro

by Hulvio Brant Aleixo

Our next contribution speaks for itself. There have been other accounts of kidnappings and abductions recorded in the UFO literature. Betty and Barney Hill, Antônio Villas Boas in Brazil, and that at Pascagoula, Mississippi, and among the incidents that have been widely publicized. This strange incident from Bebedouro in Brazil was known to only a few of us through newspaper reports, translations of which were first published in 1969 in Flying Saucer Review *under the title "Forty-Eight Hours in a Flying Saucer." Then, by the greatest good fortune, Professor Hulvio B. Aleixo of Belo Horizonte and his friends, Alberto do Carmo, Heros C. Jardin, Roberto C. Aleixo, Maria Irene Neves, Dr. Walter Buhler, Wanda M. Santos, Edson A. Moura, and Luiz Romaniello, reinvestigated the report in depth.*

The incident occurred between 1:30 P.M. *on Sunday, May 4, 1969, and 4:00* A.M. *on Friday, May 9, 1969. The events commenced at Bebedouro on the Rio dos Velhas, 50 kilometers from Belo Horizonte, and ended at a place 32 kilometers from Vitoria in the state of Espirito Santo, some 360 kilometers from Belo Horizonte.*

Professor Aleixo is chairman of the investigatory group CICOANI (Caixa Postal 1675, 30000 Belo Horizonte, M.G., Brazil). The account of the abduction was published in Flying Saucer Review, *Volume 19, Number 6 (November–December, 1973), with the translation from the Portuguese by Gordon Creighton.*

At 7:25 A.M. on the morning of May 10, 1969, train No. NF-32, coming from Pedro Nolasco, Vitória, in the state of Espírito Santo, arrived at the Belo Horizonte station of the Central Brazil Line.

Senor Geraldo Lopes da Silva, a railway security official, observed among the passengers descending from the coaches a young fellow who was poorly clad, with a stocking wound round his head, and carrying something wrapped in a cloth. It was precisely this package which had at first drawn his attention to the young man, because thefts of copper wire from the railway were frequent occurrences. Challenging him, the security man asked for his identity papers. "No, Chief, I haven't got any papers, because they were taken from me," he replied, "But I am a soldier." The security agent persisted in his inquiries and took the young man to one of the booking halls, where he proceeded to examine the contents of his bundle. It contained fishing tackle, some food, and articles of clothing. Under pressure from the security agent, José Antônio da Silva said he had a story to tell, and identified himself as the orderly to Major Célio Ferreira, Deputy-Commandant of the Guards Battalion of the Military Police of Minas Gerais.

After hearing the story through several times, trying to find contradictions in it, the security agent finally accepted it, strange as it was. Then he called for a reporter from the Rádio Guarani local broadcasting station and, after a quick interview by the latter, the soldier was sent off to his barracks.

Major Célio Ferreira, struck by the extremely poor physical condition of the soldier, isolated him for 24 hours in his own home so that he could have food, rest, and medicine.

On the morning of Sunday, May 11, with great difficulty, the soldier made his way up the hill on which his home stands, to rejoin his family. They found him thin, burned by the sun, bearded, and lame in one leg. His absence from home for almost a week had been worrying them, for José Antônio had never before been away from home so long without informing them. Major Célio Ferreira had indeed gone so far as to organize search parties, on the day preceeding, to look for him.

On the night of Sunday May 11, CICOANI secured their first interview with José Antônio and, from then on, there followed a whole series of other interviews without any significant variations being observed in either his account or in his behavior.

A week after his return, a reconstitution of the scene was enacted at the actual site of the occurrence at Bebedouro.

The Abduction

On the evening of Saturday, May 3, 1969, José Antônio da Silva left his home to go fishing. At the bus station in Belo Horizonte he caught a bus bound for Pedro Leopoldo. Before they reached the latter place, however, he got off, and walked along the Jaguara road to the place known as Bebedouro (formerly the old "Fazenda dos Ingleses"), in the municipal district of Matozinhos. At about midnight he reached the banks of a small lagoon, took his gear out of his cloth bundle, and with the cloth he set himself up a little tent. Then he went off to fish for a while before turning in to sleep.

At daybreak on Sunday, the 4th, José Antônio awoke, folded up his tent, and then began fishing again, but with no success. He stopped for a while at midday to make a meal of a tin of sardines, and then went back to his fishing.

At about 3:00 o'clock in the afternoon, looking away to one side, he was vaguely aware of figures moving about behind him, and the sound of voices. Then he heard a cry "seemingly like a groan coming from deep down in the chest" and he felt his legs struck by a "burst of fire" coming from the direction of a form that was partly hidden by bushes. Seized with cramp and a feeling of numbness in the legs, he automatically knelt down at the lakeside, dropping his fishing rod.

"The burst looked like fire, but it wasn't, because it didn't burn my leg," he said. It was a beam of light, greenish in the middle and reddish at the edges, and fanning out slightly from its point of origin.

In a matter of seconds he found himself between two individuals in masks, who seized him under the armpits and dragged him off through the swampy thickets which they negotiated with great ease. With his knees scraping the ground, José Antônio gave up resisting as he thought of what would befall him if a further jet of light were to be fired at his head.

When they had gone only 10 meters or so from the lake, he saw, in the long grass, a third individual who was identical with those accompanying him. This one made no move as they passed by, and remained behind. All three, he observed were carrying a sort of weapon, but he thinks this third one was the one who had fired at him and had uttered the deep sound like a groan.

The Captors

José Antônio was dressed at the time merely in a pair of brief yellow leather shorts, with a big rosary tied round his waist and, on his head, a cap made from a woman's stocking, under another cap of black mesh.

The little fellows, as he noted, were about 1 meter 20 centimeters in height and they were completely covered. Their bodies were clad in a shining, light-colored garment, with articulated segments at the elbows and knees. Their heads were covered with masks[1] of a dull gray color, "like dull aluminum." The masks were rounded at the back and squared off at the front with sharp edges, and were flattened all the way down from the forehead except at the level of the nose, where there was a corresponding projection. At the level of the eyes there were two round holes about 2 centimeters in diameter. The mask, seemingly rigid, descended wide on to the shoulders and was not connected to the clothing. From the lower part of the mask came a tube of material resembling plastic which, passing over the chest and under the armpit, ended in a small metal container affixed to the back of each little man.

The latter had human proportions and were robust in relation to their small stature. Their legs seemed to be thick. José Antônio remarks: "I think I could have taken on two of them, if I had wanted to." At this stage in the affair he still felt more curiosity than fear.

The Machine

As soon as he had gone past the third individual, he caught sight of a machine. They were carrying him toward it through the trees. It was standing, slightly inclined, on a small dirt road. It consisted of a vertical cylinder joined at the bases to two lenticular or flattened pieces, both of them having a diameter greater than that of the cylinder, and the upper one being wider than the lower one. In order to describe this shape, José Antônio made use of a tumbler with its base set on a saucer and with a large saucer, upside-down, placed on top of its mouth. From the edges of the upper platform, at regular intervals, ran rods which were set obliquely into the base of the cylinder (and not into the rim of the lower platform). In the cylinder there was an opening resembling a door, some 1.30 × 0.60 meters in size. The external height of the machine was about 2 meters, the upper platform being about 3 meters in diameter and the lower platform, which rested on the ground, being some 2.5 meters in diameter. The cylinder was of a gray color, and the two platforms were black.

Taken into the machine through the door, José Antônio found himself in a quadrangular compartment, each side being about 2 meters long and the height about the same. The walls, the ceiling, and the floor were a dark gray, reminiscent of a stone surface and the seats, which had no legs, were of the same color. Near the wall containing the door was the longer of the seats, on which his two companions and he took their places. In the center of the room was the smaller seat, which later was to be taken by the third crew member who was still outside.

The lighting in the compartment was intense, "of the mercury vapor type," but he was unable to detect any sources for the light,[2] nor any openings or salient parts on the smooth surfaces.

When they had him seated in the center of the hard bench, the two beings accompanying him placed on his head a helmet similar to the ones they were wearing, and to get it on him they pushed his head through an opening in the back of the helmet.[3] This helmet likewise had a tube which led round toward his back, but José Antônio was unable to see whether they fixed on him a container like the ones that the crew were wearing on their own backs. He agrees that this item may have been put on him across the seat, but he did not detect it.

The two crew members, seated one on each side of him, next fastened his feet, and then his waist, with a "dry," rough material. Then they made themselves fast, and at that point the third crew member came in and sat down in front of him, on the single seat, and also fastened himself down.

At this stage José Antônio could only see out through the two holes in the heavy mask, the sharp edges of which were beginning to hurt his shoulders.

The Journey

As he sat there, facing the other three, the single crew member who was on the small seat by himself moved sideways a small lever set in the floor on his left. Immediately, José Antônio heard a humming noise coming from the upper part of the machine and felt the sensation of taking off. Then, when the pilot operated a bigger lever which was above, to his right, the soldier heard a hum in the lower part of the machine, and had the impression that the machine was accelerating vertically.

Immediately after the takeoff the strange beings began talking animatedly among themselves, glancing frequently at José Antônio, who of course understood not a word. In the incomprehensible language the phoneme *r* predominated at the end of many of the words, which were uttered in an arrogant fashion, in a deep, guttural tone.

The higher the machine seemed to rise, the more difficult did breathing seem for the soldier, and at one stage, in addition to his state of low morale, he felt as though his whole body was physically tired out, almost paralyzed. He felt more and more uncomfortable in this position, owing to the hardness and the shape of the seat, the numbness in his legs, and the weight of the helmet, the corners of which were bruising his shoulders and neck.

After a long period of traveling—to him it seemed interminable—he noticed that the light inside the cabin was growing stronger and was pulsating, and although he had the helmet on, he was forced to close his eyes. Then, after what seemed about an hour or so, he realized that the light was diminishing, and was able to open his eyes again.

Then the journey continued, with no other features of note, until the machine seemed to rotate 90° on its lateral axis.[4] To illustrate this maneuver, José Antônio took a tumbler, to represent the central cylinder of the machine, and laid it on its side. The seats adjusted themselves to this new position of the machine, "and seemed to have swung over themselves." Then, after another lengthy period, the machine and the seats reverted to the normal positions. And finally, after yet another long period, the machine landed somewhere. "I felt the jarring sensation," says José Antônio.

The Landing

The little men unfastened themselves and then the soldier. They put a band over the holes in his mask, so that now all he could do was hear. Up to now very talkative and seemingly cheerful, they fell quiet. They took him again by the armpits and carried him with his legs drawn up and his knees dragging on the ground.[5] His legs were still numb, but José Antônio thinks that, had he tried, he would have been able to stand up at that stage. The little men were extremely strong for their small size.

As they carried him along, José Antônio, still in total darkness as the eyeholes in his helmet were covered, heard footsteps and the sound of many people talking. He wanted to look, and at this point even managed to feel cheerful. All the voices he could hear were speaking the same language of his companions, who now were silent. Some of the voices were deeper, and others less so. None of the voices, however, seemed to him to be feminine.

He felt them set him down on a backless seat. Then they removed the bandage from the holes in his helmet, but still left the helmet on him. Through the eyeholes he saw that he was in a very large quadrangular room, measuring some 10 to 15 meters on each wall. His attention was at once caught by the figure of a being who was standing in front of him, at a distance of about 5 meters, with his gaze riveted on him.

This individual was a little taller (1.25 meters) than the rest, and also more robustly built. He was wearing no helmet and no spacesuit, and was eyeing José Antônio with apparent satisfaction. Meanwhile, his three captors were taking off their respective helmets and were talking very animatedly with this new one whom José Antônio took to be their chief. Like the others, he was extremely hairy. His long tresses, reddish and wavy, fell down behind past his shoulders to his waist; his beard was long and thick and came down to his stomach. He had wide-set eyebrows, two fingers thick, running right across almost the whole forehead. His skin was light-colored, very pale. His eyes were round, larger than is the norm with us, and of a green shade like the color of green leaves beginning to wither. The orbital cavities of his eyes were deep, the sclerotica was darker in color than his skin, and his pupils were dark. His eyes scarcely ever blinked. José Antônio did not notice any eyelashes.

José Antônio says: "I started praying when I saw *him*. I thought I'd never come back."

The little man's nose, long and pointed, was "bigger than ours." His ears were bigger too. The lower part of the ears was the same as ours, but the upper parts were more rounded than ours. His mouth was wide, with some resemblance to ours, but, said José Antônio: "They looked like fishes' mouths[6] I didn't see a tooth in any of them. When they opened their mouths, I didn't see one."

The little chief, surrounded by the three companions who had brought José Antônio, seemed extremely happy, and gesticulated with his hands as he talked. Meanwhile, the soldier's fear was now beginning to abate, because the little fellow "seemed to be nice."

Meanwhile, José Antônio saw others, of identical appearance, arriving from behind him, until at one point there were as many as ten or twelve of the homuncules present, gathered around the one who seemed to be their leader. When they came into, or vanished from, José Antônio's limited field of vision, it was always from or to a point behind him, where he supposed there must be a door in the wall. However he did not see this wall, as his position and the helmet he was wearing did not permit. He was only able to see three of the walls of the room and the floor. He did not notice the ceiling, owing to his inclined position, with his legs extended. The seat he was on was very low.

José Antônio was astonished and terrified when he caught sight of a sort of low shelf, apparently of stone, on which the bodies of four men were stretched out, side by side. This was to one side of him and near the left side-wall of the room. The bodies were lying on their backs, naked—wearing no masks—and seemed dead, their eyes being closed, and they had the rigidity of corpses. One of them was dark-skinned, "indeed a Negro," and another was of a light-brown color. Both seemed very well built. The other two bodies were lighter in color and thin. One of these was very blond, "like a foreigner." The bodies seemed to be of men resembling us, and they displayed no visible injuries. ("Unless they had them on their backs, which of course I couldn't see," added José Antônio.)

The little men paid no heed to the corpses. In José Antônio, however, the sight of the latter had aroused gloomy and pessimistic thoughts on the matter of his ever getting home again. Nevertheless, he does not think that the corpses were of men who had been killed by the homuncules. "Perhaps they couldn't stand up to the experience, or perhaps they pulled their helmets off," he thinks.

The walls and floor of the big room seemed to him to be of stone,[7] in view of the uniformly gray color. The lighting was also uniform, and was intensely bright, of the mercury vapor type, but no lamps were apparent anywhere.[8] No windows[9] or doors were visible. On the wall to his left—the wall beside which was the shelf with the corpses—were colored pictures of many things that were familiar to José Antônio or of which he knew: there were animals, such as the jaguar, the monkey, the elephant, the giraffe. There were pictures of houses and of a small town; there were pictures of trees, forests, the sea. There were pictures of vehicles: trucks, like the FNM (Alfa-Romeo); a propeller-driven two-engined aircraft, and an automobile. These pictures, arranged separately along the wall, covered that side of the room only. There was nothing on the wall facing him or on the wall to his right.

Standing on the floor, a little to his right, was a strange apparatus which put José Antônio in mind of a racing car. It was an approximately cylindrical construction, 2 meters long and 0.80 meter high, and had no openings. On either side of it, in the positions corresponding to those of the wheels of a car, there were round things sticking out, four of them in all, which were not touching the ground, and which reminded him of turbines. Try as he might, he was unable to form any idea as to the purpose and the method of operation of that machine.

Some 5 meters or so from him, in front, there was a small cubical seat, with no legs, on which the "chief" sat from time to time. On the right-hand side of this seat, and almost at floor level, there was another slab, several meters long, with a white surface. It seemed to him to be about 3 meters, and it was used later as a slate, for the drawing of sketches.

Amid all the confusion attendant upon the coming and going of the little men, and their gesticulating and their weird language, and the animation evident in their faces, José Antônio finally concluded that his presence there was a source of great satisfaction for them. The various individuals were all extremely alike, despite the variations in size, features, skin coloring, length of beard, and color of eyes.

José Antônio was surprised to see that one of them was carefully undoing the cloth bundle in which he had been carrying his fishing tackle. When he was captured on the bank of the lake, this cloth was lying open in a small clearing, and his objects all scattered around it. He had no idea who had rolled it up, with the tackle inside, and brought it to this room, but he now thinks this must have been done by the third member of the crew who remained behind among the trees while he was being carried toward the craft.

In any case, there the little men now were, taking out and examining, with much animation, one by one, his various possessions contained in the bundle. From hand to hand they passed around his collections of hooks, his knives, his boxes of matches, his other angler's tools, a tin of sardines and other foodstuffs, as well as his pieces of clothing. And in the meantime he himself was feeling cold, for he was still wearing only his shorts. He was, however, breathing better.

He observed how, immediately after all the objects and garments had been closely inspected, they set aside one specimen of everything of which there was a duplicate. Thus, the little men took one specimen of each type of fishing hook; they took one of the three big knives; a box of matches; one of his changes of clothing; and a 100-Cruzeiro banknote (old Cruzeiros) from the total of CR$35,100 which they had found in one of his pockets. All the objects for which there was no duplicate—such as the tin of sardines, for example—were put back into the cloth and this was then rolled up again and carefully fastened. The only exception was his identity card, which they had also found in one of his pockets, and which was passed round for all to see. This, his only identity card, they did not return to him, and it caused many problems for him after his return.

He thinks that the little men had perceived, from his identity card, that he belonged to the military.

For, immediately afterward, one of them pointed his weapon toward the wall and fired a beam of light which caused a discoloration of the affected area of the wall. And, in addition to that, the first part of José Antônio's "conversation" with the leader subsequently was to revolve around the subject of weapons.

The weapons carried by all the little men were standardized but of various sizes. A good deal smaller than a rifle, their barrels were very much wider and shorter than those of a rifle and, made of one piece, widened out toward the rear to form the butt. On the top of the central part of each weapon there was a sort of trigger which, when pulled backward, caused the emission of a luminous beam of the type by which he was struck before being captured.

Attempts to Communicate

Into the short, thick fingers of the "chief" one of the little men passed a small black cylindrical object which he used later as a pencil for writing on the smooth, light-colored "slate" beside him. Turning now directly toward José Antônio, he accompanied his incomprehensible speech with wide-sweeping gestures. He pointed at the soldier, then upward, then downward, then to his companions, and, after each combination of words and gestures, he seemed to be awaiting an answer from José Antônio. As this series of attempts continued, the soldier thought he began to understand some of it: thus, that the gesture pointing downward meant: *your country;* the gesture upward meant: *this room, here,* or *our country,* and so on. His understanding was amplified by the illustrations, in the form of rough sketches, made by the leader on the white "slate" and by his accompanying words and gestures.

In the first sketch, José Antônio thought he could see "an army camp." It was a circle with armed figures around it, like sentries. The leader pointed to the weapons in the sketch, and then to José Antônio, and then downward, and then finally upward, from which José Antônio understood that he wanted to get some of our weapons through him, José Antônio. To this José Antônio gesticulated negatively, and, as the leader still kept insisting on this type of theme, he began to lose all hope of returning home alive. *(José Antônio has repeatedly refused to reveal to us other passages in the "conversation" on this subject.)*

One of the little men, carrying in both hands a cube which seemed to be heavy and made of stone, came up to José Antônio. The cube was hollowed out on the upper side and contained a dark-green-colored liquid. The leader indicated to him that he should drink it, while one of the subordinates loosened his helmet from behind and raised it with a certain degree of violence. José Antônio resisted and made gestures of refusal. Then, later, seeing that one of the little men was drinking the liquid himself he decided to take some too, for he felt very weak and had had nothing to eat. The liquid had a bitter taste and was contained in a pyramidal-shaped cavity in the cube. From that moment he began to feel better and had more life in him. And, furthermore, he thinks that after that he began to understand better what the leader wanted to say.

The Leader's Proposition

Among all the various aspects touched upon in the attempts at communication, there is one point on which José Antônio is in no doubt: these individuals were insisting that he help them in connection with their purposes vis-à-vis our society.

Using the big pencil on the horizontal "slate," the leader patiently traced two big circles, side by side. Then he blackened one of them, leaving the other circle white. He pointed first to one circle and then to the other, and then finally to José Antônio and downward, and José Antônio finally grasped that the white circle corresponded to the terrestrial day and the black circle to our night. After the considerable period of time which it had taken for José Antônio to arrive at this conclusion, he nodded his head affirmatively, and the leader continued with his sketches.

He next outlined an enormous series of small circles with white insides, linking them, by gestures, with the bigger white circle. As he had stopped referring to the blackened circle, José Antônio understood that the small circles corresponded to "days." As he drew each small circle, the leader of the little men paused, and drew José Antônio's attention by gestures, so that he began to count them. Very patiently, the leader completed a great mass of small white circles and then drew around them all another larger circle. José Antônio lost count when he had got beyond 300 with the number of small circles, but concluded that the whole lot taken together signified a year, or 365 days. When he had given his affirmative gesture to the leader, the latter went on to draw nine more agglomerations of small circles, linking them by gestures to the first agglomeration, and drawing the attention of José Antônio, who now perceived that he was talking about a unit of *ten years,* as each agglomeration of small white circles was circumscribed by another larger one.

Then the little man drew a thick line separating off three of the agglomerations from the remaining seven, and then began pointing, first at the group of three agglomerations of circles, and then at José Antônio, and then downward. After that, he again pointed to the soldier and then upward and then at the group of seven large agglomerations, and made still more gestures, thus giving José Antônio to understand the sequence of his message as follows:

> "He is proposing to take me to the Earth, where I shall remain for three years, collecting information for him. Then he will send for me to come to them, where I shall remain studying for seven years. And then finally they will land on Earth, with me as a guide."

José Antônio's reply to this was a gesture of negation, indicating his refusal. At that moment he was already fingering the rosary which he had been wearing rolled round his waist, and he was praying aloud. When he had got as far as the fourth "mystery" of the first part of the telling of his beads, the leader stepped toward him and, displaying irritation for the first time, seized the crucifix and snatched it from him. One of the beads rolled onto the floor and was picked up by one of the little men, who showed it to the others. The crucifix was passed round in the same way, arousing the curiosity of all of them.

A Vision and a Secret

Suddenly, while the little men were involved in a lengthy discussion, José Antônio saw appear, almost right in front of him, and as though out of the void, a human figure. It took up position in front of him and remained there immobile, with a firm and friendly demeanor, and looking straight at him and speaking to him in a very clear Portuguese. José Antônio at once concluded that this vision was exclusively for *him*, because, despite the favorable position of the figure in the room, it was apparently not perceived by the little men, who went on talking among themselves, while getting more and more angry.

Despite the way in which the apparition had arrived it was quite clearly the figure of a man of about 1:70 meters in height, lean, with long fair hair and beard. His complexion was pink and white, his eyes clear and serene. His dark clothing reached to his feet, which were bare. His robe had wide sleeves the collar was turned down, and he wore a sort of thick white cord around the waist, with a knot at each of the hanging extremities, like a friar's cassock.

José Antônio, who until that moment was in sore distress and without hope, felt relief coming at once from the presence of this person whom he identifies as "a good person, one of our people" and, in particular, took heart from certain revelations that the vision made to him. These revelations were to be imparted to nobody else, so José Antônio tells us, until he had received fresh instructions, and that might perhaps not be before two or three years have passed.

On the matter of this vision, the soldier has displayed tremendous resistance to questioning, especially as regards the message received by him, which he considers to be a secret. Even these details of the physical description of the individual seen in the vision were given by him only with the greatest reluctance, for he maintains that these details could suffice for the identification of the person.

We asked him how it could be possible for the secret to be discovered merely from a simple description of the features of someone whom we did not know and would never meet. He gave us to understand, however, that it *would* be possible to recognize the person, and that it *would not* be impossible that we should meet him. Asked whether the vision was of Jesus, José Antônio promptly replied that it was not. As to whether it was some saint, he was unwilling to reply, merely smiling and changing the subject of conversation. After repeated interviews we managed to obtain some indications regarding the contents of the message. (See the concluding part of this report.)

The Return Journey

The tall individual vanished in just the same way as he had appeared in the room—suddenly. And, at precisely the same moment, the little men began to show signs of irritation against each other. The leader came over to the two custodians, who had never left José Antônio's side. Then the eyeholes in his helmet were covered again with a blindfold. And, in the same fashion as he had been brought, the soldier was now taken under the arms and carried to another place which, when the blindfold had been removed, he discovered to be the inside of the machine that had brought him.

Then began the long return journey, with the same three crew members and with the same incidents as when he had been brought, that is to say, with the machine changing position for a time, and with the light increasing and pulsating for a certain period.

Immediately after he had felt the shock which meant that the machine had touched down, his companions loosened and then removed his helmet. Then he suffered an almost total loss of consciousness, being merely aware that they were dragging him into the darkness. He thinks he remained in this condition of semiconsciousness for about an hour, after which he began to notice the first signs of the approaching dawn. Then he became aware of the sound of running water nearby and, impelled by intense thirst, he crawled along on the ground until he came to a brook. He had his bundle, from which he drew out his water bottle, which he filled twice. He estimates that he drank 1½ liters of water, yet still his thirst was not entirely quenched. Then he got out his fishing tackle and managed to catch a few small fish, which he ate.

When the sun came up he was able to take a better look at his surroundings, which he found to be a landscape that was totally strange to him. He had been left on the edge of a small stone quarry, beside a ravine. Lame, confused, exhausted, and unkempt, with his great growth of beard, he started to walk, and soon came to a paved road where he approached somebody who was passing along it. He asked them where he was, and was told that he was 32 kilometers from Vitória, the capital of the state of Espírito Santo, and that he was on the road leading from there to the state of Minas Gerais. On hearing this he was amazed, and asked what day it was. This time it was the turn of the unknown passer-by to be amazed, for he told the soldier it was Friday, May 9.

Making a quick mental calculation, José Antônio concluded, with great alarm, that he had been away for four-and-a-half days. He asked in which direction Minas Gerais lay, and then set off along the road, absorbed in his own thoughts. He came to the conclusion that he had better not return to Minas Gerais, since he would be unable to account for his absence: nobody would believe his story. So he decided that he would prefer to make for the woods and try to live off fruit and fish. He was especially afraid of being picked up by the police of Espírito Santo, as he had no longer any identity card that he could show them.

Nevertheless, while his thoughts followed this trend, his route was bringing him back ever nearer to the Minas Gerais state-line. Several times motorists, seeing he was having difficulty walking, stopped to offer him a lift, but he refused them. His right leg was the one more seriously affected, and seemed to be swollen at the knee. In addition to that, he had three open wounds on his shoulders and below the nape of the neck, caused by the action of the helmet rubbing against him.

At last, however, overcome by fatigue, he gave in and accepted a lift, which brought him to near the town of Colatina. But he remained extremely careful to conceal his story, and when people asked him questions he gave the excuse that he was "fulfilling a vow."

Setting out again along the road, he met a group of children and asked them the shortest way which would bring him to the nearest station on the Vitória-Minas Gerais line. He complains that, after having told him the route, the children pelted him with stones and jeered at him, maybe because of his strange appearance.

Following the railway line, he finally came to a small station, which was in fact Colatina. There he stopped and asked the station agent when the next train to Belo Horizonte would come, for he had already changed his mind by now, and was resolved to return home and face the consequences.

As it would be quite a long time yet before the train arrived, he remained in the station talking to the agent, with whom he struck up a friendship, with the result that he went to the agent's house and had something to eat, and met his wife and children. He also met a settler who lived nearby and who offered him a job, which he did not accept. Grateful to the agent for the way in which he had treated him, he gave him one of his two remaining knives. In addition, he paid for the ticket of a youth who had no money. The little men had put back CR$35,000 into his pocket out of the total of CR$35,100 (old Cruzeiros) that he had been carrying.

At 7:25 A.M. on Saturday he got out of the train at the Belo Horizonte station of the Estrada de Ferro Central do Brasil (Central Brazil Railway Line), where he was approached by the railway's security man, Senor Geraldo Lopes da Silva. Finally, he told the security man the whole story[10] and was sent by him to the barracks, from where he was taken to the home of Major Célio Ferreira.

In the course of our interviews with him, José António was very insistent that we should go with him to the spot where the machine had landed when it brought him back, for so he said, we should probably still find there a little fish swimming about in a small pool in the rocks into which it had fallen when he threw it back, after having eaten enough. He also said that the railway agent at Colatina would know him and would show us the large knife which he had given him.

NOTES

1. At times Senor Hulvio Brant Aleixo describes this headpiece as a mask (Portuguese: *mascara*) and at other times as a helmet (Portuguese: *capacete*).
2. I draw attention once more to this very important feature of the compartment's brilliant lighting, coming from no visible source. It is a feature that has appeared in numerous claims made by individuals who say they have been inside landed UFOs, and, since these people are not usually students of the UFO literature but rather unsophisticated folk with no previ-

ous knowledge of our subject, it strikes me as arguing strongly for the truthfulness of their stories.

3. As I pointed out in *Forty-eight Hours in a Flying Saucer,* this feature of the helmet which they placed on their prisoner's head reminds us strongly of the case of Felipe Martinez of Argentina who told a Buenos Aires newspaper in October, 1965, that, in one of his several encounters with small beings from landed UFOs, they had tried to put a "spacesuit" on him but that it had caused circulatory disturbances. He also claimed that they had once produced a numbing or paralyzed effect in his legs. But this too is a feature that has been claimed very often, as is the upright shaft said to be running through the center of the UFO. (On Felipe Martinez, see Case 44 of "The Humanoids in Latin America," being Section 4 of *The Humanoids,* Neville Spearman, London, 1969.
4. Compare Charles Bowen's article "Fantasy or Truth?" on the "Salzburg-Mars Express," in *Flying Saucer Review,* Volume 13, Number 4 (July–August, 1967). The anonymous Austrian who claimed to have been paralyzed and kidnapped by a small being, and abducted in a saucer, said that soon after takeoff the vehicle seemed to reverse poles and that a second motor, previously below the "floor" and now above the "ceiling," took over from the other motor.
5. This recalls the scuffing of the toes of Barney Hill's shoes (See John G. Fuller: *The Interrupted Journey*. Dial Press, New York: 1966).
6. This too we have heard before.
7. Everything—walls, floor, shelves or slabs, and even the drinking vessel—appears to be of *stone*. Perhaps there is a valuable clue here.
8. See Note 2 above.
9. And here, maybe, is another clue.
10. Finally, as regards the setting of this extraordinary alleged experience of a Brazilian soldier, it should be noted that it lies not very far to the north of Itaperuna, which has figured so often in our reports of late. And the creatures described in the Itaperuna episodes also seem always to be around the 1 meter or 1 meter 20 size.

    Moreover there is another place quite close which has even more sinister connotations. This is Diamantina, not far from the Rio das Velhas, near which stream José Antônio da Silva said he had been captured. It was at Diamantina (see Case 29 in my "The Humanoids in Latin America") that, in the early hours of August, 1962, the diamond prospector Rivalino Mafra da Silva (no relation of José Antônio, so far as we know) was abducted on the very doorstep of his hut, and before the eyes of his small son, seemingly by two mysterious balls, following upon a night of terror during which weird small forms had appeared inside the hut and inspected him and his sleeping children. We understand that Rivalino da Silva was never seen again.

Bebedouro Postscript: The Little Men Return for the Soldier

Since the publication of the foregoing piece on the Bebedouro abduction, Professor Húlvio B. Aleixo and his colleagues conducted further investigations. A translation of their report, which was first published in Portuguese in Dr. Walter Buhler's SBEDV Bulletin *Number 94–98 (September, 1973, to June, 1974) was published under the professor's signature in* Flying Saucer Review, *Volume 21, Numbers 3–4 of 1975 (a double issue). As (almost) always, the translation was by Gordon Creighton, and here, by way of a conclusion to the first article, are the opening paragraphs of that later report.*

In the course of our investigations we have gathered a great deal of additional information about the incident and about the central figure, the soldier José Antônio da Silva who, as we reported in Part I, claimed to have been abducted from May 4 to May 9 of 1969 by small red-bearded creatures who took him aboard their machine.

Further Details on the Soldier

José Antônio da Silva, aged 24, is an unmarried man, the second eldest in a family of 12 children. His father is still alive, but his mother died two years ago. As regards his education, he has had only the primary course of education, and even that not completely. For the past five years he has been an enlisted man in the military police of the state of Minas Gerais. He appears to be of a sound and healthy constitution. His social-economic situation is a modest one, and he lives with his family in a suburban house that he helped to build. He gave part of the land to some of his brothers and sisters. He spends little money on himself, and has been able to acquire three other plots of land in the town for his brothers as well. He takes the initiative in the home and decides most family matters. His friends and superiors regard him as a person worthy of all confidence. Apart from his work in the military police, which he enjoys, he has few other interests. He is very religious but does not attempt to ram it down anybody else's throat. He belongs to no Catholic brotherhood or religious association, but is a faithful practising churchgoer. His father agrees that it is José Antônio who is the leader in the family. He is full of praise for his son and says José Antônio gets on well with everybody and has no weaknesses or vices.

The Soldier's Symptoms after His Return

In addition to the three marks on his shoulders and neck, and the slight swelling of his right knee, already reported in Part I, José Antônio also displayed other symptoms. When he arrived back home his family and his superiors in the military police all noticed that he was thin, sunburned, unshaven, and downcast. They noticed, moreover, that he had difficulty in walking, had little appetite, and that he complained of constipation, which lasted for a week.

During the month following our report, we also heard him complaining of a burning sensation in the eyes[1] and a reduction in the sharpness of his vision. Subsequently, he began to speak of intermittent stomach pains involving a well-defined transverse zone of the lower abdomen. This was accompanied by headache in the frontal region and by an increase in the burning sensation of the eyes, which now began to water. He said this sensation in the eyes resembled the sensation he had felt inside the little men's machine, when the light in the cabin increased and pulsated. He is convinced that he has not been able to see properly since his experience.

He seems to be alarmed over these symptoms and says that nothing like this had ever happened to him before. His family agree that prior to the experience his health was normal in every respect. When we suggested that he get himself examined at the military hospital, he replied that he would not do so, as it might be interpreted as meaning that he wanted to get off work.

With the passage of time, all his symptoms have gradually abated and disappeared.

Reconstruction of the Incident on the Spot

On thc morning of May 26, 1969, we went to Bebedouro, scene of the episode, accompanied by José Antônio. The CI-COANI Investigation Group were represented by myself and by Luiz Romaniello. Colonel Prazedes, Major Célio, and Captain Edem were there on behalf of the military police (the two first-named being, respectively, the commandant and deputy-commandant of the guards battalion). Lieutenant Vitorino represented the CIONAI UFO Investigation Group.

After we had determined the precise spot and photographed it, the soldier reenacted the incident from the initial abduction episode beside the lake up to the point where he was forcibly taken aboard the strange craft. At all stages of the reenactment José Antônio's behavior and reactions appeared to us to be consistent and coherent with his previously given account of the episode.

In the short time left, we used the opportunity to make a superficial inquiry among members of the sparse population of the district, whom we encountered on the road, asking them about the presence of strange aerial objects in the region. The results of our inquiry were positive. One of the brief accounts we received came from a boy who said he had seen a silent, high-flying machine which resembled an umbrella.

On the homeward journey we noticed that José Antônio had fallen silent, and we tried to find out what was worrying him. After a great deal of resistance he finally replied that he was concerned about the possibility that the green liquid he had drunk in the chamber where they had questioned him might have given the little men power over him.

For, he said, they had come back to look for him in the garden of his home.

He explained that at about midnight on May 21 (twelve days after his abduction), when he was already lying in bed, he had a sudden impulse to go out into the garden to see to his goats. And there to his astonishment he saw the three little men, dressed in their flight suits, standing motionless in the garden, looking at him.

His automatic reaction was to step back into the house and bolt the door, without saying a word or hearing anything from them. When we asked him why he had reacted in this fashion, José Antônio replied: "So you think, do you, that I'm going to work against my own people?"

Then he gave us to understand that the little men might represent a threat for all of us in the future. But, as he was not sure whether the danger came from the particular type of individual who had abducted him or from other unknown types, he was at present prepared to have a further meeting with them in order to clarify the matter. In any case, he said, he was certain that the world was in great danger, without, however, knowing from where this danger would come. The danger had been revealed to him by the fair-skinned individual of friendly mien who had appeared mysteriously before him in the chamber, unperceived by the little men. The danger would involve the whole of mankind, and would possibly include intervention by unknown beings, in addition to other calamities. This danger might, however, be avoided if mankind changed their present behavior.[2]

NOTES

1. These physical symptoms, particularly the watering and stinging of the eyes and the headaches and intestinal disturbances, should be carefully compared with those mentioned in Dr. Olavo Fontes' "Medical Report on A.V.B." (See: "The Amazing Case of Antonio Villas Boas," in *FSR*'s famous and much-translated classic, *The Humanoids,* now available again, this time as a paperback edition, published by Futura Publications Ltd., 49 Poland Street, London, WIA 2LG.)
2. Warnings of this kind run like a red thread throughout the whole of the UFO phenomenon since 1947, and are also a fundamental ingredient in the Marian Epiphanies of the nineteenth and early twentieth centuries (which are not generally held to form an integral part of the UFO phenomenon, though some of us feel sure that they are).

Escorted by UFOs from Umvuma to Beit Bridge

by Carl Van Vlierden

This selection, a report from South Africa about an incident said to have taken place in Rhodesia, could well be one of the most important yet to have appeared in the annals of ufology. It has many of the features associated already with other cases in this collection, and much of what is believed to have gone on, as in the case of Betty and Barney Hill, had to be released from the subconscious memory of the prime witness during hypnotic regression.

We learn of aerial objects tracking the witnesses' car, beams of light, control, teleportation, humanoids and "them," and an insight into what "they" may be up to. "They" could be the mysterious invaders of our airspace and our privacy; the hoverers over housetops at night and schools by day; the putters-on of displays and the dispensers of gibberish and gobbledygook, of varied messages and *apparent good sense as well.*

This remarkable account was transcribed and edited from Mr. van Vlierden's taped interview, and the tape of the session under hypnosis, by Charles Bowen, and it was published in Flying Saucer Review, *Volume 21, Number 2 (March–April, 1975).*

Introductory notes with a brief and partial comparative phenomenology, and a preliminary newspaper report of the UFO encounter claimed to have been experienced by Peter and Frances,* with suspected levitation of their car, were

* Names and addresses on file with *FSR.*

presented in the last issue of *Flying Saucer Review* by Charles Bowen in his article "Car Teleported by UFOs in Rhodesia."

The incident occurred on the night of May 30-31, 1974, during a journey that Peter and his wife were making from Salisbury via Fort Victoria and Beit Bridge on the border, to Durban, Natal, South Africa. The young couple were puzzled by the affair, but having given little thought previously to the subject of UFOs, and not having read books on the subject—although it will be seen that Peter, a young man with unusual gifts, had had an earlier UFO experience—they had no idea to whom to turn, to whom to report the incident. Then one day when they had been settled in the republic for more than five months, they read a seriously treated news item about a UFO report in *The Natal Mercury*. They approached the newspaper, and science columnist Bill Faill listened to their account and referred them to me.

On November 28, 1974, Peter and Frances completed sighting report forms for me in my capacity as MUFON representative (as well as *FSR* correspondent) in South Africa. On December 1, 1974, I interviewed them in their Durban home, going over all the points, in depth, that they had made in their written reports. With their permission I recorded the interview, and the following account is based on, or quoted directly from that recording.

The Encounters

The night of May 30-31, 1974, was cloudless, with 100 percent visibility, although there was no moon.

The strange events started at a point about 10 kilometers to the south of Umvuma, when both witnesses saw a policeman, at least they thought at first that it was a policeman, sitting at the side of the road, and holding a "walkie-talkie" in his hand. This is what he seemed to be to Peter, who was driving his Peugeot 404 well in excess of the 100 km./p.h. speed limit. As that stretch of road is noted for speed traps, he slowed down. The pair of them then began to think in more detail about the policeman. Peter remarked that the metallic-looking suit seemed queer for a policeman, as they normally wore khaki. Frances described the suit as "plasticky."

Frances looked back but could see nothing behind them.

The UFO appeared at 2:30 A.M. Frances is quite sure of the time, because she thought the light was from a house on a hill and, looking at her watch remarked that it was very late for someone to be up in that part of the world. Then the idea occurred to her that it might be a communications tower beacon. The light was like a spotlight and it started to revolve like a lighthouse in such a way that it was like a spotlight being switched on and off.

The light was on the passenger side of the vehicle (left-hand side). It appeared fairly close and seemed to keep pace with the car. For a brief while they wondered whether or not it might be a helicopter.

It had a bluish tinge, was bright and steady, on for 5 seconds, off for 2 seconds.

Next the car lights began to fade. This was pointed out by Peter, and although they were again driving at 140 km./p.h., the maximum for the Peugeot, the lights inside and outside slowly dimmed out. At the same time the radio continued to function perfectly as they listened to L.M.'s (Lourenco Marques in Mozambique) light jazz program.

Peter said, however, that there was an immense light around the car, as if from neon lights, and enough to cast shadows.

As they drove along, it suddenly became very cold in the car, unseasonally so, and they had to wrap up in coats, woolies, and blankets, and switch the electric heater on (that, like the radio, was still operating). The ignition too must have been normal, for the engine was running well. Then, said Peter, he took his foot off the accelerator, but the car continued to motor at 150 km./p.h.! It seemed the battery had plenty of "juice" in it, and after all, the radio (powered from the battery) and cigarette lighters still worked.

The cold in the car was very unusual. Peter had traveled the route several times, and said he'd never known such cold. It was just like the inside of a refrigerator, and he estimated the drop in temperature to have been about 20°–30°F., down to less than 50°F.

I took Peter up on his statement that he had taken his foot off the accelerator and that there had been no associated reduction of speed. He confirmed that he'd driven from a point 18 kilometers outside Fort Victoria, until entering the filling station at Fort Victoria, without headlights, and with no control. He couldn't stop the car, as there was no power over braking. At the same time he couldn't steer or control the engine. The car was traveling at about 160 km./p.h., and when he took his foot off the accelerator to apply the brake, the car just continued without interruption.

I observed that as he'd moved his leg and foot he wasn't "paralyzed" and he retorted that he certainly wasn't, for he had been lighting cigarettes, and so on.

Peter: "I only did it (took foot off accelerator) once. I was petrified, but said nothing to Frances, for she seemed on the verge of hysteria as it was, seeing all this happening."

Frances: "The car seemed perfectly controlled. As the passenger I saw nothing untoward. The car wasn't veering all over the road. The driver just sat doing nothing: it was as though we were on 'automatic pilot.' "

Peter: "I tried to move the steering wheel, but nothing happened. I was petrified, but Frances remarked: 'How can you sit there so calm?'

Frances: " 'Oh,' he said, 'it's only a UFO,' and I said, 'What are you going to do about it?' He replied, 'What *can* I do about it?' "

The solitary UFO switched from the left (Frances's side) to Peter's side of the car for about 1 kilometer and then switched back. The one UFO stayed with them until they were a few kilometers from Fort Victoria.

At about the time of the switching of station, they passed what appeared to be an African bus parked in a lay-by outside an African trading store. There was not a soul in sight. All lights in the bus, and its headlights, were blazing, but it was empty. Usually, said Peter, these buses were crammed with passengers and luggage, with bikes, bags and trunks, and chickens, on top, and many passengers sit throughout the journey guarding their possessions, even relieving themselves in the bus rather than leaving their personal chattels. On this instance there was not a person to be seen. "Very weird," said Frances.

This first bus was on the left, and pointing in the direction in which they were traveling. The next two African buses, with lights on and engines running, were on the other side of the road and facing in the other direction. The second bus was 7 kilometers beyond the first bus they'd seen, and then there was a third a further 5 kilometers along the road. Both were empty. Both were parked at the roadside, a thing drivers of buses do not do in Rhodesia as heavy fines are inflicted on the proprietors for such offenses. If a bus breaks down, it is incumbent upon the driver to place a warning red triangle on the road behind the vehicle. None of these buses were accompanied by red triangles.

Peter and Frances were particularly interested in the buses as they carried the livery of a firm in the group for which Frances worked.

There was a beam of light from the UFO to the horizon or (asked Frances) was it from the horizon to the UFO?

When they were some 10 kilometers from Fort Victoria the UFO shot off like a shooting star.

At 4:30 A.M. they drove into the garage in Fort Victoria without lights. (Peter switched off the engine and when, an hour later he switched on again, and started, the lights responded normally to the switch.)

The petrol pump attendant remarked that there was something wrong with their headlights. As he was filling the tank up to the brim with petrol, Frances, swathed in fur coat and woolies, said something about it being a very cold night. The native attendant, who had been sleeping near the pumps clad in only a singlet and shorts, looked at her in surprise and denied that it was cold.

The car was only warm again when they got back in, after a fruitless endeavor to buy hot coffee, but after a welcome wash at the hotel, they drove away from Fort Victoria at 5:30 A.M.

About 10 kilometers out of Fort Victoria Frances once again alerted Peter to the appearance of a/the UFO on the left-hand station, but this time they also saw another one move into position above the car. They were either small, or a lot higher. This time they did not come up from behind a hill like the first one had done. Suddenly, for example, the one on the left was there, traveling at the same speed as the car. Its light was steady, and there was no twinkle.

Another strange aspect of the journey was that apart from the "policeman" and one native at the Fort Victoria filling station, they recalled seeing no one else during the journey. Nor were there any vehicles other than the three buses, seen in most unusual circumstances and condition. Peter said that this was normally a busy route. [*Especially as, in view of the daytime heat, people probably prefer to drive through the night; also, this was the night before a South African public holiday, National Day, and as this was the main route to South Africa, one might expect additional travelers*—EDITOR.]

Now they came upon most unexpected terrain. Frances had fixed her attention on the UFO which she could see pacing them to the left, but she does recall seeing many low bushes and masses of high grass, and the land appeared wet. Which was strange, for vegetation in that region is sparse, with a few "umbrella trees" and scattered low scrub on very dry ground. Peter was more specific: "There were large expanses of swamp, and water on the surface, which I could see reflecting the light from above."

This light was the same color as before, and the car lights were now normal, and Peter could see lush foliage. The road was stone dry, yet the sides of the road, the verges, and the country beyond were wet. Lots of water and tropical vegetation.

Frances reminded us that normally there is a constant noise of crickets and cicadas. There was no noise from the engine, and no sound of crickets and cicadas. It was like traveling in a dream with all the sounds switched off—except the radio still plugging away with the same old program.

As they were leaving Fort Victoria their speed was of the order of 120 km./p.h. It was now up to, or even above the 190 km./p.h. region (limit of the graduated scale).

Peter said he himself had no control over the car at 200 km./p.h., or more, yet ". . . the car was not lacking control at all: it 'did its own thing.'" And he admitted that inwardly he was scared out of his wits. "I tried to ignore the phenomenon at first as being an optical illusion, but then found that I was losing control, as though someone else was operating the car: *I wasn't driving!*"

He felt shocked, indeed petrified. He just couldn't drive, and there was no response when he tried to. He said he might just as well have climbed into the back seat away from the controls.

Although the road from Fort Victoria to Beit Bridge is far from straight, that night, according to Peter, it was dead straight; straight as a ribbon until about 3 kilometers before reaching Beit Bridge.

The witnesses recalled being worried by the absence of the usual beautiful Rhodesian dawn. No rosy pre-dawn, no sunrise; just gray overcast.

It was fully light—the gray light—when Peter switched off the headlights. The two UFOs were still clearly visible, though seemingly higher. There was still no sign of life, either human or animal.

Frances fell asleep at about 6:15 A.M.

Frances: "There's a point I'd like to make: just before I fell asleep I think we'd lost all sound from the radio. Till then we'd not had to change the station at all, which is unusual for the distance traveled, and the time. Then, for about half an hour, nothing, which is why I went to sleep, for there was no radio to listen to and keep me occupied. We fiddled with it for a time but could pick up nothing."

Peter: "From 5:30 A.M. I had lost trace of time. I felt as though in a coma. Everything just disappeared. Three minutes after Frances fell asleep I can remember nothing. I seemed mesmerized by the unending, solid stream of road—it was like drivers' hypnosis."

At one point in my interview I remarked upon the fact that in his report Peter had suggested that the objects might have been solar-energized. Why?

Peter: "Because there was no sun."

CvV: "But why?"

Peter: "I don't know . . ."

Frances: "Because they rose from where the sun had set, and we thought the light coming up from the horizon was energy from the sun. No pinky dawn, and this made me think they were absorbing sunlight, because we'd switched off the car lights, and they couldn't absorb the power, if that's what they were doing. It was horrible: it was the worst bit, because we didn't know if we were still on Earth."

Peter: "Yes, there were still the swamps."

Frances awoke when nearing Beit Bridge at about 7:00 A.M. There was no sunlight, and the two objects were still visible. At the border post she did not draw the attention of the customs men to the UFOs. Furthermore, and this may have been purely coincidental, she was confused as to the time.

The clock inside the Rhodesian post showed 8:30 A.M., which was also the time on the clock on the tower of the South African post over the way, yet the car clock, and their watches, indicated nearly 7:30 A.M.

The Rhodesian officials were the first living things they had seen since leaving Fort Victoria, and they were wearing safari suits. When they saw Frances and Peter they were amazed and asked whether they had just come from the North Pole. At that point someone switched on a radio, and a time-check was given at 7:30 A.M.

The UFOs had now gone, and the sunlight was all around them in the usual manner, but they could not remember seeing it come up at all. Peter suggested that the UFOs must have gone straight up and out of sight. [*This might sound a trifle vague, but even on the strength of the account we have heard so far, the witnesses had had a traumatic experience, so it is hardly surprising they sound vague over details*—EDITOR.]

Peter was surprised, when reading the speedo trip meter, which he had reset to zero at Fort Victoria, to find that it had recorded only 17 kilometers, yet the distance by road from Fort Victoria to Beit Bridge is 288 kilometers. He had "tanked up" to the brim at Fort Victoria, and expected to take on a further supply at the Beit Bridge South African post. When he tried to do this, the tank would take only 22 cents worth, which is less than two liters—which must have been the amount used between Fort Victoria and the point where the UFOs had picked them up the second time that night.

Which was a remarkable conclusion to a remarkable and nightmarish night's drive.

Strange Experience in the Past

Peter and Frances kept their counsel. To any normal person, that is, to any lay person with little concern for UFO or other strange phenomena, their story would no doubt have sounded ludicrous. But, as will be seen, other factors may have been at work prompting their immediate silence about their experience.

Peter had entered a note about astral traveling in his report form, so I asked him about it. He told me that he was accustomed to astral travel up to four or five years ago. He had

started the practice when he was 14, at puberty, and he went on doing it until he was 19. He stopped doing it after meeting Frances because she didn't like it.
Frances: "There was one night when I got a terrific shock because he was asleep and he suddenly went . . . well, I thought he had died, because he wasn't breathing, and his skin . . . I could almost see through him, and his skin was almost transparent. I figured he must be astral traveling then because I realized his breathing was there, very shallow. I knew better than to wake him up, so I left him, and about 10 minutes later he was back to normal, and I woke him up. Since then he's never done it again and *(turning to Peter)* I don't know what happened then . . . I never asked you."
CvV: "When astral traveling have you seen the cord connecting you with your body shell?"
Peter: "Yes."
CvV: "And this recent (UFO) experience . . . ?"
Peter: "It was exactly the same sensation that one gets when one is parting from one's own self . . . like the initial stages when one relaxes and takes in oneself, preparing to astral travel: this is how I felt."

Peter, in his statement, said his mental telepathic powers were fading since the experience of May 30–31, 1974, but that his power to concentrate and absorb things has improved immensely. I asked him at what age he first realized he had telepathic powers.
Peter: "At adolescence, at about 14 years of age, I found I could do these things: astral travel, self-hypnosis, and mental telepathy. Things outside the scope of normal boys. I used telepathy as a party piece, but crudely, because I never perfected it. Now I've lost it."
CvV: "Can you still do astral traveling?"
Peter: "No. I've tried, but it's gone."
CvV: "And you, Frances, your fantastic memory?"
Frances: "Yes. I could read through a set book before an exam and remember it almost word for word. Now it's gone, completely."
Peter: (with a chuckle): "Now just a lovely dumb blonde!"

In his report Peter had added an important note. One point, he wrote, that may have had some bearing on the fact that these objects picked them up is that in July, 1964, he saw a flying saucer, which he erased from his memory, due to the opinions about those objects at that time. He also drew an excellent sketch of the object. I asked him for further details of that experience.

Peter: "It was outside Shabani. I was traveling with my father in his van. I used to bunk school to help him do his long delivery trips. He was driving. It was on a dirt road from Gwelo via Selukwe to Shabani. There was an embankment around a bend. As we came around the corner there it was, about four feet off the road and about 60–70 feet across. As it took off it shot hot-red dust around us in clouds."

CvV: "Did your father see it?"

Peter: "Yes. But he's the type of man who'd forget it."

Frances: "He wouldn't *want* to know."

CvV: "Did it make a big impression on you?"

Peter: "Yes. It made an impression on my father too, but he wouldn't mention it to anybody. The thing was only 20 to 30 feet away from us. It took off at an angle and just flew off. It was gun-metal gray, with black sections where the power unit was. Dust clung to the car for days, weeks. It was even baked into the paint of our big white van."

Frances: "What time was it? I haven't heard this story before. Was it day or night?"

Peter: "Daytime, about 11:30 A.M.

Frances: "Good heavens."

Peter: We are doing about 80 mph. We saw it there and it just shot off. We were braking hard. Dad daren't swerve on the dirt road surface."

CvV: "I see. Where is Shabani on the map in relation to your recent encounter?"

Peter: "Here. The area is in an iron belt and is rich in other minerals, gold and diamonds. Also the metal used in the bases of American spacecraft comes from Rhodesia. Everything is in that area."

CvV: "You say you erased this experience from your memory."

Peter: "Yes. My father told me to. He said: 'Don't tell anyone you've seen this.' "

CvV: "Have you told him about this latest . . . ?"

Peter: "No. He's a brilliant man with physical things, but does not want to know about the unknown."

On the July, 1964, occasion Peter and his father were carrying a consignment of electronic tuning equipment. After the experience they found that in every piece of equipment every valve and diode had been "blown" and they had to take them home to replace them.

Peter is a clever artist, and now uses his talent commercially in his work as sales manager for a furniture business, where he is also involved in interior design and decoration.

Peter wrote about a remarkable lack of wear of the tires of the car after the 1974 experience. What precisely did he mean by this, I asked.

Peter: "For the trip I bought cheap retreads. My intention was to buy new Michelins for the Peugeot when I got down here, because in Rhodesia they're about $60–$70 each [*Rhodesian dollars*—EDITOR] while in South Africa they're only R18–R19 each. So there was no point in spending good money on tires, and I put 'rubbish' on."

Frances: "Just to get us here."

Peter: "It so happens I retreaded my Michelins. If you know anything about tires you'll know it's voodoo to retread wire frames. Give them 1,200 kilometers and they'll be off. The tire people protested, but I insisted. Now, seven months later, I've still got enough tread to last . . . er . . . well, they're not wearing at all."

Frances: "We can show you."

CvV: "That's the car out there?"

Frances: "Yes. We've done 7,000–8,000 kilometers on them, and they're like new."

Peter: "I do a lot of motor sport, and I know how to punish a tire. One day I took the car to a drive-in and put it through its paces to rip the treads. They didn't budge."

Frances: "He's continually moaning about them because their road-holding isn't too good, but they're so perfect we don't want to spend money unnecessarily."

CvV: "You'd better hang on to that car. Maybe it's indestructible!"

Frances: "It's not."

Peter: "We're having lots of trouble with the electrically assisted clutch operation. And the alternator too. The only way to burn out an alternator is to run it too fast."

CvV: "I see. So the excessive speed of the car on the trip from Rhodesia . . . that could be proof?"

Peter: "I suppose so."

That was the end of my interview with this pleasant young couple. I had one important suggestion to make to them. The next step, if they were willing, would be to arrange for them to be questioned under hypnosis. This I could do through a friend of mine, a medical doctor, who had offered to help whenever I needed it. Everything would be conducted under properly controlled conditions.

Frances and Peter agreed readily to this, and to my suggestion that we should record the sessions.

Investigation under Hypnosis: Contact Revealed

The investigation under hypnosis was conducted in Durban on December 3, 1974, by Dr. Paul Obertik, M.D., in his consulting rooms.

Dr. Obertik went to South Africa in the late 1960s from Czechoslovakia, where he had studied and qualified in medicine. He is a member of the South African Society for Psychical Research (Natal Branch) and uses hypnotism in work connected with psychic studies. It was in the society that he met Carl van Vlierden, and they found that they had mutual interests in that field.

Peter was an ideal subject under deep hypnosis. As recorded in *The Natal Mercury* of January 16, 1975, Dr. Obertik explains that there are several accepted levels of hypnosis—light, medium, and deep. In the first, the subject's subconscious can probably project false beliefs and his own ideas. In the last category—and Peter was in a very deep trance—nothing can be hidden, and the truth will always be revealed. The doctor's only conclusion, in the light of his considerable medical and experimental experience with hypnosis was that Peter experienced the things he talked about.

Frances, however, had no deeper experiences than those she remembered consciously. In fact she was unconscious between Fort Victoria and Beit Bridge.

Here then is a transcript of the recording of the investigation under hypnosis: readers are asked to excuse occasional gaps where the words—in a dull, flat monotone—of the hypnotized subject, were unrecognizable.

December 3, 1974.

Dr. O: Now, Peter, you hear me. You can see everything. Tell me once more. You were traveling about 12 kilometers from Fort Victoria. What happened then?

Peter: We were about 12 kilometers outside Fort Victoria when we picked up the two objects. Two crafts together. One was about 85° off [?], the other was 90° directly above the car about 200–300 yards straight up. It sent down beams of light . . . or beams of some description, I don't know what type they were . . . [?], which gave the car a complete mind of its own, its own sense of power, direction, speed control, steering ability, lighting, everything. Even, at one stage, the car was telling me what to do, how to do it . . . smoke a cigarette . . . light the lighter . . . change . . . switch the radio off from L.M. radio to another station. This is when we heard voices on the radio which sounded like L.M. broadcasting . . . sounded like music, but it wasn't. It was direct signals from the directly-above spacecraft to the radio which was sending impulses to the car . . . to the cab, and to . . . I tried to fight it the whole journey, and this simulated screen was put in front of the windscreen, the side windscreens and the back windscreen of the motor car. This was from somewhere I don't know. We traveled along the whole journey completely off the top of the road. We didn't travel on the road at all. We went in a dead straight line from Fort Victoria to . . . to . . . 3 kilometers outside . . . Fort Vic . . . [*Beit Bridge?*—EDITOR]. Then we touched to the road again and both objects went to 2 to 3 miles directly above, again one at 80° to the motor car, the other directly above. This is very briefly what happened. More details . . . more details . . . er . . .

Dr. O: Relax, Peter. You can remember what you want to say. Say so. What are the "more details" Peter? What did you want to say about more details? Are there some more details, Peter?

Peter: We were programmed inside the motor car. My wife fell asleep, or was put to sleep by the radio which was the voice of "them," so she can't remember very much of what happened inside the car. And then the form which was beamed straight to the back seat and sat there the entire journey. It told me I would see what I wanted to see in and around, and at itself. I would only see what I wanted to see: if I wanted it to look like a duck, then it looked like a duck; if I wanted it to look like a monster, then it looked like a monster. I don't know . . . what they did . . . because I just don't know . . . I'll have to try to remember, because I must . . . they . . .

Dr. O: They . . . yes?

Peter: They took about 7 seconds to find that I had communicated with the past, and that I had control over my mind to be able to give myself post-hypnotic suggestions. They erased this . . . they tried to erase this, so I wouldn't be able to be hypnotized and tell what happened in the motor car . . . I just can't remember . . . they were very clever. I never went up to the machine, but I could see, through the beams, what went on inside and what it looked like . . .

Dr. O: How did it look, Peter? Tell me.

Peter: It had three levels. Bottom level . . . was the power unit . . . second level was . . . [*stumbled over words*] the engine . . . lev . . . room, rest centers . . . communications . . . living quarters. Top level was . . . complete flight deck . . . inter-astral control center. Whole unit was linked by two vacuum shafts. One placed oneself in the tube and was deposited on the level indicated. Transportation around the interior of the craft was by vacuum suckle . . . vacuum suc . . . inside tu . . . inside the units. It was about 80 or 90 feet across, about 60 feet high. Maximum thrust was . . . well [*much now mumbled and indistinct*] . . . horizontal planes from outer edges . . . lateral they went to [?] by thrust direct down, thrust direct up. They had a stabilizer unit to simulate both . . . in the laboratory section. This was . . . any humans who were taken up could be put into this unit and would simulate their surroundings completely . . . this is just an empty space, but using man's ability, or lack of knowledge, they could suggest what he wanted to see, or where he was.

Dr. O: What did they look like, Peter? How do they look, in fact?

Peter: They looked how I wanted them to look. They looked like a duck then it looked like a duck; if it looked like a monster then it looked like a monster.

Dr. O: Have they any real form, any real form? These are all forms that you can imagine. Have they got any real form? Are they physical beings?
Peter: Physical.
Dr. O: They are physical beings?
Peter: Physical beings.
Dr. O: Have they got any steady form in which they are normally? Any form where they appear among themselves?
Peter: The ones that were in the car and the . . . spaceship, were all . . . that I could see. Identical in size, color, looks, shape, and weight.
Dr. O: And how did they look?
Peter: Same basic form as humans, with large trunks, necks, hairless, two arms, two legs [?].
Dr. O: Same [? genetic ?] organs as we have? Male or female?
Peter: No form of reproductive organs at all.
Dr. O: How do they multiply?
Peter: I don't know.
Dr. O: How . . . where do they come from?
Peter: Outer galaxies.
Dr. O: Which outer galaxies?
Peter: They didn't give any names . . . they just said . . . outer galaxies.
Dr. O: Are they friendly toward us . . . Earth beings?
Peter: Yes.
Dr. O: They are friendly. Then why don't they make direct contact to us if they possess these great powers?
Peter: Because there are two billion people who wouldn't understand them, wouldn't know how to approach them, look at them, see them, talk to them . . .
Dr. O: Can't they make them understand?
Peter: No, because they'd have to change the world, and they don't want to do that.
Dr. O: Do they believe in God, Peter? Do they believe in God?
Peter: No God.
Dr. O: They don't believe in God?
Peter: No gods.
Dr. O: What do they believe in? Do they believe in infinite . . . believe in immortality?
Peter: They are extremely advanced.

Dr. O: Are they immortal?
Peter: No.
Dr. O: Are they mortals? Do they die, Peter?
Peter: Yes.
Dr. O: How long a time in our Earth time do they live?
Peter: . . . I don't know.
Dr. O: How far can they travel, Peter? How fast? Can they travel faster then the speed of light?
Peter: They travel by time, not by light.
Dr. O: They travel by time? What do you mean exactly by that?
Peter: They can travel on time . . . speed of light is too slow to cover billions of miles in seconds. If they want to go from point A to point B they have to come back in time to get to the Earth, so they send themselves back into time. They are time travelers, not space travelers.
Dr. O: How do they talk? Do they speak, or just communicate?
Peter: They . . . mentally . . . they know the English language perfectly, and they know every language, every language of the galaxies.
Dr. O: You want to say then that they have all knowledge of the universe?
Peter: All knowledge of the universe, but we, in the galaxies, are the size of a pinhead cut a billion times.
Dr. O: What world do they come from? Is it similar to ours? Is there oxygen?
Peter: They come from twelve planets of the Milky Way . . . and they don't fight. There are no wars, because they are about 2,000 years ahead of Earth.
Dr. O: So it takes 2,000 years for us to get there: [*Did the doctor misunderstand, and so get on the wrong tack?*—EDITOR.]
Peter: 2,000 light-years.
Dr. O: What do they say, Peter, about Earth? Is it going to be peaceful? Are we going to survive?
Peter: They will change Earth the way they changed the pyramids. They changed the [?] wars. They changed everything by introducing their way of doing things.
Dr. O: How are going to do it?
Peter: I don't know.

Dr. O: Tell me, Peter, are there any of them among us, unnoticed?
Peter: Thousands [?].
Dr. O: They are among us?
Peter: They are clerks, typists, businessmen, university students, lecturers, dustbin cleaners . . .
Dr. O: Peter, if you want to make contact and want knowledge from them, will they give it to us? Do they make contact if you want?
Peter: They make contact only when they want to. And by influencing others. They never do anything direct, on Earth . . . that would make them a figurehead, set them up as a center of attraction. They're only influencers, the schemers, and directors of a person who would do it, and be given the [?] thing, which is praise. Humans survive on praise, and they give this to our . . . [*End of recording*—EDITOR]

Postscript
by Charles Bowen

Well, that's that. It was a remarkable experience to listen to that recording. From what I have heard of the young couple speaking naturally, in their conscious states, and of Peter speaking from his subconscious, I feel that they had a very real and alarming experience. There is little doubt that Peter was aware how his car was taken over, and teleported, how the entity came down and sat beside Frances who had been put to sleep, and that he did see into something, perhaps a real, or a simulated spacecraft (note that he only uses that description, as opposed to "UFO" or "flying saucer," when talking under hypnosis) and that it confused him somewhat. As for the rest of the account given under hypnosis, we must retain open minds. Was it the truth, or was it some "spoof" history, the product of brainwashing by "them"? The fact remains that the account bears not a little relationship to some of the "messages" we have heard before. Readers, no doubt will already have spotted contradictions, like the one about the UFO entities having come from "outer galaxies" and later from "twelve planets of the Milky Way" (which to us is the innermost galaxy!). This, of course, does not mean that Peter did not have the story implanted in his subconscious by extraterrestrial, or other, agencies. Possibly it is all part and parcel of some long-term control process. Consequently this case is very important, giving as it does a close insight into the possible meaning of contact.

Beliefs

by Charles Bowen

To conclude, there follows an extract from the editorial lead article of Flying Saucer Review, *Volume 20, Number 6 (December, 1974), the issue which completed twenty years of unbroken publication of the magazine. It was entitled "More Beliefs" and was in effect an up-to-date and augmented version of an editorial that had appeared nine years earlier on the thorny topic of "belief." The gist of the earlier message had been that we do not "*believe *in flying saucers," and it is the same now, as put down for all to see in our "creed" of 1974.*

We believe that "flying saucers," or UFOs, do exist: the evidence of sight, radar, and sound indicates that some either might be metallic, or might give the impressions of being metallic.

We believe that they could be powered in ways as yet unknown to man. There is ample evidence of their effects on electronic devices and on the electrical systems of internal combustion engines. However it is realized that these effects might be produced by something quite apart from the "propulsion unit."

We believe it possible that these objects could be either of extraterrestrial origin, or that they could be coming to us from another time-space continuum, perhaps some "interpenetrating universe" (there is evidence of materialization and dematerialization to support speculation in this direction), or that they could come from both.

We believe that these objects have appeared before human

beings in a guise or a frame of reference appropriate to the period, or one that might be expected in the near future (relative to that period).

We believe that they are intelligently controlled (to support this contention there is a great mass of evidence of strange entities in landing and contact cases) and that they could be associated with, or indeed be responsible for, other psychical phenomena. We ask whether or not it is possible that some, or all, of the images and entities perceived and reported by the witnesses could be projected by the controlling powers and/or their UFOs, into the minds of the observers; that the often meaningless and gibberish messages, being more than just attempts to treat us as playthings, may or may not be part and parcel of attempts at the influencing of, or the remote control of human beings, in which many of the perpetrators could well have succeeded.

Furthermore we suspect now that they have been succeeding for thousands of years and that man, for as long as he has been able, has been recording these intrusions into his realm (viz., the important observations by Aimé Michel about the cave paintings of the Middle and Upper Paleolithic,* and the enigmatic events in the Old Testament, for example, about Elijah/Elisha, and Ezekiel). Man has been aware throughout his time on Earth of the forces of good and evil—as they apply to him—and this awareness is the cornerstone of religion.

We recognize therefore that there could be a struggle for possession by groups of entities, each with its own form of UFO manifestation, from outside the Earth's atmosphere and/or from (for example) interpenetrating universes, or from among the elementals. While it is possible that little of this is concerned with the ultimate welfare of the human race, the great source of hope for mankind is that there *are* the good forces for which he yearns, and that it is these—no doubt with their own measure of control over us—that over the centuries have kept at bay the evil forces.

We believe that great care will be needed on the part of human beings, even in chance encounters with these objects. Not only should we heed the warnings inherent in the reports of people who have experienced unusual physical and mental

* See "Paleolithic UFO-Shapes," in *Flying Saucer Review*, Volume 15, Number 6 (November–December, 1969).

effects, or have suffered physical harm, or worse, but also endeavor to avoid close contact on account of the very dangers detailed in the foregoing paragraph. There are known to be top-flight scientists who believe that "we must not answer the extraterrestrial telephone when it rings." With the prospects that any such caller may well want us as zoological specimens, or test tube samples, or even fodder, that is good advice.

We believe that the public is slowly learning that there are many people who now treat this phenomenon with the utmost seriousness, and we hasten to add that it has long seemed to us that it is a subject which calls not only for study by scientists, but also by historians, theologians, classical scholars, specialists in linguistics, anthropologists, archaeologists, and so on.

We believed it possible, in 1965, that "some of the contactee claims, complete with 'messages,' may have more than an element of truth in them, albeit in a manner that neither the contactees nor skeptical ufologists expect." Hoaxing, we feared, was not the prerogative of Earth men. We believe that that view holds doubly good today, and that the crux of the whole UFO business will be found in the contact or contactee sphere: the signs have been there for all to see, as recently as the startling business of Andrija Puharich and Uri Geller, and others like Uri.

All in all, we believe there is a very real case to examine, and that this examination calls for completely open minds. *Every* aspect of the mystery must be studied, and we must here add one important point: those who have studied the reports and evidence in depth, and have felt at any time, suddenly, that they should give up their labors as being work unworthy of their time, or as work from which there is nothing more to be learned, should staunchly resist such inner urging and ask themselves where such prompting comes from, and why. We would take long odds on the possibility that it is the future well-being of mankind, body and soul, that is at stake, It goes without saying that our main problem is to locate the good forces and avoid the others, so we must continue our work of recording the evidence, and providing a platform for the great debate, in the knowledge that this may well be for the benefit of following generations; for posterity rather than ourselves.

Appendix

European Organizations

FLYING SAUCER REVIEW
FSR Publications Ltd.
West Malling
Maidstone
Kent
England
Annual subscriptions: £4.20 or
U.S. $9 (by air U.S. $16)

UFO Investigators Network
(conducts field work in
association with *Flying
Saucer Review*)
Secretary: Miss Jenny Randles
23 Sunningdale Drive
Irlam
Greater Manchester
M30 6NT
England

Lumières dans la Nuit
(French investigative group
which publishes journal of the same name)
Mr. R. Veillith
"Les Pins"
43400 Le Chambon-sur-Lignon
France

Inforespace
(Journal—in French—published
by the SOBEPS investigating group)
Boulevard Aristide Briand 25
1070 Brussels
Belgium

GICOFF
(Göteborgs Informations Center
för Oidentifierade Flygande
Föremål)
Stobe ' egatan 28B
416 53 Göteborg
Sweden

CNIFAA
(Comitato Nazionale Independente per lo Studio dei Fenomeni
Aerei Anomali)
Via Rizzoli 4 sc/B
40125 Bologna
Italy

About the Editor

Charles Bowen is editor of *The Flying Saucer Review* and lives in England.